Management Skills for the New Health Care Supervisor

Second Edition

William Umiker, MD

Adjunct Professor of Clinical Pathology
The Penn State's Milton S. Hershey
   Medical Center
Hershey, Pennsylvania

AN ASPEN PUBLICATION®
Aspen Publishers, Inc.
Gaithersburg, Maryland
1994

Library of Congress Cataloging-in-Publication Data

Umiker, William O.
Management skills for the new health care supervisor / William
Umiker. -- 2nd ed.
p.   cm.
Includes bibliographical references and index.
ISBN: 0-8342-0398-7
1. Health facilities—Personnel management.   2. Supervision of
employees.   I. Title.
[DNLM: 1. Health Facility Administrators.   2. Personnel
Management—methods.   WX 155 U51m 1993]
RA971.35.U526   1993
362.1'068'3—dc20
DNLM/DLC
for Library of Congress
93-8096
CIP

Copyright © 1994 by Aspen Publishers, Inc.

Editorial Resources: Ruth Bloom

Library of Congress Catalog Card Number: 93-8096
ISBN: 0-8342-0398-7

Printed in the United States of America

1 2 3 4 5

Table of Contents

Objectives of This Book

This book will enable you to:

- ensure that employees know what is expected of them

- appraise performance while bolstering self-esteem

- apply leadership techniques to win commitment

- plan, organize, and delegate work for greater productivity

- sharpen communication skills to build better teamwork

- improve the performance of subordinates through better indoctrination and coaching

- motivate staff to achieve their full potential

- work with employees who do not seem to care

- augment decision-making and problem-solving skills

- manage time to meet deadlines, minimize pressure, and achieve goals

- formulate and implement a personal development plan

Foreword

I had the privilege of serving as one of Dr. Umiker's laboratory supervisors before he retired. His book reflects the importance he attributes to sound management principles. It made me recall the firm yet humane and caring manner in which he guided us.

Supervisors know that people problems are the most difficult and frustrating ones. This book is about preventing and solving people problems.

Many supervisors are promoted to supervisory roles with little or no preparation for managerial responsibilities. Even innately skilled leaders encounter situations in which they fell like screaming for help. My confidence, creativity, sense of humor, and respect for others were strengthened by reading this opus.

I particularly commend this informative and highly readable work to newly appointed supervisors and to laboratorians who contemplate moving up into management. This book will help them avoid the snares and pitfalls that can turn challenges into nightmares.

Experienced supervisors will also find this book valuable if they want to fine-tune their skills in communication, time management, problem solving, motivation, and other critical competencies. The numerous chats and lists of "helpful hints" are very useful.

The book addresses many day-to-day problems as well as broader management issues and will be a valuable "resource manual" for all health care supervisors and professionals.

Wendy George MT (ASCP), MS, SM
Microbiologist
St. Joseph Hospital and Health Care Center
Lancaster, Pennsylvania

Preface

The first edition of this book presented an overview of what successful health care managers should know about supervision. The second edition takes a giant step forward by explaining not only what supervisors should know but how they can get those essential things done. The book is now a supervisor's survival kit.

Since the publication of the first edition, many new developments have surfaced in hospitals, clinics, nursing homes, and other health care institutions. Supervisors are faced with a bewildering array of new management approaches, new laws and regulations, and other challenges. These include employee empowerment, cross-functional and self-directed teams, quality improvement, cost control, cultural diversity, and coping with disadvantaged people.

To meet these new challenges, supervisors must make many alterations in the way they select, coach, and even communicate with a changing roster of employees. Examining all this required extensive revision and expansion of most chapters. New chapters on team building, burnout, office politics, confrontation, and personnel retention have been added. Additional topics include empowerment, mentoring, downsizing, and computer use.

The Joint Commission on Accreditation of Healthcare Organizations has moved rapidly in the direction of quality improvement. Readers will find the word *customer* used throughout this book. After all, customer input and satisfaction are the keys to quality improvement. The chapter on introducing change provides useful information for implementing quality improvement measures and any of the other many new requirements that health care supervisors face.

Managers who are involved in helping form autonomous teams or shifting to a more participative management style will appreciate the chapter on team building. Also, the popularity of seminars and books on coping with difficult people led to extensive fleshing out of the chapters dealing with that subject.

Hard work and professional or technical competence alone often do not win promotions or substantial salary increases. People who want more upward mobility should find the chapters on career development, office politics, and networking helpful. You will even learn how to prepare to ask for raises and how to increase your promotability.

Preface to the First Edition

This book was written primarily for health care workers who have no managerial training but who may be, or have been, promoted to supervisory positions. Seasoned first-line and middle managers will also find many practical suggestions for improving their effectiveness.

Managers are judged not only by their personal performance but also by that of their subordinates. This book provides the information that managers need to get the maximum effort and results from their staff.

There is not a great deal of theory in this book. Also omitted are discussions of administrative responsibilities such as budget preparation and inventory control. There is only practical advice on getting things done through and with people. You will learn not only what you must do but also exactly how to do it—even the best words to use.

Acknowledgments

When I was a young boy my parents gave me a radio kit. I put all the parts together, but the radio didn't play. A kind uncle took it all apart and reassembled it, and it worked. The editors at Aspen Publishers did the same thing for this book.

I wish to thank Patricia Rush Miller and Florita A. Gaenzle for their help in my literature searches.

Part I

Do You Really Want To Be a Supervisor?

Chapter 1

"The Man (or Woman) in the Middle"

- promotion to supervisor: a major vocational change
- changing relationships
- a checklist to help you determine whether you will be happy
- definitions of *supervisor*
- the two essential facts of management
- the five critical functions of managers
- how supervisors spend their time

Promotion to supervisor is a major vocational change if you have never held a managerial position. You must exchange some tasks that you enjoy for others that you either dislike or feel uncomfortable doing. It is very likely that you were promoted because of your professional knowledge, technical skills, and seniority. You may have had little or no experience as a leader.

Of course, it is flattering to have been offered the supervisory job. You certainly can use the extra pay. Your family will be proud of you. Yet accepting the position could be a decision you will regret.

Your relationship with former teammates will never be the same. You are now part of "them," not "us." Your daily routine, your interpersonal relationships, and your self-concept all must change. Your loyalty must be with management. To some degree a supervisory position separates you from your co-workers. This will occasionally make you feel alone. Your decisions and your efforts to enforce policies and rules will not always be popular. They may create adversarial relationships. Your new peers (i.e., supervisors and other managers) may be reluctant to accept you, especially if you continue to identify closely with your old group.

If you have not thought about this role change and have not prepared for it, you must be especially careful. It is necessary to weigh the advantages and disadvantages of the change. To help you think this through, you should answer the questions on the following checklist. If most of your answers are yes, you are probably going to be happy as a supervisor.

- Do you prefer leading other people to working alone?
- Do you enjoy teaching others how to do things?

- Do you like to chair committees and to moderate meetings?
- Do you like making decisions or solving problems?
- Are you willing to take an unpopular stand?
- Are you regarded as a good listener?
- Do employees frequently seek your advice?
- Are you willing to take responsibility for the work of others?
- Do you want more responsibility and authority?
- Are you a good planner and organizer?
- Do you like sharing information with others?
- Are you willing to do a reasonable amount of paperwork?
- Are you assertive?
- Do you handle stress well?
- Do you keep up to date professionally and technically?

You should seek the advice of your present supervisor or other managers you respect. After reflecting on the many changes that must take place, you may find it helpful to list the advantages and disadvantages of this new role before you make the choice.

DEFINITIONS

Management is getting things done through people. The term *manager* is used in both a generic and a title sense. In the generic sense, it refers to any member of the management team from supervisor to chief executive officer. In the title sense, it describes someone at an organizational level below an executive but above a supervisor. Managers are granted certain powers called authorities. Thus we will use the term *managers* for all persons above the rank of supervisor and the term *executives* for members of top management; we will use the term *supervisors* only for first-line managers.

According to the Taft-Hartley Act of 1947, a supervisor is:

> any individual having the authority to hire, transfer, suspend, recall, or discipline other employees; or responsibility to direct them, or to adjust their grievances.[1]

A distinguishing characteristics of supervisors is that the people who report to them are not managers. Supervisors spend most of their time meeting goals, implementing plans, and enforcing policies; managers spend most of their time setting goals, planning, and making policies. Supervisors are more likely to be able to fill in for absent workers than managers. In small departments, supervisors may spend much of their time working side by side with subordinates.

The supervisor has been depicted as the man or woman in the middle, beset by the opposing forces of upper management and the workers. Upper management wants work quality, productivity, and low costs. Workers want higher pay, more fringe benefits, and job satisfaction. Although the supervisor's primary loyalty is to the organization, subordinates expect their supervisor to represent their needs and to be their spokesperson.

TWO ESSENTIAL FACTS OF MANAGEMENT

1. Supervisors need subordinates more than subordinates need supervisors.
2. Supervisors get paid for what their subordinates do, not for what they themselves do.

In the past, supervisors were bosses. Today's supervisors must be leaders. They are the primary source of answers, instructions, assistance, and guidance for the employees who report to them. Their primary function is to help their employees get the work done. Many employees feel that their supervisors have forgotten this. This led Drucker, the patron saint of management, to say "Most of what we call management consists of making it difficult for people to get their work done."[2] As a supervisor, you must accept full responsibility for the success or failure of your human resources.

CRITICAL FUNCTIONS OF MANAGEMENT

In addition to professional and technical duties, a supervisor is responsible for the following five functions:

1. *planning:* budgets, new methods and procedures, goals and objectives, and continuing education programs
2. *organizing:* position descriptions, locations of equipment and work stations, and inventory
3. *directing:* selection and indoctrination of new personnel, schedules, assignments, training, coaching, and resolution of employee grievances
4. *controlling:* policies and rules; standards of performance; performance appraisals; quality, safety, cost, and inventory controls; counseling; and discipline
5. *coordinating:* cooperation with other sections of the department, other departments, and services

According to one study, supervisors spend their time as follows:[3]

Assigning and supervising	15%–25%
Communicating with subordinates	15%–20%
Communicating with superiors	10%–20%
Planning and scheduling	10%–15%
Handling paperwork	5%–10%
Doing same work as subordinates	0%–10%
Handling complaints and grievances	<5%
Handling disciplinary problems	<5%
Handling safety problems	<5%

In many health care organizations, supervisors spend a higher percentage of their time doing routine procedures.

NOTES

1. Taft-Hartley Act of 1947 (Labor-Management Relations Act of 1947) Section 101, Subsection 2(11).
2. P. Drucker, *Management: Tasks, Practices, Responsibilities* (New York: Harper & Row, 1974).
3. L.E. Taglliaferri, *Creative Cost Improvement for Managers* (New York: Wiley, 1981).

Chapter 2

Needed Supervisory Skills

- the six basic skills of supervision
- activities that supervisors feel they do least well
- seven qualities of a good supervisor
- what employees appreciate in bosses

First and foremost, a supervisor must be technically and professionally competent. Most supervisors assist with technical tasks. For some, such tasks make up most of their daily routine; for others, they are only back-up duties. In either case, supervisors need professional competency for making decisions and solving problems. As a facilitator and resource person, you must have this expertise.

Your influence as a leader must not be limited to the authority granted to you by your employer. Your knowledge and experience grant you much more power. Most health care workers who are promoted to managerial posts have been selected because of their professional competency. This does not mean that they must know more about everything than their subordinates or must be technically more proficient than their subordinates. A supervisor's expertise must be sufficient to earn the respect of subordinates, however.

BASIC SKILLS OF SUPERVISION

Every supervisor needs to have basic skills in:

- communication
- motivation
- decision making and problem solving
- delegation of authority
- time management
- career development

The importance of these leadership skills is clear in the comments of current practitioners of health care supervision. In response to a questionnaire, for example, laboratory supervisors reported that their major problems involved motivation, communication, continuing education, compensation, and miscellaneous supervi-

7

sory activities.[1] Technical and fiscal matters other than compensation did not seem to pose as many difficulties for them.

The specific activities that these supervisors reported feeling least competent to do were[2]:

- preparing letters and memos
- conducting selection and disciplinary interviews
- setting goals for themselves and subordinates
- offering suggestions for work improvement
- delegating authority
- providing data for budgets
- developing job descriptions
- resolving conflicts among subordinates

It is obvious from this study that people problems are harder to solve than things problems.

The following list of traits desirable in supervisors also reflects the predominance of people activities in a supervisory position:

- *Self-confidence.* Good supervisors do not become defensive when criticized. They accept responsibility not only for their own actions but also for the actions of their subordinates.
- *Respects for others.* Good supervisors welcome input from all sources and are good listeners. They praise more than they criticize.
- *Sense of humor.* Good supervisors can laugh at themselves. They seldom lose their temper.
- *Ability to make decisions.* Good supervisors make decisions promptly, but not before careful consideration. They do not pass the buck.
- *Flexibility and resiliency.* Good supervisors adjust rapidly to changing situations and demands. They overcome setbacks without becoming bitter.
- *Energy and enthusiasm.* Good supervisors have a strong work ethic. They are optimistic and cheerful, even when under stress.
- *Creativity.* Good supervisors are always thinking about better ways to do things. They encourage others to be innovative.
- *Customer awareness.* Good supervisors know their external and internal customers and strive to exceed these customers' expectations.
- *Quality oriented.* Good supervisors insist on things being done right the first time. They support all quality improvement measures.
- *Empowering.* Good supervisors practice participative management and are great team builders.

• *Risk-taking.* Good supervisors are willing to express opinions, encourage creativity, and accept responsibility.

SUPERVISORS FROM SUBORDINATES' POINT OF VIEW

The following is a list of some things that workers like about their supervisors:

• He discusses problems with me and listens to what I have to say.
• She tells the big boss when we do a good job.
• She lets me know how she feels about my work, good or bad.
• I can trust him to go to bat for me.
• He means it when he gives me a compliment, and I know exactly what I did that he liked.
• He is always ready to listen to me.
• She tries to help me do a better job.

NOTES

1. R. Wilder, How one lab gauges job satisfaction, *Medical Laboratory Observer* 13 (1981): 35–39.
2. Wilder, How one lab gauges, 35–39.

Chapter 3

Transition from Employee to Supervisor

- when the transition is easy
- leading versus doing
- relationship with subordinates: the honeymoon phase
- relationship with other supervisors
- relationship with superiors
- adjusting to the new routines
- how to get off to a fast start
- what supervisors find most difficult

Moving up to a supervisory position in the department in which you have been working has its advantages and disadvantages. You know the people and the territory. On the other hand, you must establish a new relationship with former buddies and now identify with management. The transition is easiest if you have:

- been recognized as an informal group leader
- served in leadership roles, such as chairperson, trainer, or substitute supervisor
- performed administrative tasks
- prepared yourself for the promotion through formal educational programs or self-training

The most common reason that supervisors fail is poor personal relationships with subordinates, new peers, or superiors. So it is important to get off on the right foot.

LEADING VERSUS DOING

Many new supervisors simply cannot stop doing what they did before their promotion, partly because they did those things so well (which is probably why they were picked for promotion) and partly because they were not trained to be managers. Trying to serve as a full-time leader and a full-time worker at the same time ends eventually in burnout or supervisory failure.

Supervisors must maintain enough technical or professional expertise to be able to answer questions, to serve as a source person, and occasionally to pitch in and help with the work. Some positions, especially in smaller units or on after-hour shifts, call for hybrid leadership-worker roles.

Some supervisors become frustrated when they realize that they no longer can do everything better than each of their subordinates.

RELATIONSHIP WITH SUBORDINATES

As a supervisor, you want to be liked by and popular with the people you supervise, but you cannot continue to be part of the old gang. It is necessary to strive for their respect rather than their affection. You must be firm, fair, and consistent. You must develop your managerial skills while maintaining your professional knowledge.

If you previously earned the respect of your teammates, you are off to a good start. On the other hand, if they resent your promotion, think that someone else deserved it more, or believe that you were selected as a result of favoritism, you may experience some rough going.

The Honeymoon Phase

Right after the promotion, you and your subordinates make a special effort to cooperate. The employees congratulate you, saying that they are happy to have you as their new boss. You reciprocate with equal enthusiasm. You tell them that nothing has really changed. Together, you plan to correct all the things that have long bothered the group.

During this phase, those at organizational levels above and below you watch you carefully. Your leadership is tested. Your former pals have mixed feelings toward you; this is called the phenomenon of ambivalence. They want to like and trust you, but they resent your control over them.

After the Honeymoon

The honeymoon phase—when everyone cooperates, acts friendly, and conceals problems—lasts about as long as a marital honeymoon. The honeymoon may give way abruptly to a phase of discomfort when a sensitive problem, such as the need for a reduction in personnel, arises. More often, the honeymoon ends gradually as the new supervisor must say no or becomes ineffective. In their desire to be liked, new supervisors tend to go too far with the friendship approach. This ultimately hampers their ability to give directions, to criticize work performance, or to make unpleasant decisions. It is necessary to risk friendship to gain respect. Like it or not, you must finally realize that you are now one of "them," no longer one of "us."

Some subordinates take advantage of the supervisor's good will; the rest take a wait-and-see attitude. The chronic complainers, cynics, passive-aggressives, and negativists cannot stay silent long. They soon begin to describe all the new boss' weaknesses, compare him or her unfavorably with his or her predecessors, and point out how things have been getting worse, not better.

Work should be the primary topic of conversation. This does not rule out casual conversation, but your main job is to ensure that the work is completed. You must enforce orders from your superiors, even when these orders do not seem sensible or fair to you or to your subordinates. You will feel an urge to dissociate yourself from these orders; if you yield to that temptation, however, you will only lose the respect of your subordinates. Instead, you should discuss such an order with your superior and try to change it. At least, you should find out and explain to your people the reasons for the directive. Above all, you must not discredit management with statements such as "What do you expect from those idiots!"

If you let your authority go to your head and lower the boom on your charges, they will unite against you. It is essential to meld humility with firmness. Overcontrolling is largely one-way communication: no listening and a great deal of ordering. This may occur either because a new supervisor wants to do a good job or because he or she enjoys the feeling of authority.

Because of your new supervisory responsibilities, you must spend less time with former teammates. This should extend to time spent in social activities. Others are more likely to charge you with favoritism if you have close social ties with some of your old buddies. You are also more likely to disclose confidential information while socializing. As a supervisor, you must remember that your words carry more weight. Comments you make about others are more often repeated—and get you into hot water.

On the other hand, you should not destroy your old relationships. The temptation to please management may reduce your sensitivity to your subordinates. You should take time to continue personal, positive contacts with each subordinate, chiefly during brief encounters at the workbench or during breaks. You should not be afraid to ask questions or solicit the help of subordinates at these times.

RELATIONSHIP WITH OTHER SUPERVISORS

Your new peers, the other supervisors, will not accept you unless you start meeting with them. This contact is important for other reasons. Sharing problems and ideas with other supervisors enhances your growth as a supervisor, that is, your horizontal development. In the health care industry, there is too much emphasis on strictly professional growth, that is, vertical development. We identify with fellow professionals rather than with fellow managers.

Another reason for moving closer to fellow supervisors is the need for coordinating work. Sharing equipment and services requires close cooperation among departmental sections and among departments.

RELATIONSHIP WITH YOUR BOSS

If you have been promoted from the ranks, you already know something about the boss. You know (1) whether the boss prefers to communicate verbally or by memo, (2) how to interpret the boss' body language, (3) when to stay out of the boss' way, and (4) what pleases the boss. If you are new to the department, you must learn these things as soon as you can.

Good supervisors help the boss manage his or her time by handling trifles themselves. They give the boss all necessary information, even if the news is bad. They admit their mistakes, and they do not make the same one twice.

ADJUSTMENT TO THE NEW ROUTINE

You must know your responsibilities, priorities, performance standards, and authority. If these are not spelled out clearly in your position description, you should ask your boss to clarify them for you.

It is a mistake to make too many changes too soon. You should use the first few weeks to become more familiar with your job and your subordinates. Given a little time, you can assess the abilities of the people you work with and learn to recognize the signals that they send when you question them or assign them work. Initially, it is better to adopt a formal approach because it is much easier to go from formal to informal than vice versa.

A review of the position description and most recent performance appraisal of each subordinate is necessary. These items should be discussed with subordinates in one-on-one meetings. The work definitions probably need updating, and these meetings make it possible to discover changes that subordinates would like or that could benefit the work section. Training or experiential needs are also elicited.

Even in larger work groups, supervisors must fill in for absent workers. As a nonsupervisory worker, you undoubtedly had tasks you enjoyed or took pride in doing better than anyone else. You may feel more comfortable being an individual contributor than getting things done through others. It is essential to give priority to managerial tasks, however, because these tasks pay the largest dividends.

In your first few weeks as a supervisor, you should also:

- have the courage to make decisions and take action
- keep your subordinates well informed
- keep your boss well informed through his or her favorite communication channel
- ask for input from your people, and show your appreciation for it
- defend your subordinates against outsiders
- accept responsibility for the mistakes of subordinates

Supervisors often find the following requirements of their job difficult when they first become a supervisor:

- breaking away from old friends
- controlling subordinates
    —saying no
    —criticizing
    —disciplining
- controlling their tongues
- giving up old tasks that they enjoyed doing.

Part II
Planning

Chapter 4

The Position Description

- uses of position descriptions
- position evaluations
- position title and classification
- position summary
- hierarchical relationships
- scope of authority
- degrees of supervision or independence
- special demands and working environment
- responsibilities, duties, and tasks
- effects of the American with Disabilities Act on position descriptions

Employees must know what they are expected to do and how well these tasks must be carried out. Then they must be told how well they are meeting these expectations. Position descriptions provide the what, and performance standards provide the how well.

Position descriptions inform employees about their responsibilities and ensure compliance with legal, regulatory, and accrediting mandates. Hiring practices must have validity, and that validity is based principally on position descriptions.

Position descriptions determine exemption or inclusion of personnel under provisions of collective bargaining agreements. The Americans with Disability Act (ADA) has forced employers to update their job descriptions (more on the ADA at the end of this chapter). Major uses of position descriptions are listed in Exhibit 4–1.

JOB EVALUATION

Job evaluations provide the basis for equitable compensation systems. Job analysis uses the information found in position descriptions to provide the foundation upon which jobs can be evaluated fairly. Factors considered in any job analysis include education, experience, physical and mental demands, hazards and other working conditions, degrees of authority, and how much harm could result from failure to discharge one's responsibilities.

Exhibit 4–1 Uses of Position Descriptions

Legal
- Protect against affirmative action and discrimination violations, including ADA violations
- Establish basis for pay grades
- Provide framework for performance standards
- Perform job evaluations (salary administration)
- Grievance handling

Staffing
- Inform job candidates about job qualifications, work conditions, authority, and responsibilities
- Serve as a guide for job posting
- Orient and train new employees
- Set parameters for performance appraisal
- Establish a basis for career planning
- Perform work flow analysis

Controlling
- Coaching
- Counseling
- Disciplining
- Performance appraising

The Joint Commission on Accreditation of Healthcare Organizations mandates that job descriptions specify standards of performance and delineate the functions, responsibilities, and specific qualifications of each classification.[1]

JOB TITLE

Job titles are important for prestige and self-esteem. Often a title change with or without a few additional responsibilities can result in a pay raise. Even without pay increases, the more prestigious titles are appreciated by the recipients. The titles in the right-hand column below are usually preferred by incumbents.

Supervisor	Technical director
Secretary	Administrative assistant
Technician	Specialist
Technologist	Scientist
Director	Vice president
Salesperson	Sales associate

CLASSIFICATION

Positions are classified as salary or hourly (exempt or nonexempt) and part time or full time and on the basis of job grade and wage range. The position classification indicates whether an employee is permanently assigned to a particular shift or rotates among shifts, and it documents after-hours or weekend work. If call-backs and compulsory overtime are required, that should be noted in the position classification.

POSITION SUMMARY

Other terms are *position analysis, function statement, purpose statement,* and *mission statement.* The position summary consists of a brief statement that summarizes the purpose of the job. It may include the number of people supervised, the size of the person's budget, or the impact of the job on the organization. The following is an example:

> The employee plans, directs, and controls a ten-person hematology/blood collection section of the clinical laboratory. He or she also teaches students and new employees.

QUALIFICATIONS

Qualifications refer to the requirements of the job, not the qualifications of the job holder.

For some jobs, such as physician, registered nurse, and emergency medical technician, certification or a license is required. In other instances, detailed prerequisites relating to temperament, aptitudes, specialized knowledge, or experience are needed.

Qualifications should not be set too high for the following reasons:

- To avoid charges of discrimination by the Equal Employment Opportunity Commission, you must be able to justify the qualifications because they will be used in employment selection and promotion. To avoid violations, these criteria must be justifiable. The risk of such violations can be reduced by using minimum mandatory requirements and adding desired higher qualifications. For example, at least 2 years of formal training and 1 year of related experience are required; a college degree is desirable.
- The higher you set the qualifications, the more difficult, slower, and more expensive the recruitment process, and the higher the salary.
- Good candidates may be lost.
- Overqualified persons are more likely to become dissatisfied and leave.

HIERARCHICAL RELATIONSHIPS

Because health care organizations are complex and interdepartmental cooperation is essential, the position description should indicate horizontal as well as vertical relationships. The following questions are important: To whom does the incumbent report, and how available is that person? How many employees report to the incumbent, and what are their professional, technical, or other categories? With whom must the employee coordinate or cooperate within and outside the department?

SCOPE OF AUTHORITY

Delineating levels of authority goes a long way toward avoiding misunderstandings and embarrassment, especially related to taking disciplinary actions or incurring large expenses. Three levels are recommended for each major responsibility. Level one, the highest, gives one unlimited power to make decisions and to take action without consulting one's superior. Level two has some limitations. For example, a supervisor may be authorized to assign overtime but must inform his or her superior of the action on the next day. At level three, one has no authority to act before obtaining supervisory approval.

A global statement may suffice in some situations. For example, the manager has authority to discharge the responsibilities of the job within the constraints of the law, organizational and departmental policy, and the labor contract. He or she has signing authority for up to $1,000 for instrument repair.[2]

DEGREES OF SUPERVISION OR INDEPENDENCE

These are important for nonsupervisory positions. For example:

- detailed written instructions are available
- written instructions are available only for new or difficult tasks
- employee and superior jointly establish objectives, procedures, priorities, and deadlines
- only expected results are specified

The position description may list the documented guidelines that are available to the incumbent. These may include policy or safety manuals and budget process descriptions or specific aids such as procedures manuals.[3]

The type of supervision provided by incumbents is important. Here is one such classification:

1. no responsibility for directing others
2. serves as team leader or senior professional (technical) worker; performs essentially the same work as employees being supervised; functions chiefly as trainer, instructor, and resource person

3. responsible for work unit or team; performs functions of planning, directing, controlling, assigning, and scheduling; has authority to counsel, reprimand, and discipline

4. similar to (3) except that supervisors or other managers also report to incumbent

5. same as (3) except that senior managers report to incumbent

SPECIAL DEMANDS AND WORKING ENVIRONMENT

Working conditions include physical space, temperature extremes, and exposure to infectious agents, chemicals, radiation, and other hazards. The type of safety equipment and attire may be spelled out.

Physical demands have assumed new significance with the passage of the ADA (see later) and must be based on current requirements of actual incumbents. Most professional and technical positions make special demands on incumbents. Such demands include absolute integrity and accuracy in reporting observations, discretion with patient information, willingness to alter work schedules, and the ability to work under stress.

RESPONSIBILITIES, DUTIES, AND TASKS

The responsibilities and duties must justify the salary for the position. Responsibilities are activities in their broadest sense, duties are more specific and may be broken down into their task components. For example:

- Responsibility
  1. Teach radiology students.
- Duty
  1. Provide at least 10 lecture hours and 40 hours of practical instruction for 4 to 6 students.
- Tasks
  1. Prepare agenda.
  2. Explain principles and methods.
  3. Prepare and administer examinations.
  4. Grade student performance.

For managerial and professional positions, only major responsibilities may be documented. The approximate percentage of time needed for each is usually indicated.

Whether to divide the responsibilities into duties is a matter of choice. Because of the ADA, it is now necessary to divide responsibilities into essential and nonessential categories.

Description of tasks is recommended for low-level jobs, where detailed instructions are needed. Delineation of specific tasks is also informative for job candidates who would appreciate more information regarding unfamiliar jobs.

Only for the simplest, most repetitive, and most rigidly structured jobs is it possible to capture every probable task in a position description. Employees must understand that many of the odd tasks that arise will be one-time tasks that will not appear on the list of duties or will occur so infrequently that it makes little sense to include them. Thus it is not without reason that an apparently catch-all statement such as "other duties as assigned" appears at the end of most lists of duties.

In describing duties and tasks, some personnel experts recommend the use of descriptive phrases that add prestige to the activity. This boosts self-esteem and gets more favorable consideration when jobs are re-evaluated for salary considerations. Here are some examples:

- consult with physician (instead of "ask physician")
- evaluate clinical status (instead of "observe patient")
- generate data (instead of "report results")
- implement quality control measures (instead of "check for errors")

Other authorities frown upon the above practice and urge the use of specific phraseology. They shun words such as *coordinate* and *participate*. Instead of "Coordinate schedules with the medical staff," they would use "Check with medical staff secretary before posting schedule." Instead of "Participate in quality assurance activities," they would say "Notify supervisor when variances are noted." Exhibit 4–2 gives a list of verbs that are often used when describing supervisory duties.

Position descriptions reflect more professionalism if repetition of verbs is avoided. Examples are as follows:

- plan (use *establish, set, maintain,* or *ensure*)
- monitor (use *observe, compare, investigate,* or *resolve*)
- develop (use *instruct, appraise, provide,* or *coach*)
- schedule (use *assign, post, establish,* or *rotate*)

Customer-oriented position descriptions use phraseology that favors customer service (e.g., "Make visitors feel welcome" is better than "Greet people").

When responsibilities are accompanied by descriptors that relate the type of behavior or outcome that identifies successful job performance, we have performance standards (more on that in the next chapter).

Exhibit 4–2 Verbs That Reflect Professionalism

Medical knowledge and patient care	Education and training
• Correlates	• Applies principle
• Integrates	• Instructs/lectures/demonstrates
• Empathizes	• Evaluates
Biomedical instrumentation	**Research and development**
• Calibrates	• Investigates
• Standardizes	• Proposes
• Troubleshoots	• Justifies
Analytical and quality assurance skills	**Supervision**
• Evaluates	• Coaches/counsels/disciplines
• Modifies	• Facilitates/supports
• Develops	• Motivates

EFFECTS OF THE ADA ON POSITION DESCRIPTIONS

The ADA protects individuals with physical or mental disabilities that limit major life activities. Included are persons with acquired immunodeficiency syndrome, rehabilitated drug and alcohol abusers, obese persons, and those with cosmetic disfigurement. The law prohibits employers from discriminating against these people with regard to hiring, firing, salary, training, promotion, and any other condition of employment.

According to the law, people with disabilities who can otherwise qualify for a job may not be disqualified because they may have difficulty in performing tasks that bear only a marginal relationship to a particular job.[4]

This new law will have a major impact on hiring and promotion. It will also force employers to make changes in the work environment. For example, the ADA requires that reasonable accommodations be made on behalf of physically and mentally challenged employees. Such accommodations may be physical, such as installing ramps, repositioning work stations, widening doors, and installing grab bars in toilet stalls. They may also involve deletions of certain nonessential tasks from position descriptions.

The ADA is concerned with factual determinations of essential functions, such as the percentage of time spent on the function and the consequences of not requiring the incumbent to perform the function.

We have already mentioned that duties now must be designated as essential or nonessential. The essential functions of a job are those that, in the employer's judgment, constitute business necessity.[5] If a person cannot carry out essential responsibilities, that person is disqualified for the job. Employers are not required to lower qualification standards tied to the essential functions of a job.

An example of a reasonable accommodation would be to delete a task that is performed only occasionally and to assign that task to another employee. For example, if a job calls for occasional driving of a car, that responsibility may be assigned to a co-worker, or someone could transport the person with the disability.

The physical requirements portion of the position description is critically important in terms of ADA compliance. It must spell out the actual level of physical demands. Information includes kinds and amount of lifting, types of work surfaces, and any auxilliary devices used, such as ladders. Deciding whether the overall physical demand level is occasional, frequent, or constant is a key factor.[6]

Rewriting job descriptions requires going beyond the basic task-oriented listing to develop a functional job description with a performance evaluation parameter (e.g., "Task requires average or above-average hand coordination skills" or "Horizontal lifting and carrying capability of 40 pounds for 10 feet is required").[7]

NOTES

1. Joint Commission on Accreditation of Healthcare Organizations; *Accreditation Manual* (Chicago, IL: Joint Comission, 1992).
2. R.J. Doyle and P.I. Doyle, *Gain Management* (New York: AMACOM, 1992).
3. C.R. McConnell, The position analysis: Single source for multiple applications, *Health Care Supervisor* 6 (1988): 72–84.
4. S. Greenberg and R. Bello, Rewrite job descriptions: Focus on functions, *HR Focus* 69 (1992): 10.
5. Greenberg and Bello, Rewrite job descriptions, 10.
6. K. Shingleton, Audits as interviews: Define physical requirements, *H.R. Focus* 69 (1992): 11.
7. Greenberg and Bello, Rewrite job descriptions, 10.

Chapter 5

Performance Standards

- the four key questions that employees want answered
- definition of performance standards
- uses of performance standards
- kinds of performance standards
- characteristics of a good standard
- coupling techniques
- tips for formulating descriptors
- use of percentages and weights
- pitfalls
- the monitoring process

For a performance appraisal to have validity, an employee must be evaluated objectively. Position descriptions and performance standards can provide that validity. Performance standards state how well the work must be done. Performance standards also provide the linchpin for pay-for-performance systems.

Although the following four employee questions are not often verbalized, effective supervisors know those questions are there, and they respond to them:

1. Exactly what do you want me to do?
2. How well and how fast must I do it?
3. Will you show me how to do what I can't do?
4. Will you tell me how I'm doing?

DEFINITION OF PERFORMANCE STANDARDS

A performance standard is a statement of expected results, behavior, or attitude. A minimum level standard (i.e., meets expectations) provides a pass-fail situation. Performance below the specified level is unacceptable, signaling a need for remedial or administrative action. The appropriate remedy may be as simple as clarifying the supervisor's expectations. In other instances additional training or counseling is needed. When performance remains below the minimum level despite the combined efforts of the employee and the supervisor, administrative actions such as transfer, demotion, or termination follow.

Except in the case of new employees or marginal performers, a pass-fail level provides little challenge. Challenge is introduced by superior level standards (i.e., exceeds expectations). Employees who consistently perform at this level earn the right to share in rewards.

> **A caveat:** *Superior levels should not be too high; they must be realistic. If only a few employees can attain that degree of excellence, morale plummets.*

Avoid using a level of average, for two good reasons. First, few employees think they are only average, and very, very few believe they are below average. Pity the poor supervisor who must designate each employee as either above or below average. Second, average does not provide any basis for administrative action. How far below average must performance drop before it becomes unacceptable?

USES OF PERFORMANCE STANDARDS

Supervisors use performance standards to:

- facilitate the orientation of new employees
- enable employees to appraise their own performance
- provide a solid basis for performance appraisals, counseling, and disciplinary actions
- support pay-for-performance and promotion selection strategies
- identify training and development needs
- satisfy the requirements of accrediting and licensing agencies
- avoid charges of discrimination and protect against grievance actions

KINDS OF PERFORMANCE STANDARDS

Performance standards may be expressed in terms of bottom lines or results, operational performance, or customer satisfaction. They may be based on:

- results—These standards represent hard data. They include objective descriptors such as output, time, quantity, and cost. Examples are turnaround time, infection rates, and compliance with budget.

- behavior—Work habits, initiative, creativity, knowledge, and reliability are referred to as soft data. They are often difficult to tie directly to specific duties. More important, they are more difficult to quantify.

Standards that concern compliance with policies, procedures, and rules are usually covered in employee handbooks, procedure manuals, and other documents. Berte[1] recommends that a statement such as "Meets the conditions of employment as set forth in the policy and procedure manual" be included in position descriptions.

Sometimes exceptions from a generic standard are needed. For example, the appearance and interactive skills required for employees who have direct contact with patients and other external customers may be more stringent than for other employees.

Examples of behavioral competencies for supervisors are given in Exhibit 5–1.

CHARACTERISTICS OF A GOOD STANDARD

- It describes a level either below which a performance is not acceptable or above which a performance is superior.
- It provides a challenge but is attainable by a majority of incumbents.
- It is results based and quantifiable whenever possible.
- It is specific, objective, and measurable.
- It deals with performance over which the employee has control.
- It excludes imprecise words such as *professional, suitable, timely, attitude,* and *ethical* unless these words are accompanied by descriptors.
- It limits the use of absolute terms such as *never, always,* or *100 percent* to actions that are life threatening or in some other way serious (e.g., issuing compatible blood for transfusions).
- It is understood and agreed to by both employee and supervisor.
- It does not discriminate against any member of a group protected by the Equal Employment Opportunity Commission.
- It directly or indirectly benefits an external or internal customer.

COUPLING TECHNIQUES

The coupling techniques and format of performance standards are a matter of individual preference by different employers; supervisors may have little or no input into this choice.

Exhibit 5–1 Examples of Managerial Competencies

Demonstrates an "I care" attitude and service
- knows who the external and internal customers are, and what they need or want
- meets or exceeds customers' expectations

Practices the principles of quality management
- is a leader in any organizational movement toward service and product improvement
- models ethical, moral, and compassionate behavior

Maintains contemporary professional knowledge
- keeps up to date on professional and technical information
- includes management self-development in personal continuing education programs
- regularly attends professional and managerial seminars and workshops

Shows initiative, innovativeness, and flexibility
- is regarded as an effective change agent
- demonstrates problem-solving ability
- offers frequent suggestions and ideas

Maximizes use of resources
- keeps materiel costs within authorized limits
- evaluates, selects, and maintains equipment and supplies skillfully

Communicates effectively
- is regarded as a good listener and communicator by superiors, subordinates, and peers
- makes effective and efficient use of meetings

Displays leadership abilities
- selects new employees carefully, and trains them thoroughly
- coaches, counsels, and disciplines skillfully
- obtains employee work improvement from performance reviews
- maintains high morale and motivation
- empowers and delegates effectively
- plans, organizes, and staffs skillfully

Is a good team player
- encourages teamwork among staff members
- plays an active role in special projects and task forces
- cooperates with other departments

Here are some questions that executives must answer:

- Will the standards be included in the position descriptions or in a separate document?
- Will there be standards for all responsibilities or only for major ones?
- Will standards be coupled with responsibilities, key results areas, duties, tasks, or criteria such as quality, quantity, and knowledge?[2] Examples of each of these are illustrated in Exhibits 5–2 to 5–5.
- Will comprehensive, behavior-anchored standards be used?[3]

- Should detailed lists of procedural steps, accompanied by indicators, be included; or is it better to record these in procedural manuals?
- How many tiers of performance will be represented? The two most common are three- and five-tiered systems.

Example of a three-tiered system:

1. does not meet expectations
2. meets expectations
3. exceeds expectations

Example of a five-tiered system:

1. unsatisfactory
2. meets most minimum standards (or "needs improvement")
3. meets all minimum standards (or "average")
4. superior (or "above average")
5. outstanding

Exhibit 5–2 Sample Format for Duties and Performance Standards for a Medical Technologist

PERFORM ROUTINE BACTERIOLOGY PROCEDURES INCLUDING READING OF PLATES, IDENTIFICATION, AND ANTIBIOTIC SUSCEPTIBILITY TESTING OF SUSPECTED PATHOGENS

a) Cultures must be planted on appropriate media within 15 minutes of receiving the specimens.

b) Stat Gram stains must be prepared and interpreted within 30 minutes of receiving the specimen.

c) Plates must be read and necessary tests set up by 3 p.m.

d) Must advice technicians on identification workup of unusual isolates.

e) All procedures in the department must be performed according to laboratory specifications.

f) There shall be no more than three complaints (incident reports) a year from physicians or nursing personnel regarding bacteriology results and procedures.

PERFORM ROUTINE AFB WORK INCLUDING SPECIMEN PROCESSING AND STAINING

a) Process, culture, and prepare smears of specimens within one hour.

b) Interpret stains within 15 minutes, and notify the proper authorities when positive.

Source: Reprinted from *Performance Standards for Laboratory Personnel* by W.O. Umiker and S.M. Yohe, p. 99, with permission of Medical Economics, © 1984.

The duties are capitalized. The standards follow in lower case.

Exhibit 5-3 Sample Format for Coupling of Duties and Performance Standards

Duties	Standards
Orient new employees.	Submit schedule and agenda to office 1 week before arrival of new hire.
	Notify trainers at least 1 week before arrival of new employees.
	Complete orientation within 5 work days.
	Return check-off list to office within 1 week of completion.
	Receive favorable evaluations from indoctrinees more than 90 percent of the time.

Exhibit 5-4 Performance Standards for Phlebotomist

Duty: Draws blood from patient, and returns tubes and requests to clinical laboratory.

Standards:
1. Greets patient by introducing self and calling patient by formal name.
2. Verifies correct patient by checking name on requisition form against name on patient's wrist band.
3. Explains procedure to patient.
4. Follows infection prevention instructions in phlebotomist's procedure manual.
5. Performs phlebotomy. No more than three unsuccessful attempts are permitted. Calls supervisor if help is needed.
6. Labels blood tubes immediately after blood is obtained by following procedure in manual.
7. Disposes used needles in accordance with procedure in manual.
8. Returns tubes and requisitions to the blood collection station within the time allowed by supervisor.

TIPS FOR FORMULATING STANDARDS

Start by upgrading the position descriptions, particularly the segment on responsibilities. This is the skeleton for the standards. If you have long lists of duties, group them into segments of related topics. Call these key results areas, significant job segments, or some similar title.

For example, in the case of an administrative assistant, all activities that relate to preparing for a meeting can be grouped under meeting preparations. This results in relatively few categories, to which standards are then coupled. For a nursing unit supervisor these could consist of the following:[4]

- personnel functions
- financial functions
- unit operational functions

Exhibit 5–5 Sample Format of Behaviorally Anchored Performance Standards

Meets Expectations	*Exceeds Expectations*	*Fails To Meet Expectations*
Quality assurance		
Performs required reagent quality control each day; records results, dates, and initials. Notifies supervisor of discrepant results or bad reagents. Changes temperature graphs and charts promptly when needed and makes sure pen and graph are working properly. Performs equipment QC according to predetermined time schedule greater than 90 percent of the time; records dates, initials, and results on proper forms. Notifies supervisor of discrepant results or nonfunctioning equipment. Follows established lab safety regulations.	Consistently performs reagent QC and temperature checks prior to testing. When there will not be enough reagent to last until the next day, assists other shifts by checking extra bottles. Volunteers to do required equipment QC and follows through without reminders. Completes QC records accurately. Notifies supervisor and/or biomedical department of discrepant results or broken equipment after attempting to identify and fix problem. Follows established lab safety regulations and encourages others to do so.	Forgets to change temperature charts, or perform temperature of reagent QC, more than twice per year. Does not notify supervisor of equipment or reagent problems or discrepant results. Needs reminder more than once per year to perform scheduled equipment QC. Does not follow established lab safety regulations.
Result reporting		
Efficiently and accurately reports results manually and via computer. Always writes neatly and legibly. Forms always include date, technologist's initials, and completion time. No more than 2 uncorrected transcription errors (undiscovered before they go into patient records) per year.	Meets expectations and reports results manually and via computer with no uncorrected transcription errors.	Makes more than 2 uncorrected transcription errors per year. Reports are found to be illegible or incomplete, or lack required information.

Source: Reprinted from *Medical Laboratory Observer,* Vol. 19, pp. 33–39, with permission of Medical Economics, © November 1987.

- patient care functions
- professional growth and development

Use a KISS strategy: Keep It Short and Simple. In health care, new technologies, services, and responsibilities translate into frequent changes in position descriptions. If you spend too much time developing comprehensive standards, you find yourself back at the drawing board. Most authorities believe that only six or seven major responsibilities of professional or technical specialists need descriptors.

Remember what your two goals are: (1) to provide the information incumbents need to know what is expected of them; and (2) to give supervisors a valid instrument for evaluating performance. How detailed you get depends entirely on how much is needed to achieve these two goals.

Solicit the help of incumbents when deciding what should and should not be included. Incumbents are also helpful when selecting the degree of difficulty for standards. Contrary to what we may expect, employees tend to peg expectations higher than their supervisors.

When working on minimum standards, be sure you know what level of performance is acceptable and what is not. If descriptors are too low, sooner or later you will find you have accumulated deadwood and cannot get rid of it. To use the old quality assurance cliche, "Do it right the first time."

If you subsequently raise those standards, you had better negotiate the changes with the concerned employees. Do not forget to raise the same standards for all the other employees who hold that position.

It is helpful to recall what kinds of problems your borderline performers have had or are having. Perhaps they tend to forget a step in a complicated procedure or have difficulty dealing with certain customers. Composing standards based on such practical knowledge gives great standards.

When pondering descriptors for superior levels, watch one of your best employees at work. What does he or she do that makes the difference? These observations give you clues to good indicators.

USE OF PERCENTAGES AND WEIGHTS

Try to indicate the level of excellence desired by using percentages for those activities that do not demand perfection. An example would be "Reports of performance evaluations submitted on time 90 percent of the time."

This does not mean that supervisors have to keep tallies of such percentages. Their function is to let the employees know just how much tolerance is permitted and how "meets expectations" differs from "exceeds expectations." Assigning weights to different responsibilities also lets employees know the relative importance and priorities of various responsibilities.

If a five-tiered evaluation system is used, it is better to use only three levels for rating each responsibility and to base the five classes on the grand total of weights rather than try to award five different values for each responsibility.

It is difficult to explain to an employee the difference between a third and fourth, or between a fourth and fifth level of performance for each responsibility or duty.

It is difficult enough to convince a person that his or her performance only rates a "meets expectations" level.

Considerations when assigning weights include the following:

- importance to overall job
- time spent on responsibility
- consequences of errors
- impact on other people

PITFALLS

When you review the completed standards, keep in mind the following pitfalls:

- The list of responsibilities (duties) is incomplete or too exhaustive.
- Average performance level is used.
- The level is not labeled as minimum or superior.
- Responsibilities are not under the employee's control.
- A standard is based on invalid or unreliable data.
- Expectations are too low or too high.
- Too few of the standards are based on results (bottom line).
- The supervisor or employee is unwilling to renegotiate the level of a standard.
- There is little or no commitment on the part of, or input from, the employee.
- There is inadequate monitoring of subsequent performance.

THE MONITORING PROCESS

Much of monitoring is simply a matter of reviewing records maintained for other purposes (e.g., customer complaints, attendance records, dates of reports, etc.). Supervisors who practice management by wandering around have no difficulty with the monitoring process. They know what is going on at all times.

NOTES

1. L. Berte, *Developing Performance Standards for Hospital Personnel* (Chicago: ASCP (American Society of Clinical Pathologists) Press, 1989).
2. W. Umiker and S. Yohe, *Performance Standards for Laboratory Personnel* (Oradell, N.J.: Medical Economics, 1984); 99.
3. L.B. Bachert, Performance standards for the transfusion service, *Medical Laboratory Observer* 19 (1987): 33–39.
4. Berte, *Developing Performance Standards,* 61.

Chapter 6
Policy Making and Implementation

- definition and importance of policies
- uses of policies
- supervisory responsibilities
- seven steps for formulating a policy
- implementation of policies
- potential problem policy areas

Policies are broad guidelines for reaching goals or meeting standards. They reflect the philosophy and values of an organization. Generally, the higher the level of its origin, the less specific a policy will be. This permits managers to be flexible, an advantage that supervisors who complain about vague policies fail to appreciate.

A sound policy is one that is needed, achievable, flexible, enforceable, acceptable, understandable, and fair.

IMPORTANCE OF POLICIES

Unnecessary or vague policies create red tape and Mickey Mouse rules that frustrate employees and supervisors. Poorly worded policies lead to confusion. Inappropriate, ill-conceived, unfair, or illogical policies are obstacles to effective performance and require numerous exceptions.

The absence of policies results in management by crisis. Managers waste time making the same decisions and answering the same questions over and over. Confusion, uncertainty, and conflicts become pervasive.

When actual practices stray from policies and procedures, or when practices turn into unwritten policies, trouble brews. Lax adherence to policies may cause legal problems and endanger staff morale.

Although there are always legal risks involved in documenting policies, it is more dangerous not to have an employee handbook written at a level that is understood by all employees and covers important policies, rules and regulations. Policies must be updated constantly because of changes in laws, services, and personnel matters. Examples include modifications of benefits packages, job sharing, flexible scheduling, work-at-home programs, employee exposure to hazardous agents, precautions regarding care of patients with acquired immunodeficiency syndrome (AIDS), sexual harassment, employment of people with disabilities, and new Joint Commission on Accreditation of Healthcare Organizations standards.

USES OF POLICIES

Well-formulated policies have several important uses.

- to enhance communication—they promote understanding, clarity, and consistency; employees know what is expected of them; feel more confident, and police themselves
- to eliminate repetitive decision making, to standardize responses, and to save time
- to help in the orientation of new hires
- to provide documented controls as required by licensing and accrediting agencies

THE SUPERVISOR'S RESPONSIBILITIES

Policies from Upper Management

Supervisors must know, interpret, promulgate, and enforce policies. Being able to quote from an employee handbook is not enough. Supervisors must understand the purpose of each policy and know how much freedom they have in modifying or originating policies. For example, Supervisor Sue says to one of her employees, "Sally, I don't think you look up to it today. Take the rest of the day off with pay, and it won't count as sick time." This is good faith and legal, but what is your organization's policy regarding it?

Policies must be enforced uniformly and fairly. Often, supervisors must implement policies that they had no hand in developing. They might not comprehend the rationale behind, or even agree with, some of these policies, but they are still obliged to enforce them.

Insecure managers divorce themselves from unpopular policies by making statements such as "Don't blame me for that stupid policy" or "Management expects you to. . . ." Even worse, they may ignore the policy or depend on others to enforce it. The result is a loss of respect for both the organization and the manager who takes this approach.

When supervisors feel that a policy is inappropriate or is causing problems, they should discuss the problem with their superiors. Usually there is a rational explanation for it.

There are times when supervisors must bend or even ignore a policy; this is a matter of risk taking. For example,

> Hospital A has a strict policy that prohibits employees from bringing young children into the clinical laboratory. A blood bank technologist receives an urgent call late one night to return to the hospital because of an emergency. She has no one to leave her 6-year-old daughter with, so she brings her in with her and has her sit in the laboratory while mother helps with the work.
>
> Should this technologist be reprimanded or thanked for this behavior?

Policies Formulated by Supervisors

New policies or changes in old ones should be considered:

- when a new service is introduced
- when there have been customer complaints
- when the same question is asked repeatedly, especially when questioners are getting different answers
- when there are administrative problems (e.g., conflict over work or vacation schedules)
- when there are frequent violations of a policy
- when operational, safety, legal, personnel, or fiscal problems are encountered

Before constructing a policy, supervisors should make certain that they have the authority to do so. It is also wise for them to discuss proposed changes with their superiors.

Here is a procedure for formulating a policy:

1. State the need for, and describe the purpose of, a new policy or a revision of an old one.
2. Determine whether the need is great enough to warrant a new policy or change.
3. Consider alternative solutions (e.g., a notice on the bulletin board or a memo).
4. Gather data and input from others, especially the people affected by the policy.
5. Check the rough draft for the following:

- compliance with institutional philosophy, mission, values, ethics, and established policies, rules, and regulations
- completeness, clarity, and understandability
- answers to questions of what, when. where, who, how, and why
- anticipated acceptance by persons affected
- enforcement problems

6. Circulate a rough draft, and/or discuss it with others. Get approval of superiors. Have a legal expert check whether there are liability aspects.
7. Make any necessary modifications. Ask yourself whether the policy meets the following criteria:
   - it is needed
   - it will be understood
   - it is achievable
   - it is flexible and fair
   - it will be acceptable
   - it can be enforced

IMPLEMENTATION OF POLICIES

Publish the finished document. Ensure that everyone gets a copy. Get each employee and new hire to sign on.

Enforce the policy fairly, firmly, and uniformly. Unenforced policies become meaningless. Supervisors have a tendency to overlook transgressions by their more valued employees. Unfairness of this type often translates to the filing of grievances. Furthermore, supervisors must make certain that they themselves comply with the letter of the policies. They serve as models for their staffs. The old cliche "Do as I say, not as I do" does not work.

Heavy-handedness in enforcement can be counter-productive. Employees are more skillful in avoiding compliance than managers are in enforcing policies. Sometimes the violating of rules becomes a game, especially when the supervisor is unpopular or autocratic.

Be willing to admit when one of your policies turns out to be a dud. Modify or eliminate such policies when appropriate. Do not regard the policy as written in stone. Give your policy manual an annual check-up.

POTENTIAL PROBLEM AREAS

As stated earlier, when practices stray from policies and procedures, or when practices turn into unwritten policies, trouble brews. Particular hazards include the following.

Employee Selection

Usually the human resources department screens candidates for employment, but the actual selection is left to supervisors. Hazards include questions of illegality, lack of basis for excluding candidates, and inaccurate or incomplete job descriptions or performance standards.

Orientation and Training

Personnel departments may be responsible for orientation and training, but a portion of this task still is left to supervisors. Supervisors may be responsible for proper completion of forms by new hires. They may have to answer questions about payroll deductions, benefits packages, sick or bereavement leave, and cumulative leave.

Hazards include incomplete or poorly supervised indoctrination programs and overrating poor performers at completion of their probationary periods.

Schedules

Vague or unwritten policies about schedules can destroy morale and lead to the filing of grievances, especially in unionized organizations. Hazards include discrimination in assigning work, vacation, overtime, or call-back schedules.

Safety and Health

With the explosive increase in worker's compensation claims, supervisors must be emphatic about reporting, correcting, and following up on suspected safety or health hazards. Failure to follow established policy, including the careful documentation and the prompt handling of injuries, can be costly to organizations and damaging to the careers of supervisors who have been negligent in this responsibility.

A touchy situation is that of AIDS. First there is consideration for the employee who has the disease, and then there is consideration for the co-workers who are concerned about being infected. This is particularly acute in health care, where there is an increased risk of workers contracting AIDS from patients, and where problems of confidentiality are involved.

The policy should indicate that employees with AIDS be treated as any other person with a disability. It must spell out the rights of both employees with AIDS and co-workers, and it must be known and understood by all employees.

Supervisors should be ready to cope with workers who object to working with an employee who has AIDS. Training programs for managers as well as workers are essential. The inadvertent mishandling of an employee with AIDS can leave an organization liable for discrimination, invasion of privacy, or unauthorized disclosure.

Handling Problem or Special Employees

Grievances usually are filed after disciplinary measures have been taken. Poor leadership leads to poor followership, which leads to reprimands or other disciplinary actions, which then leads to grievances.

Mishandled severance procedures can be costly in both dollars and feelings. Supervisory botching of charges of sexual harassment or discrimination can be embarrassing and expensive for employers.

Effective resolution of personnel problems starts with good policies and ends with skillful implementation of these policies. In the case of sexual harassment, the blanket grievance procedure usually calls for the immediate supervisor to be the first person contacted. In sexual harassment, the immediate supervisor is often the perpetrator. A separate policy for sexual harassment is mandatory.

Policy must spell out limits on drug testing. Is it routine or random? Who will be tested? How about the invasion of privacy issue?

The Special Case of the Americans with Disabilities Act

Policies must address the new federal regulations regarding hiring, assigning, promoting, and accommodating people who have physical or mental disabilities. This translates into making changes in position descriptions, performance standards, and recruiting, testing, and interviewing of candidates.

A particularly sensitive area of concern to supervisors is accommodating. Reasonable accommodations under the Americans with Disabilities Act include making existing facilities accessible to individuals with disabilities; job restructuring; job reassignment; part-time or modified work schedules; granting unpaid leave; acquisition or modification of equipment; providing qualified readers or interpreters; and adjustment or modification of examinations, training materials, or policies.[1]

Reasonable accommodation requires employers to modify examinations, training materials, and policies. Jobs must be restructured so that marginal or nonessential duties that exclude people with disabilities are eliminated when possible. Employers must be able to justify exclusionary qualifications or capabilities. Candidates may not be tested for functions and knowledge that are not essential to the job. Supervisors must know, however, that bumping another employee out of a position to create a vacancy for one of these candidates is not required.

NOTE

1. *Federal Register* 35,736 (July 26, 1991). EEOC regulation pertaining to ADA under Title I—Employment (Title VII, Civil Rights Act of 1964).

Part III
Organizing

Chapter 7
Organizing, Staffing, and Coordinating

- vision, mission, values, goals, and strategy
- culture and structure
- authority and other powers
- unity of command and span of control
- staffing and assigning
- the informal organization
- new management trends
- coordination

Organizing is gearing up to carry out the decisions made in the planning phase. It is concerned with delineating tasks and establishing a framework of authority and responsibility for the people who will carry out these tasks. It involves analyzing the workload, distributing it among employees, and coordinating the activities so that work proceeds smoothly.

Supervisors carry out these functions through the general structure designed in the executive suites. Tables of organization illustrate this structure, showing the flow of authority.

Essential organizational tools include policies, procedures, rules, and position descriptions.

VISION, MISSION, VALUES, GOALS, AND STRATEGY

Before managers can organize effectively they must have a vision; that is, they must be able to visualize what their organization will look like and be doing in the near and the distant future.

The mission is a larger purpose that gives meaning to work. It is the foundation upon which decision makers can build corporate strategic planning processes.

The mission statement answers the question of why the organization exists. It provides the overall framework and philosophy of the organization by broadly defining the organization's purpose and by identifying the organization's operating domain in terms of product, market, and technology selections.

In developing mission statements, employers try to answer five key questions[1]:

1. What business are we in?
2. Who are our customers?
3. What are our products or services?
4. Who are our competitors?
5. What competitive advantages do we have?

Many mission statements are too long, too vague, uninspiring, or lacking in sense of purpose. Can you and each of your employees paraphrase the mission statement of your organization?

Values are things that employees can commit themselves to, are willing to stand up for, or cherish. Some key values are respect for the dignity of each person and for human life, ethical practices, and quality care. **Goals** state what is to be accomplished. **Strategies** enunciate how the goals will be reached.

Culture consists of the visible and invisible forces that shape life within an organization. It encompasses the philosophy, leadership style, communication, organization charts, mission statements, policy manuals, protocols, rituals, and taboos that create the uniqueness of the organization. Put simply, culture is "the way we do things around here."

The complement of culture is **structure,** which starts with job design and work flow patterns and includes policies, procedures, spans of control, reporting relationships, and other factors that dictate how work is to be done and business conducted. Many supervisors are called upon to design or redesign the structure of a work unit or a new program.

A **functional structure** is subdivided on the basis of what duties must be performed. A department may have more than one function (e.g., maintenance and security). A **divisional structure** is subdivided on the basis of product and market. An example of a divisional structure is the categorization provided by the diagnosis-related groups which is affecting the organizational structure of hospitals.[2] Within a divisional structure, a level is reached at which the subdivision will have to be made on the basis of function.

A **matrix structure** superimposes a horizontal association directly over the vertical hierarchical structure. This permits the functional organization with its pool of specialists to retain its traditional vertical flow of authority while assigning employees to leaders of projects or special work units. For example, staff physicians and nurses often share the leadership of nursing floors and direct the activities of social workers, dietary employees, physical therapists, and other specialists, and these specialists still report to the heads of their respective departments (Figure 7–1).

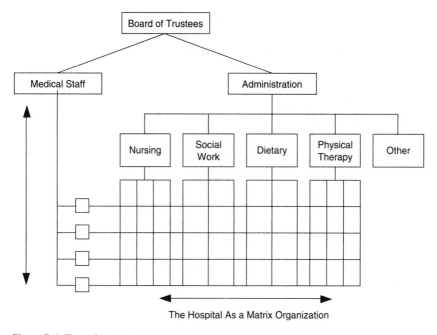

The Hospital As a Matrix Organization

Figure 7–1 The patient care team

AUTHORITY

Authority is a delegated or formal power that is passed on down the hierarchy. It is the power needed to carry out responsibilities. It is axiomatic that people should not be given responsibilities without enough authority to get the job done. Although authority is that power that makes a managerial job a reality, it does not amount to much unless it is supplemented by powers such as the following:

- the power of expertise (e.g., licensure, certification, knowledge, skill, and experience)
- the power of credibility (e.g., trust and respect)
- the power of natural or acquired leadership skill
- the power of persuasiveness or charisma
- the power of influence (e.g., whom one knows or is related to)

Ideally, the extent of supervisors' authority is spelled out in their position descriptions. Some of the more important activities over which supervisors may have much, little, or no authority include the following:

- personnel administration
  1. selecting, orienting, and training new hires
  2. assigning or delegating
  3. scheduling and approving overtime
  4. coaching, counseling, and disciplining
- fiscal administration
  1. selecting or approving purchases of supplies and equipment
  2. selecting vendors
  3. determining inventory levels
- procedures
  1. selecting or modifying methods
  2. enforcing or formulating policies and rules
  3. participating in administrative matters (e.g., quality management, safety, and education)

UNITY OF COMMAND

The principle of unity of command originally meant that each employee reported to one and only one superior. Matrix structures and other complex organizational structures have eroded that concept. Now unity of command means that for each task that an employee performs he or she is accountable to an individual leader.

STAFFING

The staffing process starts with human resource planning, recruitment, personnel selection, and orientation of new hires. It continues with training and development, performance control, and appraisal and may lead to promotion, transfer, demotion, or separation.

Avoid staffing with overqualified people. The personnel costs and turnover are excessive. Underqualified candidates, on the other hand, may represent good investments when they can be trained without great cost or loss of time. These individuals, when trained, are less likely to be bored with routine tasks and are motivated, and their turnover is low.

Personnel availability is enhanced and morale increased when work hours suit employees. Health care workers are predominantly women; many prefer work hours that permit them to care for their families. Part-time employment, flextime and job-sharing opportunities can be powerful incentives. The use of these staffing strategies also helps provide the needed flexibility in jobs that have peaks and troughs.

ASSIGNING AND DELEGATING

Assigning and delegating have one thing in common: If they are not done, the supervisor does all the work. Assigned tasks are those described in position descriptions. They are activities ordinarily performed by employees in that particular category, and the employees have limited or no choice in the specific assignments. A delegated task, on the other hand, is one that is transferred from a supervisor to a subordinate. Delegation is discussed in a subsequent chapter.

The composite list of qualifications of all your employees is like all the pieces in a set of Tinker Toys. All the pieces and all the qualifications are not used; some are left over, and some may be missing. Your task is to match the expertise and available staff-hours to the requirements of your unit. Make maximum use of strengths, and make weaknesses irrelevant.

Supervisors who maintain an inventory of their employees' skills find such charts helpful in ensuring back-up services and in organizing training programs, especially those for cross-training.

Supervisors make the specific assignments and ensure that the work is performed. To do this effectively, supervisors must:

- know the what, where, who, when, how, and why
  1. what must be done
  2. what equipment and supplies are needed
  3. what authority the supervisor has
  4. what quality and productivity are needed
  5. what the cost constraints are
  6. where the tasks are to be performed
  7. where supplies and service supports are located
  8. where help can be obtained
  9. who does what
  10. when must work be done (e.g., deadlines and turnaround time)

11. when changes must be made
12. how the work is to be performed (e.g., methodology)
13. how well, fast, and inexpensively work must be done
14. why the work is done (employees must know how their work affects the big picture)

- ensure a good match between the assignment and the assignee's ability
- make certain that the assignee has sufficient time to finish the work
- provide necessary training and experience
- explain the assignment without overloading the explanation with trivial details
- ask the assignee to repeat the instructions or perform the work under observation to ensure understanding
- put complicated orders in writing
- alert assignees to pitfalls or constraints
- tell assignees when and how to seek help or to report problems

Whenever possible, assignments should be holistic, that is, they should consist of a complete task. For example, most nurses prefer being responsible for all the nursing care of an individual patient rather than providing only a part of that care (e.g., passing out medications).

SPAN OF CONTROL

Span of control refers to the number of employees who report to a leader. With the advent of computerization, increased delegation of authority and responsibility to workers, elimination of layers of management, various cost-control measures, and decreased need for guidance on the part of today's professional and technical employees, the span of control has been greatly expanded.

Each supervisor can best lead a certain number of staff, however. When that number is exceeded, the employees are deprived of leadership support. When that number is too low, supervisors either are underutilized or will tend to oversupervise, much to the discomfort of the people who report to them.

THE INFORMAL ORGANIZATION

Every organization has an informal network that is not represented on organization charts but is nevertheless powerful. It even has its own communication system: the grapevine.

There are the teams composed of co-workers or colleagues who have no formal power over other members and who must negotiate for what they want. Much of this is interdepartmental and may be represented on organization charts by dotted lines. There are also committees, task forces, and focus groups. Finally, we have within formal work groups cliques that select informal leaders based on those leaders' expertise, personality, persuasiveness, or physical power. Often these informal leaders have more power than the formal leaders; union leaders are such an example.

Members of coteries exert power over fellow members by ostracism, sabotaging work stations or equipment, blocking work flow, starting malicious rumors, or inflicting physical harm.

Supervisors must be aware of these informal networks, learn to tap into the grapevine, and use it to their advantage. They must recognize the informal leaders and make special efforts to get along with them.

NEW MANAGEMENT TRENDS

Current management trends feature the elimination of layers of middle management (flattening the pyramid) and decreasing the number of supervisors (increasing span of control), with more responsibility and accountability being shifted to frontline workers or teams. Empowerment of employees and team building are discussed later.

THE COORDINATION PROCESS

Coordination is the process of synchronizing activities and participants so that they function smoothly. When coordination fails, conflict and confusion run rampant. Proactive coordinating involves activities aimed at anticipating and preventing problems and improving the articulation of the parts of the organization without regard to specific problems. Reactive coordinating consists of regulatory activities aimed at the maintenance of existing structural and functional arrangements and corrective activities that rectify errors or dysfunctions after they have occurred.[3]

The more steps and the more gatekeepers involved in a work flow process, the greater the need for coordination. Joint projects and services that require interdepartmental cooperation also demand coordination.

Breakdowns in coordination are largely due to faulty communication, personality conflicts, turf battles, job design problems, training deficiencies, ill-conceived physical arrangements, conflicts of authority, and lack of appropriate policies or procedures.

Work flow coordination is facilitated when each employee interaction is regarded as a customer service with a provider and a service user (customer), who is encouraged to provide feedback to the provider as to the quality of service or who makes suggestions for improving transactions.

Coordinating Requires Persuasive Ability

The definition of management can be expanded to include not only getting things done through people but also getting things done with people. This addition signifies the importance of influencing persons who are neither bosses nor subordinates. These relationships are lateral, or collegial, rather than hierarchical. As organizations grow more complex and more highly specialized, supervisors spend less time with superiors and subordinates and more time with their peers. Peers are found both inside and outside the department and the organization. These peer groups include internal and external customers, vendors and other outside providers, and individuals who precede or follow in work flows.

Most managers and supervisors are involved in both intradepartmental and interdepartmental coordination. The inability to function effectively and efficiently as a coordinator can result in career fatalities.

The Tools of Coordination

Committees

One of the major purposes of committees is to increase coordination, but this tool is costly, time consuming, and often ineffective. The strength of committee action comes through a synthesis and integration of divergent viewpoints.[4]

Coordinators

As interdepartmental coordination becomes more and more important, new coordinating and facilitating roles have been established. Examples of activities that use coordinators are quality management, employee safety, risk management, customer service, staff training, and cost containment.

Communication Modalities

Up-to-date tables of organization, policy and procedural manuals, standard operating procedures, computers, memos, reports, and newsletters are important, as are all verbal communication channels. The latter include telephones, intercoms, voice mail, and meetings.

Tips for Better Interdepartmental Coordination

- Make service requests direct and clear. Whenever possible, make the requests directly to the person who provides the service.
- Anticipate negative responses, and be ready to respond.
- Get an agreement on date or time of action when the initial request is made.
- Follow up verbal requests with written ones.
- Listen to employees' problems, and empathize.
- Seek collaborative (win–win) solutions, but be prepared to compromise.
- Treat people as collaborators. Use the word *we* instead of *you.*
- Place teamwork above competition.
- Be patient and reasonable, not demanding or critical.
- Avoid getting upset or upsetting the other person.
- Eliminate all kidding and sarcasm from your repertoire.
- Get to know your staff and colleagues and their work better.
- Express sincere appreciation for their efforts.

We will discuss other aspects of coordination, including project management, delegation, job descriptions, empowering employees, and team building, in other chapters.

NOTES

1. W.G. Callerman and W.W. McCarny, The supervisor's place in strategic planning, *Supervisory Management* 34 (1989): 7–11.

2. D. Pointer, *Organizational Design Puzzle: Selection and Assembly* (Los Angeles: Health and Sciences Network, 1984).

3. B.B. Longest, Jr., *Management Practices for the Health Professional*, 3d ed. (Reston, Va.: Reston Publishing, 1984).

4. Longest, *Management Practices,* 179.

Chapter 8

Personnel Selection

- the three imperatives
- legal constraints in the recruiting and hiring process
- how you can help in the recruiting process
- tools for evaluating candidates
- who should conduct the interviews?
- computer-assisted interviews
- preparing for the interview
- steps in the interview
- the questioning process
- kinds of questions
- lists of recommended questions
- handling sensitive issues
- clues to untruthful candidates
- how to get applicants to want the job
- closing the interview
- organizing the report
- comments on evaluating candidates
- getting references
- how to conduct a telephone reference check
- notification of candidates

> *"It's a lot easier to hire the right people to begin with than to try to fix them later."*[1]

Of all supervisory responsibilities, the selection of new employees ranks near the top in importance. Motivational problems, personnel turnover, difficult people, and susceptibility to unionization are all reduced by hiring the right people. Better selection of new employees is an integral part of improved customer service, team building, and successful quality management strategies.

Poor recruitment and selection are expensive. The eventual cost of a mis-hire is probably several times that employee's annual salary.

To get the kind of employees we want, there are three imperatives. First, there must be an effective recruiting program: We want a lot of good candidates to pick from. As Goldzimer writes, "Cast a very wide net and carefully sift through what you catch in it."[2(p.109)]

Review the qualifications for the job. If they can be lowered, there will be more candidates to choose from. Separate the must-haves from the nice-to-haves. Does the person really need a college degree and 3 years of experience? If the requirement is challenged by a candidate from a protected group, could you justify the requirement in court? Instead of stating that something is mandatory, say that it is highly desirable.

Second, the selection process should enable us to pick the best candidate with a high degree of confidence.

Third, we must persuade the candidates of our choice to accept our offers.

LEGAL CONSTRAINTS RELATED TO THE HIRING PROCESS

The thrust of federal and state legislations is to ensure that hiring, retention, and promotion decisions are made only on the basis of an employee's ability to do the job.

Affirmative Action (Civil Rights Act of 1964)

Organizations must establish objectives for hiring a certain percentage of women and racial minorities so that these groups are given the same opportunity as white men and to reflect the same proportions as the general labor market.

Supervisors must be aware of the legal requirements of Equal Employment Opportunity (EEO) regulations and of their organization's policies and practices related to EEO and the Americans with Disabilities Act (ADA). They must recognize and eliminate stereotyping and preconceptions of women and minorities and provide clear and achievable expectations for all their employees.

Unlawful Inquiries (Title VI of the Civil Rights Act of 1964)

Each state also has its own requirements, so ask your personnel department for a copy. Here is a partial list of questions that are interdicted by the Equal Opportunity Employment Commission:

- age, nationality, and marital status
- spouse's occupation or place of employment
- pregnancy or plans for pregnancy

- child or baby-sitting arrangements (you may ask whether there are problems in getting to work, such as call-backs)
- military record except as related to the job
- arrest record (you may ask whether the person has been convicted of a crime but not whether he or she has been arrested)
- membership in organizations other than work-related ones
- religious affiliation
- nature, severity, or existence of physical or mental impairments; avoid questions about use of sick leave (you may ask how often the person was absent from work as long as the question is not limited to absences resulting from illness or injury)
- worker's compensation history (this may be obtained after hiring)
- questions asked only of members of a protected group (if you want to ask women whether they can lift a 50-pound child, you must ask male candidates that same question)

The Age Discrimination in Employment Act of 1967

As amended in 1986, this act prohibits employers from placing an age limit on candidates for employment except for those occupations in which age is a bona fide qualification (e.g., police officer or firefighter).

The Rehabilitation Act of 1973 and the Americans with Disabilities Act of 1992

There are two major aspects of these laws; those that relate to hiring and promotion practices, and those that require reasonable accommodation.

The cardinal rule is that any question asked of candidates should relate to the job in some way. You can ask whether an applicant is able to perform all job-related functions and can meet attendance requirements, but you may not ask about an applicant's current or past medical or health conditions.

If an applicant reveals that he or she cannot perform an essential function, do not probe into the medical history. Instead, tailor the questions to identify how the disability renders the applicant unable to perform the job's essential functions and how any requested accommodations would enable the applicant to do the job.[3]

Reasonable accommodation refers to measures that an employer may take to enable a person to perform essential functions. This could be physical changes such as wider doors or magnified displays, or it could be the elimination of some nonessential or infrequently performed tasks. For example, if a job requires occasional typing and the candidate lacks the mechanical ability to type, that activity could be assigned to other employees.

How You Can Help in the Recruiting Process

- Provide maximum opportunities for promotion from within.
- Solicit the help of your staff and resignees in finding candidates. Make it a team effort. Some experts recommend that recruiting be part of everyone's position description.
- Provide your recruiters with a condensed position description of the job. Include a list of the desirable features of that position.
- Suggest the best publications in which to place ads.
- Obtain a list of technical or professional schools where candidates train.
- Offer to answer questions from potential candidates and to provide tours of your department.
- Participate in career programs.
- Accept volunteers, and offer summer internships.

Tools for Evaluating Candidates

Resumes

Resumes are the public relations sheets of candidates—balance sheets without liabilities. As Dortch states, "Some of the best fiction writing in the world is in the form of resumes."[4]

When studying resumes, look for signs of customer service (e.g., volunteer work and membership in social organizations), team work, and responsibilities that exceeded job requirements.

Frequent job changes call for close questioning of candidates. Look also for job gaps of a month or more. When moves are to jobs with lower pay or less responsibility or to those requiring less competency, watch out. Equally significant are job changes attributed to personal reasons or explain as "My boss and I had different chemistries."

Outside interests are generally favorable, but some may interfere with attendance.

Avoid the halo effect. Because a person was successful in one type of job does not ensure his or her success in another.

Credentialing

There must be confirmation of licensure, certification, or registration.

Preemployment Tests

Role simulations and other tests can be helpful. They are underutilized because of the time and effort required and the fear that they may violate antidiscrimination laws.

Employers must be able to prove that the tests possess validity and reliability. As long as the tests are based on a major required skill or knowledge as documented in the job description, however, there is only one concern, and that is the affirmative action requirement that preemployment tests must have freedom from adverse impact. This means that the test must pass protected groups at a rate of at least 80 percent of the rate for unprotected groups.

Examples of good tests are as follows:

- Clerk-receptionist candidates are asked to take some incoming phone calls.
- Candidates for jobs involving teaching responsibilities are forewarned that they all must give a short lecture on a subject of their choice.

Special Questionnaires

Many questionnaires have been designed to replace the polygraph tests that are now illegal in most jobs. These paper-and-pencil tests are purported to measure honesty, loyalty, and other positive attitudes, but the jury is still out on their usefulness. Even handwriting analysis (graphology) is making a comeback via computerization.

Drug screening is still a controversial subject, and fortunately it is not a decision made by supervisors.

Who Should Conduct the Interviews?

These interviews are so important that the principal interviewer should be someone who has received special training in this skill. One such person achieves more than a battery of untrained or marginally interested interviewers.

The two most important characteristics of good interviewers are being good communicators, especially skilled at asking the right questions and at active visual as well as auditory listening, and being enthusiastic about their organization, their staff, the job, and the interviewees.

One or more of the candidate's future peers should serve on the interview team. Colleagues have a vested interest in new associates and can often spot people they would like to have (or not) on their team.

Computer-Assisted Interviews

Business corporations that use expert computer systems report improvement in the quality of new employees and claim beneficial effects on turnover, absenteeism, theft, and productivity. Candidates seem to be more willing to feed information to computers than to interviewers. A typical program consists of about 100 multiple-choice questions and takes about 20 minutes.

THE INTERVIEW

Preemployment interviews serve three purposes: to help pick the most appropriate candidate for the job (not necessarily the most qualified candidate), to sell the job to the candidate of your choice, and to create good public relations by treating candidates as potential customers.

Preparations for the Interview

- Prior to the meeting, send each applicant:
    - —a updated copy of the position description
    - —directions for finding your office
    - —an offer, if any, of travel reimbursement
    - —a brief agenda, and the total time allotted
    - —a description of any testing procedures
    - —one of your business cards

> **A caveat:** *Avoid Mondays if your schedule is hectic.*

- Familiarize yourself with the position description, especially the duties and mandatory qualifications.
- Review the applications and resumes (don't write on them; they are legal documents).
- Check the list of questions you plan to ask, and modify your generic list to fit the specific job. Review the questions interdicted by law.
- Select the testing procedures, if any.
- List the positive features of the job to mention when you try to impress candidates of your choice.
- Visualize the tour of your facilities that you will provide, and alert the people you want the candidate to meet.
- Prepare a rating sheet with a list of the major ranking factors.
- Schedule a time and place that will provide privacy and avoid interruptions. Your office may not be the best location.

The Interview Steps

Ice-Breaking

This nonthreatening introduction is to make the visitor comfortable and to get him or her to relax. You must be enthusiastic and persuasive yet be perceived as honest and sincere. You only get one chance to make a good first impression, so start off right.

Also, your first impression of candidates is important. What you see is what future customers will see when they first meet this person.

Be on time, and greet the interviewees by name. When you introduce yourself, include your title. Thank them for coming. Offer a rest stop or coffee.

Don't greet them from behind a desk. Seat them next to your desk rather than across from it. Maintain relatively equal eye level. Do not stand or sit on the edge of your desk.

Make small talk (the dialog lubricant). Use it to get candidates into a talking mode and you into a listening one. Ask them how they learned about the job or what their understanding of the job is. Ask whether they had a parking problem or whether someone is going to pick them up. Ask about an outside interest mentioned in their resume. Watch out for illegal questions. Attempts at small talk may include questions that violate EEO restrictions (see above).

Review the agenda, assuring interviewees that they will have an opportunity to ask all the questions they wish. Ask whether the allotted time poses any problem. They may be scheduled elsewhere after your interview. Then briefly describe the job being offered.

Chronological Review

Have the candidate start with college (high school, if there was no college). Inquire about his or her academic standing, study habits, jobs held, attendance record, athletic and social activities, and leadership roles.

Move on to the work history (e.g., "Tell me about your jobs. For each job you've held, I'd like to know your starting and final salary, duties, successes, setbacks and how you handled them, most and least enjoyable aspects, reason for leaving, and what your supervisor was like"). In some instances, ask the candidate to describe a typical work day.

Ask probing questions using the list you prepared. Finally, sell the job, and answer the candidate's questions or concerns.

THE QUESTIONING SYSTEM

The questioning system has two equally important components: process and content.

The Questioning Process

Use probing sequences. These start with an introductory question that is followed by a series of probes.

Example:

Introductory question: "Tell me about a work crisis you faced."

Probing questions: "How did that situation arise? Why was it allowed to happen? How did you respond? In retrospect, how could it have been handled better?"

Use hypothetical situations.

Example:

"If you suspected that one of your co-workers had a drinking problem on the job, what would you do?"

Early in the interview, ask some knockout questions. The wrong answer to such questions eliminates a candidate before you both have wasted a lot of time.[5]

Example:

"Would you be available for weekend assignments?"; the assumption is that weekend assignments are mandatory.

Don't ask loaded or leading questions. The former are those that force a choice between two undesirable alternatives. A leading question is one that gives away the answer you seek.

Examples:

Loaded Question—"Are you anti-union?"

Leading Question—"You're willing to serve on committees, aren't you?"

Prepare a written menu of questions, and use it for each candidate to ensure completeness, uniformity, and fairness.

Kinds of Questions

Closed-ended questions are those that can be answered in one or a few words (i.e., "When are you available?"). These questions are used to get basic data but should not be used to elicit detailed information. You will not learn much from a question such as "Did you like your last supervisor?"

Open-ended questions cannot be answered with a few words and are much better for getting detailed information. Change the above question to "Tell me about your last supervisor" and you will learn a lot more.

Reflective questions restate what the person said. For example, in response to "I could have accomplished more if I had been given more authority," an interviewer could ask "You really think it was lack of authority that held you back?"

Directive or probing questions are used to solicit more information and are usually tag-on questions. For example, an interviewer might say "If you think that more authority would have helped, just what kind of authority did you seek? Did you ever come right out and ask for it?"

Questions about general responsibilities can use the position description and job specifications to inquire about education, training, experience, knowledge, and skill. There are some excellent books listed at the end of this chapter regarding questions of this kind.

Questions to evaluate service attitudes and interactive skills are quite useful. Novice interviewers tend to ask questions that deal more with technical skills and experience rather than people skills.

Recommended Questions

We want questions that evaluate competency—"Can do"—and motivation—"Will do." We hope to flush out people who are potential problems and to spot those who possess creativity or other wanted characteristics.

Questions To Determine Professional or Technical Competency

These questions should be criterion referenced, that is, related to duties and responsibilities as documented in the job descriptions. Use hypothetical situations or pose questions such as the following:

- How would you . . .?
- Describe your technique for . . .
- If you encountered . . . , what would you do?
- Tell me about your experience with . . .
- Explain your role in . . .
- What aspect of this job would you find most difficult?
- What competency would your former boss recommend that you strengthen?

Questions To Measure Motivation

In every department, there are clock watchers and other marginal performers who could do better if they wanted to. The following questions will help you spot goof-offs:

- What have you done that demonstrates initiative and willingness to work?
- What did you do to become more effective in your position?
- Tell me about a time when you went the extra mile.

Questions To Evaluate Teamwork

Teamwork demands communication skill, congenial relationships, cooperation, the ability to compromise, and a lot of healthy give and take. The following questions help evaluate that important trait:

- Do you like to assume responsibility for your own work or to share the responsibility with others?
- What kinds of people do you get along with best? What kinds of people do you find difficult? How do you deal with them?
- What other departments did you have dealings with, and what difficulties did you encounter with any of these?

Questions To Determine Customer Orientation

- What does superior service mean to you?
- Who do you think external and internal customers are?
- Give me an example of how you made an extra effort to serve a client.

Questions To Evaluate Followership Skill

Although you're not looking for a clone of yourself, and you want people who complement your strong points, you do not want problem followers. Award bonus points to candidates who speak well of previous employers. These questions should help you pick a congenial teammate:

- Describe the best boss you ever had. Describe the worst. (Watch the body language.)
- What are some things you and your boss disagreed about?
- Give me an example of how you handled unjust criticism.

Questions To Evaluate Stress Resistance

All of us have variable stress thresholds, and different jobs generate different amounts of stress. If the position is a stressful one, include questions such as the following:

- When was the last time you got got angry at work? What caused it, and how did you react?

- What was the most difficult situation you faced at work? What feelings did you have and how did you react to them?
- What are some of your pet peeves?

Questions To Determine Retention Potential

Because one of the goals of personnel selection is to improve employee retention, questions such as the following are worthwhile:

- What do you want to be doing 5 years from now?
- What do you expect to be earning 5 years from now?
- Let's discuss your career goals and plans.

Candidates Who Have Had No Previous Jobs

Most college graduates have had part-time or summer jobs, were employees before attending college, or interrupted their education to work for a spell. Inquiries into these employments can be made. The following questions assume greater importance when the employment history is skimpy:

- Describe a teacher you had problems with. How did you handle that situation?
- What are some of the problems you faced at school or at home? If you had it to do all over again, what would you do different?
- What have you done that shows initiative and willingness to work?

Handling Sensitive Issues

Be tactful when you probe into the soft spots. Start by stating that one of the ways you evaluate maturity is by the ability of people to recognize and talk about performance areas that could be improved. Point out that such people have already taken the first step toward career improvement.

Avoid strong words such as *weakness* and *deficiency*. Substitute *area of concern, need for more experience,* and *need to enhance full potential.* Use questions such as "Is it possible that . . . ?" or "How did you happen to . . . ?"

Clues to Untruthful Candidates

- Their resumes and comments seem too good to be true.
- You have difficulty believing what they say they did or earned. They exaggerate or falsify their educational achievements (e.g., "attended" becomes "graduated from").

- Their answers to challenging questions are weak.
- Their body language gives them away. They show signs of discomfort or restlessness when closely questioned, and they avoid eye contact. You note blushing, sudden heavy perspiring, a change in voice (pitch, volume, or rate; stammering), squirming or fidgeting, and blinking.
- The information you get from their references does not correlate with what they told you.

How To Get Applicants To Want the Job

Remember that the better the candidates, the more competition there is for their services. Here are some practical tips to help sell the job[6]:

- Send a map and directions for getting to the interview site. Include a copy of the position description. This demonstrates a caring attitude.
- Provide a tour of your facilities. Show off the pleasant environment, efficient arrangements, modern equipment, and access to other departments and facilities. Point out that the personnel smile a lot and don't seem harassed. Introduce the candidate to one or two key people (but don't overdo this).
- Create a positive vision in the candidate's mind by matching what the job offers with what you have learned the candidate wants. Focus on any special features that are attractive to the person, using the position description as a guide.
- If the person has indicated a special interest (e.g., in research or teaching), discuss what you have to offer. Create a positive picture of the daily routine in the candidate's mind.
- Don't forget spouses. Frequently they cast the deciding vote. It's wise to have them sit in on part of the meeting. How do they feel about the community and the job opportunity? Are they, too, looking for new employment? What can you offer or suggest?
- Answer questions completely and honestly. Don't conceal negative aspects of the job. Refer to these aspects as challenges. On the other hand, don't dwell on the bad features or say that it has been difficult to keep people in that slot.
- Avoid salary negotiations until you make an offer. If the person expects more money, keep the door open. Say that you will give more thought to it and report back.

Closing the Interview

Ask for the person's level of interest (e.g., "Although neither of us is in a position to make a decision at this point, what's your level of interest?")

Explore doubts or reservations. If the person is noncommittal but is a good candidate, set a deadline for his or her answer.

State when the selection decision will be made and how the notification will be done. Make certain that you have the person's current phone number and address.

Take candidates to their next interview, to another on-site destination, or to the exit closest to their transportation. Thank them for coming.

Organizing Your Report

Eyeballing your rough notes is not the preferred approach. Use your previously prepared ranking form and match your findings with the list of criteria you had established.

Review information from other sources (e.g., application form, resume, and references).

Avoid subjective words such as *cocky, pompous, abrasive, personable, ideal, immature, practical,* or *sarcastic.* Instead, be objective. Record observations such as the presence of tattoos and ear pieces, type of clothing worn to the interview, amount of eye contact, and questionable responses to certain questions.

Prepare a summary of three sentences: list of strengths, list of weaknesses, and your recommendations. Consider using a weighting system to evaluate the candidate's major assets and liabilities. If multiple interviewers are used, compare notes.

Subsequent meetings with the more promising candidates are often desirable.

Comments about Evaluation of Candidates

- Assume that people will change only if they have demonstrated this ability in the past.
- Weigh negatives more heavily than positives. A lack of negatives is one of the most important factors in success.
- Watch for strong feelings and beliefs. They indicate rigidity and intolerance.
- Note where the emphasis is. Customer-oriented people talk about service and interpersonal relationships. Task-oriented individuals focus on duties. Burned-out workaholics use the word *stress* frequently.

The Notification

Don't wait too long before offering the job (24 hours is usually too short, and a month is too long). For jobs where there are few candidates and many competitors (e.g., licensed practical nurses in nursing homes), you must make a decision immediately. Notify your top choice first, and wait for that person's response before notifying the others.

The job offer is usually made in a formal letter from your human resources department. It may be preceded by a phone call. The candidate should be told how much time he or she has to respond.

Obtaining Reliable References

Getting information from references is growing more difficult because employers want to avoid legal problems that may arise from comments they make about former employees. With a little persistence and diplomacy, however, much can be learned.

The past or present immediate supervisor of a candidate is best qualified to comment on performance. Permission is important. In addition to getting authorization from candidates, ask them to call their references to alert them regarding your intended inquiry. The references are much more likely to talk to you if this is done.

If a candidate is reluctant to have you talk to supervisors, the caution flag is up unless the candidate has not yet left his or her current job. If that is the situation, ask for the name of a previous supervisor, or request a copy of the candidate's last performance appraisal.

Here is a strategy for getting the information you seek from a reference. After introducing yourself, state, "I would like to verify some information given to us by. . . , who has given us permission to talk to you." This introduction—merely asking for confirmation of information—will usually elicit a positive response.

Ask whether this is a good time and place to talk. The person may want to go to another site for more privacy or may want to call you back later.

If the person is reluctant to say anything, or states that it is against company policy to furnish such information, say that the lack of such information may exclude the candidate from further consideration. Ask whether an exception to their policy can be made in this case. If the answer is negative, ask to speak to the person's supervisor.

Ask for confirmation of data supplied by the candidate, such as title, dates of employment, responsibilities, and salary. Then move on to the same key questions you asked the candidate, after assuring the respondent that the information is confidential. Save sensitive questions for last.

Note how respondents talk about the person. If their comments are brief, hesitant, or guarded, the caution flag is up once more.

On rare occasions, you can't find anything wrong, but you still have a strong feeling that you would not hit it off with this person. This is a good time to get input from other observers. Schedule a couple more interviews for that purpose.

NOTES

1. B. Smart, *The Smart Interviewer* (New York: Wiley, 1989).
2. L.S. Goldzimer, *"I'm First": Your Customer's Message to You* (New York: Rawson, 1989), 109.
3. A.C. Goldberg, What you can and cannot ask, *HR Focus* 69 (1992): 6.
4. C.T. Dortch, Job-person match, *Personnel Journal* 68 (1989): 46.
5. H.S. Swan, *How To Pick the Right People* (New York: Wiley, 1989).
6. R. Half, *Half on Hiring* (New York: Crown, 1985).

SUGGESTED READING

Arthur, D. 1986. *Recruiting, Interviewing, Selecting and Orienting New Employees.* New York: AMACOM.

Cook, S.H. 1988. Playing it safe: How to avoid liability for negligent hiring. *Personnel* 65:32–36.

Parks, D.G. Employment references: defamation law in the clinical laboratory. *Clinical Laboratory Management Review* 7:2 March/April 1993, 103–110.

Stanton, E.S. 1988. Telephone reference checks. *Personnel Journal* 69:123–130.

Yate, M. 1990. *Hiring the Best: How To Staff Your Department Right the First Time.* 3d ed. Holbrook, Mass.: Bob Adams.

Chapter 9

Orientation and Training of New Employees

- the objectives and assumptions of orientation
- what upper management should provide
- how to prepare your program
- the first and second days
- show, tell, and assign
- meeting people
- get help from your specialists
- training of new employees
- preparations by preceptors
- how to stimulate innovativeness
- how to criticize while preserving self-esteem
- tips for better training
- graduation
- feedback from trainees
- better use of the probationary period

"Too many organizations feel that giving a good company handbook to a new employee is a sufficient orientation."[1(p.i)]

The quality of an orientation program has a profound effect on employee performance, loyalty, morale, and retention. For example, turnover reductions of 40 to 69 percent have been reported as the result of improving orientation procedures.[2] Thorough indoctrination is a major cost-saving process.

Michael Rindler, a hospital chief executive officer (CEO), emphasizes the importance of inculcating the values of honesty (not calling in sick when one is not), pride (personal appearance and the neatness of work areas), work ethic (punctuality and not abusing breaks), communication (knocking on patient's doors before entering and not calling patients "honey" or "dearie"), and customer service (going the extra mile).[3]

New employees receive the first phase of their indoctrination before they are hired, that is, in their employment interviews. At this time they learn about the organization, the position, work hours, benefits, and opportunities.

THE SIX OBJECTIVES OF A GOOD ORIENTATION PROGRAM

1. Create a favorable impression of your organization, your department, and yourself. Newcomers should feel that they have made a good choice of their new employer.
2. Provide a hearty welcome, and satisfy indoctrinees' need to be accepted by other members of the work team. Orientation is a socialization process.
3. Ensure that new employees know what is expected, what the ground rules are, and what opportunities the future holds.
4. Not only train new employees but also provide initial experiences that result in early successes. This creates a sense of self-value, instills confidence, and promotes positive attitudes. Most athletic coaches like to begin their season against weaker teams for that same reason.
5. Identify external and internal customers, and emphasize the importance of meeting or exceeding customer expectations.
6. Initiate the newcomers into the rites and rituals of your quality management program.

FIVE IMPORTANT ASSUMPTIONS

1. Early impressions are critical. At no other time is there a better opportunity to open lines of communication with new hires. They are free from the distortions of peer groups; they have not yet formed strong opinions about the job, company, or boss; and they are so eager to please.[4]
2. The first days are crucial. On the first day, make newcomers feel like honored guests. By the end of the first week, they should feel like members of their new work family.
3. The responsibility for learning is shared jointly by the new employees and their immediate supervisors.
4. New employees must visualize the big picture and where they fit in.
5. Information is timed to employees' needs.

WHAT UPPER MANAGEMENT SHOULD PROVIDE

New employees are usually enrolled in an orientation program directed by the education or human resources department. Most programs start with the history, mission, and philosophy of the organization, but attendees would rather hear about things that affect their job survival, such as opportunities for educational support and other benefits, where to park, and when the snack shop opens. All too often, the orientees are sound asleep by the time these topics are presented.

A typical agenda includes information about fires, disasters, safety and security, infection control, resuscitation procedures, uniforms and clothing, badges, pay procedures, disciplinary rules, benefits, grievance procedures, union relations, suggestion systems, performance appraisal, and advancement opportunities.

The CEO proudly discusses the mission and values of the organization and expounds on the latest management strategy (e.g., customer satisfaction, empowerment, team building, quality management, cost control, or future plans). There is usually a tour of the facilities, a distribution of employee handbooks or policy manuals, and an opportunity for newcomers to complete necessary employment paperwork.

If you are in charge of your unit's orientation process, you should know what is and is not covered in these sessions. You want to reinforce the important aspects, avoid contradicting what is presented, and provide anything not included.

HOW TO PREPARE YOUR PROGRAM

The conceptualization and implementation of a unit program should be based on what the new employee needs. Each new employee is different and so has a different set of needs. Individualize your program as much as you can. Give new employees some options: for example, ask what they would like to learn first.

Send a letter of welcome to indoctrinees. Include verification of date, time and place of reporting, the first day's agenda, and any special instructions or suggestions, such as what they should bring or wear.

Have a welcoming party before they report (why do we have parties for people who leave but none for the new arrivals?).

Prepare an orientation packet or handbook with an attractive cover. Include the following:

- departmental philosophy, mission statement, and goals
- organization chart
- position description
- policy and procedures manual
- orientation and training schedules
- checklists of tasks that must be learned
- performance appraisal forms
- probationary evaluation form (if this is not same as the performance appraisal form)

- safety, infection control, and quality improvement policies, procedures, and rules
- names, titles, and offices of trainers
- key telephone numbers or a condensed telephone directory
- orientation program evaluation form (Exhibit 9–1)

Make your policy manual readable. Break it down into sections to be studied at assigned intervals. Still better, prepare a list of important questions, and make orientees look up the answers, or review the highlights with them.

Arrange your schedule so that you can devote most of the first day to the orientee. Review the orientation and training check-off lists.

Prepare an agenda for the first week. Schedule around the employee's work schedule if the orientation and work activities interdigitate.

THE FIRST DAY: THE WELCOME WAGON

Plan to spend as much time with the newcomers as you can, and without interruptions. Hold a breakfast meeting to relax them and show that they are important.

Greet them as you would welcome visiting friends. Be on time! If the first person they meet is a receptionist, make certain that the receptionist greets them warmly and offers them coffee.

Sit down and, after assuring them that they made the right decision in joining your group, give them your best pep talk. The following is an example:

> Lucy, one of the reasons we selected you is that you demonstrated the kind of attitude we look for. As you know, we are really customer oriented. Our customers include patients, patient's families and visitors, clinicians and other care providers, third party payers, teammates, students and trainees, and other departments and officials served by our department.
> Lucy, your past experiences indicate that you are a team player and have a flair for innovativeness. We like that. We also know that you appreciate the importance of quality, timeliness, and safety.

Review the agenda, and give the new employees their indoctrination packets or handbooks. Start them on initial tasks or training. Emphasize the consequences of carelessness or errors. Tell them who they are to go to for directions when you are absent. Make certain that they have met that surrogate.

Take them to lunch, alone or with a small group of associates. Enlist the help of your teammates to see that new employees are always invited to join in at lunch or during breaks.

At the end of the day, spend some time with them to review what was accomplished, to reassure them that the confusion will diminish, to answer questions, and to discuss the next day's activities.

Check to see that all the paperwork for payroll and health benefits has been filled out and they have their identification cards, keys, desks, or lockers. Walk them to the door, and say something positive such as how glad you are to have them on board.

> **A caveat:** *Do not try to cover too much in any one day, especially the first day, when new employees are nervous and confused. Let things percolate gradually, and repeat key points.*

THE SECOND DAY: THE NUTS AND BOLTS

Review briefly what was accomplished on day one, then discuss the employee's position description and performance standards. Refer to these documents as informal contracts that represent a working agreement between you and the employee and that must be honored. Encourage the employee to ask questions. If you do not have the answers, get them yourself. Go over the organization chart, indicating where the orientee fits and what positions he or she would eventually be eligible to attain.

Then get into survival information, such as work hours, overtime, compensatory time, vacation and sick leave policies, and work rules. When you discuss sick leave, comment that you do want people to take advantage of the policy but not of the organization. Comment that attendance and showing up on time are significant factors in performance ratings.

Now is a good time to describe some of the other things you like and dislike. Tell the person how you want to be addressed (i.e., formally or on a first-name basis). Indicate that you expect everyone to be innovative, that your door is always open, and that you welcome suggestions and insist on hearing about any complaints or comments from customers. Say, "In this department we do not kill the messengers of bad tidings. We expect and appreciate them."

Mention the things that bug you, for example people slipping in a little late each day, untidy clothes, or verbal expressions such as "That's not in my position description" or "I only work here." It's better to prevent what you do not like than have to correct it after the fact.

SHOW AND TELL

Knowledge is the antidote to uncertainty, but avoid information overload. Do not try to cover everything during a single tour of the premises; that is too confusing for new persons. Point out the physical facilities. Do not stop to introduce all the people; that comes later.

On a subsequent tour, follow the sequences of various work flows. For example, in a laboratory or radiology department, trace a work request from its point of origin to the posting of results or the provision of a service. Have indoctrinees diagram some of these work patterns. Illustrate how customer service is affected by glitches at each step of these work flows. Relate examples of superior customer service that have been rendered by some of your employees.

Devote one session to a discussion of budgets, charges, and operating costs. Orientees should be shown how charges appear on patients' bills and how they can respond to customers' questions about them.

Direct attention to the communications systems, and demonstrate their use. Stress the importance of proper telephone etiquette; include the intercom, bulletin boards, mailboxes, and message centers. Point out where schedules for work, off-duty assignments, and vacations are posted.

Stress the importance of internal and external, horizontal and vertical communications and cordial relations with internal customers. Show them how the different shifts communicate with each other. Demonstrate how photocopying, faxing, and filing are done. The location and use of safety equipment is best covered separately.

Note that in larger departments it may not be feasible to complete all the above by the end of the second day. Before the employee leaves on the second day, again review what has been accomplished, review the schedule for the rest of the orientation program, and end with another question-and-answer session. Compliment the employee on the progress that he or she has made.

On subsequent days, continue with the following activities.

ASSIGNING

Most new employees are eager to demonstrate their expertise, so get them involved in routine work soon. Early accomplishments provide satisfaction and bolster self-esteem. Praise at this point is important.

MEETING CO-WORKERS

We recommend against a lot of introductions during the tours of work stations. Employees do not like to be interrupted in the middle of tasks, and this may be misinterpreted by the orientees as unfriendliness. Also, the new folks get confused by all the faces, names, and titles when these are presented in rapid succession.

Make the introductions during breaks, when people are relaxed and more inclined to be amiable. Also present newcomers at staff meetings. Encourage them to talk about their educational and recreational interests at that time.

When you introduce someone, indicate how that person's responsibilities or interests relate to the newcomer. An introduction might go like this: "Joyce, I'd like you to meet Sue Smith. Sue is in charge of our main storeroom. If you can't find something there, see Sue."

The new employee should meet with each senior member of the staff, preferably in his or her office.

MEETING OTHER IMPORTANT PEOPLE

Introduce new employees to key people in units or departments served by yours and in those who provide you with services. Examples may include vendors and departments such as housekeeping, maintenance, finance, personnel, marketing, public relations, education, risk management, infection surveillance, and materiel management.

If the employees will be involved in ongoing special projects or teams, introduce them to the leaders of these groups.

GET HELP FROM YOUR SPECIALISTS

In many larger departments, some staff members have special expertise that makes them better qualified to cover certain topics. Here are some special people:

- *The trainer or educational coordinator:* If you delegate the training, have the new employee meet the trainer early on in the orientation program. Pick trainers with care. Prerequisites include teaching ability, professional or technical expertise, sufficient time, willingness, and loads of enthusiasm. Trainers should be aware of the qualifications and experience of the indoctrinees so that they can tailor the training to the particular needs of each individual. The orientee's supervisor should also participate in this planning process. Trainees may be given folders in which to keep their continuing education records. Many departments have requirements for a minimum number of hours to be spent annually on each job category. The trainees are instructed about how these records should be kept and are reminded that it is their responsibility to do so.
- *The safety coordinator:* Your staff may include a specialist in safety and preventive medicine. This person often serves on the hospital infection control committee. This official shows new hires the location and proper use of safety equipment and reviews safety policies and regulations. New people often have questions about the dangers of hepatitis, acquired immunodeficiency syndrome (AIDS), and other infectious diseases. The safety expert can allay these fears and demonstrate the techniques for minimizing such dangers. When discussing AIDS, the expert warns against disclosure of confidential information.

- *The information service specialist:* Most health care departments are now computerized and have at least one staff member who serves as instructor and troubleshooter. Orientees are taught the use and abuse of this equipment.
- *The quality management coordinator:* This person may be chairperson of or recorder for a departmental quality improvement committee. The coordinator may limit his or her discussions to the global aspects of the programs, leaving specific details for the orientee's immediate supervisor.
- *Mentors and "buddies":* Mentors are experienced people who willingly share their wisdom and/or political clout with their proteges. They are unofficial advisors, supporters, and confidantes. New employees are encouraged to establish alliances with these individuals. In some departments, the buddy system is used. Each new arrival is assigned to an experienced employee in the same work section.

MONITOR PROGRESS

Meet regularly with the new employees during the first few weeks to answer questions, evaluate progress, and keep the program on schedule.

THE TRAINING OF NEW EMPLOYEES

"Companies that produce superior service strike a balance between social training . . . and technical training."[5(p.134)]

Training is aimed not only at building skills but also at instilling healthy mental attitudes. Teaching a clerk how to answer the telephone is skills training. Teaching that person how to please callers is part of attitude development. Positive attitude tends to piggyback on skills improvement. Strike a balance between social and technical training.

Without special training, the necessary bonding for customer satisfaction is left to chance. Customer service skills, like technical skills, are acquired.[6] Don't forget the internal customers. Cross-train to increase employees' abilities to solve customer problems on their own.

For training to take, the first-line supervisor must know what needs to be taught and must help, reward, reinforce, and support the new behaviors.[7]

PREPARATIONS BY PRECEPTOR

- Review the position description and the resume of the trainee.
- Prepare a check-off list of procedures to be learned.
- Identify teaching methods to be used.

- Prepare teaching aids, including equipment, specimens, lists of questions, handouts, and references.
- Check your notes, and update if necessary.
- Prepare a daily teaching agenda.
- Make certain that a classroom or benchwork area is available.
- Make necessary changes in the daily routine to allow sufficient time for the training.

HOW TO ENCOURAGE INNOVATIVENESS

As newcomers become familiar with your procedures, they compare your equipment, methods, and practices with those of previous employers or with what they were taught in schools and other places of learning. Trainers who are self-confident and know how to encourage innovation will not only accept well-intentioned criticism but will invite questions and comments. You do not want preceptors who slough off suggestions with remarks such as, "Just do it our way and you'll get along fine," "That would never work here," or "That's a rather stupid idea." These comments are creativity destroyers, especially when uttered sarcastically.

Unfortunately, creativity is often sacrificed for conformity during the training process. Shift from a "Do as you are told" approach to a "Now think" approach. Start by asking for an employee's opinion before you give advice.

HOW TO CRITICIZE

A common weakness of benchwork instruction is the tendency to be generous with criticism but stingy with praise. Well-meaning preceptors, concentrating on correcting faulty techniques, tend to point out only the things that trainees do wrong. There are lots of "No, not that way. Let me show you again."

A common complaint from trainees is that they only get negative feedback. Actually, there are abundant opportunities to praise performance. Even the trainee who is all thumbs does most things right.

There are three helpful techniques. The first is to maintain a positive ratio of praise to criticism. At the end of a learning session, reflect on what comments you issued. How many were positive and how many negative? By paying attention to this ratio, you will find that you increase the number of positives. You become a better supporter, and your charges respond with more enthusiasm.

The second method is the enhancing value technique. When a procedural error or cognitive lapse is noted, the trainer says, "Sue, I like the way you greet our new patients, (at this point avoid the word *but*), and if you would————you'd be right on target." The first part of that statement lets Sue know that you are her supporter, so that she becomes more receptive to the criticism that follows.

The third tactic is to explain why something must be done differently. For example, add to the statement "Answer the phone within three rings or apologize to the caller" the explanation "because it saves the caller's time and shows that we value his or her service."

SIX TIPS FOR BETTER TRAINING

---

1. Plan a highly structured process. The trainee should know what is to be learned each day, who will do the instructing, and how to prepare for the next day's work. Use an outline for each learning segment.
2. Develop a success habit by working on easier skills first.
3. Correct errors before they become habits, but don't nitpick.
4. Address errors, not traits or personality. Regard errors as learning experiences.
5. Expect to have to repeat things. Avoid that exasperated facial expression when you do.
6. Treat trainees as knowledgeable adults.

   Some managers like to give a written quiz to orientees. This has merit. It may reveal deficiencies on the part of the trainee or the program.

GRADUATION

A good indoctrination program involves much mental effort and psychological stress on the part of trainees. Therefore, the last day should be a special one for them. Three events are appropriate:

1. Their supervisor meets with them to:
   - review the check-off lists and critiques to ensure that everything has been covered
   - schedule any incomplete or omitted activities
   - discuss any last minute problems or trainee suggestions
   - congratulate them as one would congratulate new graduates
2. The department chief meets with them. Before this meeting, the chief reviews all the indoctrination reports and meets with the "faculty." At this meeting, members of the group point out needs for additional experience, behaviors to watch out for, and special accomplishments or attributes that had been manifested (e.g., "Steve made several helpful suggestions, for example . . .").

The boss likes to be able to say something complimentary and specific to show that he or she knows what's going on. Also, favorable comments from the top brass carry added weight. It also indicates to the trainee that favorable reports do go up the chain of command.

3. The event is celebrated at the next staff meeting or at a special social event. The boss makes a nice speech, and the trainees take their bows and revel in the applause (it may be the last they'll get for a long time).

Thank all the staffers who helped. Encourage the trainees to voice their appreciation. Make sure that no one has been excluded. You may be surprised at how many people helped.

FEEDBACK FROM TRAINEES

Evaluate the program by holding frequent informal chats with the indoctrinees and trainers.

Written critiques by trainees are important. Surveys taken after trainees have been performing their new duties long enough to be able to pass judgment on the training they received are even more valuable. See Exhibit 9–1 for a sample form.

Exhibit 9-1 Form for Evaluating Orientation Program

Check the items with which you agree:
1. On the first day, I was welcomed with enthusiasm.
2. By the end of the first week, I knew I had been accepted by the team.
3. My immediate supervisor spent a lot of time with me.
4. The entire program was well organized.
5. Everyone was patient and encouraging.
6. I quickly learned what was expected of me and how to do my job.
7. The new employee handbook (packet of information) is very helpful.
8. They made it easy and relatively painless to learn about important policies and rules.
9. My fears of infection and other safety factors were alleviated quickly.
10. I was made to feel important.
11. I received a lot more praise than criticism. When my work had to be corrected, they always explained why.
12. During the first few days, I met not only my colleagues but also important people in other departments.
13. I now understand how my job fits into the big picture of what our organization is all about.
14. I know how the communications systems work and how to make full use of them.
15. I had plenty of opportunities to ask questions and express my opinions.
16. I am familiar with the salary and benefits package and how performance is evaluated.
17. I understand my role in the quality improvement program.

Use this opportunity to decide how to determine future assignments and to reward each person individually. You may want to use the following questions to prepare an in-house resume for each employee.

- What do you like most about your job? Least?
- What would you like to do more of? Less of?
- What do you want to learn now?
- Would you like any changes in your work hours?
- Are there other work stations in our department that you would prefer?
- Whom do you enjoy working with most?
- Who would be a good mentor for you?
- What can I do to make your day more enjoyable?
- Would you like to be involved in any of the following:
  1. teaching
  2. service on committees, focus groups, special projects, or research
  3. administrative or supervisory duties
  4. work station rotation
- Describe what you want to accomplish by the end of your first year with us. By the end of 5 years.

Comments by trainers and other observers can be added.

SUGGESTIONS FOR BETTER ORIENTATION

DO:
- assume that trainees want to do a good job
- take full responsibility for each trainee
- have an agenda for each day
- express your expectations clearly
- be patient, available, and empathetic
- provide the why as well as the what and how
- make certain that trainees understand
- provide reassurance and encouragement
- minimize criticism, and maximize praise
- encourage creativity and innovation

- encourage questions, and ask for trainees' opinions
- treat them as colleagues, not children
- check on their progress periodically

DO NOT:
- assume that trainees can live up to their resumes
- assume that they know what you want
- overwhelm them with information
- nitpick or lecture
- destroy their self-esteem
- ignore or make fun of their suggestions
- overlook mistakes
- make rash promises
- provide unearned praise
- fail to get rid of them if they cannot or will not do justice to the job or are obvious misfits

THE PROBATIONARY PERIOD

Instead of calling this the probationary period, substitute the term *provisional.* The former term turns people off.

A universal failing of managers is to give marginal performers the benefit of the doubt at the end of their probationary period, only to regret it later. The excuse that is usually given is that the person just needs more experience or that the rough edges can be smoothed out later.

There are at least two effective ways to avoid this pitfall. The first is to pay more attention to the performance of new hires, to provide frequent feedback to them, and to evaluate their ability and willingness to shape up. All too often the time slips by, and one dreary morning your human resources department calls for your evaluation of that new person.

The other tactic is simply to request an extension of the probationary period, either citing marginal performance to date or stating that the complexity of the job demands a longer period of observation. Most human resources departments will permit this. During the extended observation period, make every effort to determine the new hire's "can do" and "will do" capabilities.

NOTES

1. C.M. Cadwell, *New Employee Orientation: A Practical Guide for Supervisors.* (Los Altos, Calif.: 1988), i.

2. R. Zemke, Employee orientation: A process, a not a program, *Training* 26 (1989): 33–40.

3. M. Rindler, *Putting Patients and Profits into Perspective* (Chicago: Pluribus, 1987).

4. W.B. Werther, Jr., *Dear Boss* (New York: Meadowbrook, 1989).

5. W.H. Davidow and B. Uttal, Total Customer Service: The Ultimate Weapon (New York: Harper & Row, 1989): 134.

6. L.S. Goldzimer, *"I'm First": Your Customer's Message to You* (New York: Rawson, 1989), 175.

7. Goldzimer, *"I'm First,"* 181.

Chapter 10

Team Building

- definition of a team
- importance of team building
- benefits of team building
- disadvantages of teams
- characteristics of effective teams
- why teams fail
- team dynamics
- stages in team maturation
- group norms
- importance of rituals and status symbols
- responsibilities of team leaders
- leadership style
- characteristics of good team leaders
- when you inherit a team

DEFINITION OF A TEAM

A team is a highly interactive group of people who share a common goal and who work together to achieve that goal.

Self-directed (autonomous or empowered) work teams are small groups empowered to control the work they do without a formal first-line manager. Typically they plan and schedule their work, make operational and personnel decisions, solve problems, and share leadership responsibilities.[1]

IMPORTANCE OF TEAM BUILDING

As enterprises become more complex, they depend more on the effectiveness of group efforts and cross-functional activities. In health care, few individuals work as solo practitioners anymore. In the old days, an emergency department was staffed by a physician and a nurse. Now that suite features dozens of professionals and technicians representing diverse skills and experience and working as a team to save lives.

Other examples include setting up satellite facilities, introducing new computer systems, developing new services, implementing changes to comply with legal and other mandated requirements, adjusting to cultural diversity, and establishing departmental and interdepartmental quality improvement programs. In the so-called partnership health care paradigm, the patient becomes a senior partner of a health care team.[2]

BENEFITS OF TEAM BUILDING

- **Greater overall expertise:** Although team development is not a panacea, it does refine a unit's diagnostic skills and increases the unit's ability to devise solutions.[3] Teams are especially useful when they deal with methods, procedures, relationships, quality, productivity, problem solving, and decision making.
- **Synergy:** The total results are greater through team effort than what would be achieved by each member acting independently.
- **Higher morale:** The motivational needs of affiliation, achievement, and control are all satisfied.
- **Greater personnel retention:** Employees are less prone to leave when they are members of teams.
- **Increased performance flexibility** is possible because there is less dependence on individuals.

DISADVANTAGES OF TEAMS

Teams are not always needed. There are many responsibilities that can be handled as well or better by individuals. Persons who have unique professional or technical know-how or experience can handle specific situations faster without consulting others or getting a series of approvals.

Work groups require start-up time, have a tendency to become bureaucratic, and may waste much time. When an enthusiastic focus group or task force turns into a standing committee, the topics often become repetitious and boring.

When quick action is needed, someone must take charge and get things rolling. When someone yells "fire," it is not the time to call a meeting.

CHARACTERISTICS OF EFFECTIVE TEAMS

An effective team:

- is not limited to a departmental work group. Its members include vendors, customers, people from other departments, and key staff personnel.

- possesses all the necessary knowledge, skill, and experience required to get the job done.
- searches for excellence in quality, productivity, and customer service. It removes factors that inhibit quality performance.
- welcomes innovation, new services, and new techniques. It is willing to take risks.
- is democratic—there is an absence of rank or formal authority. It has a leader who refers to his or her co-workers as associates, colleagues, or teammates, not as subordinates.
- has great multidirectional communication. It demonstrates openness and candor.
- is inspired by a vision of what it is trying to accomplish. Its goals are clear, and all members aim for the same goals.
- actively constructs formal and informal networks that include people who can help it.
- has power that is based not on formal authority but on the team's credibility.
- has members who trust each other and are sensitive to each other's needs.[4] They understand their roles, responsibilities, and degrees of authority.[5]
- minimizes conflict with other teams or non-team employees through collaboration, coordination, and cooperation.
- adheres to ethical and moral considerations.
- is optimistic and has fun.

WHY TEAMS FAIL

There are many reasons why teams can fail. Although unrealistic mandates from upper management, insufficient resources, understaffing, low pay, or an adverse work environment may be at fault, the first-line manager is usually to blame.

Breakdown in communications is common. Communication is more than just exchanging information. Most interactions are much more complex than that.

Another flaw is the failure to teach leadership skills to members of the team. The result is that, when a crisis occurs in the absence of the supervisor, the team is unable to respond to the need. Here are some other causes:

- Players with higher status, greater knowledge, or more aggressiveness may dominate others. Other problem members are the pessimists, negativists, obstructionists, prima donnas, and goof-offs.
- Lack of support, internal politics, hidden agendas, conformity pressures, favoritism, and excessive paperwork all take their toll.

- Too much closeness and team spirit may shut the team off from the rest of the organization.
- Competition among individuals for promotions, merit raises, bonuses, budgets, turf, resources, recognition, and access to superiors can be destructive.
- Interdepartmental competition may be self-defeating when there is deviation from organizational goals.
- Unrealistic expectations result in discouragement.
- Procedures, equipment, supplies, or environmental factors may be major barriers.
- Disapproval or lack of action on suggestions or recommendations of team members quickly quenches team enthusiasm.
- Lack of progress, failure to meet deadlines, setbacks, and bad results may be disheartening.

TEAM DYNAMICS

Dynamics implies action; team dynamics refers to interactive forces brought to bear by individuals singly or collectively in a group activity.[6]

How favorable the group dynamics is depends largely on how willing the team leaders are to share authority, responsibility, information, and resources with the team members. This kind of sharing is what participative management is all about.

STAGES IN TEAM MATURATION

Stage 1: Orientation (or Confusion)

This represents the transition from a group of individuals to a team. Participation is hesitant as members wonder what is expected of them. Suspicion, fear, anxiety, and low productivity are often manifested.

Stage 2: Bickering and Dissatisfaction

Polarization of members occurs.[7] Some members display negativity, hostility, or resistance. Others are overly zealous. Infighting, defensiveness, and competition are common. Low productivity persists.

Stage 3: Resolution

Group norms and roles emerge.[8] Dissatisfaction and conflict diminish, and a sense of cohesiveness develops. Dependence on formal leaders is decreased. This cohesion is achieved when individuals feel responsible for the success of the team. There is now moderate productivity.[9]

Stage 4: Maturation

Productivity is high and performance smooth. Members have developed insight into personal and interpersonal processes. Team members have learned how to resolve their differences and give each other constructive feedback.

All this takes time, and progress is up and down, not in a straight line.

GROUP NORMS

Group norms may be functional or dysfunctional. A positive form is expressed when team members defend their organization; a dysfunctional form is exhibited when members feel that their organization is taking advantage of them.

In dysfunctional forms, members struggle so hard to reach conformity and to avoid conflict that team decisions and judgments may be faulty.[10]

Some conflict is essential to effective problem solving. Cohesion does not mean the absence of differences of opinion, arguments, or disagreements. Members of great teams can frequently be heard debating heatedly among themselves.

IMPORTANCE OF RITUALS AND STATUS SYMBOLS

Rituals are important to team success. Positive rituals include signs of appreciation (trophies, awards, parties, picnics, and special dinners). A negative ritual is the hazing of new employees. Even some positive rituals may change their polarity. For example, the employee of the month award is regarded with scorn when there are few candidates or when the awardee is a known goof-off.

Team status symbols can also be important. Take uniforms for instance. For years the long white hospital coat was worn only by attending physicians and senior house staff members; now it is ubiquitous. More recently, the green scrub suit and stethoscope necklace have become a uniform of choice. The time-honored nurse's cap has all but disappeared.

TEAM LEADERSHIP

> *"A team is like a wheel in which each member is a spoke.*
> *It's the team leader's responsibility to have enough spokes*
> *and to keep the spokes the same length."*[11(p.3)]

Many health care managers use a laissez faire approach. They state what has to be done, provide technical specifications, and set deadlines while ignoring team-building measures. The result is a work group but not a work team.

Health care leaders must develop dual professional and supervisory skills. Team players must be given opportunities to develop their professional or technical skills (task skills) and skills that pull teams together (maintenance skills).[12]

The five major responsibilities of team leaders are described below.

Plan

Team leaders must know how to make their team effective and efficient, that is, how to make the team work smart. This cannot be accomplished without planning. Managers in concert with their team members should ask the following questions:

- What do our customers want or need?
- What additional information do we need?
- What past successes have we had in meeting these wants and needs?
- What are our strengths, and what needs improving?
- What new objectives and strategies do we need?
- How can we do it faster or less expensively?
- What are the barriers, and how can they be eliminated?
- Should we find out how others are doing it?

See Chapter 34 for more on planning and problem-solving tools.

Develop People

Every work team player, like a member of an athletic team, has certain competencies and the ability to develop more. After writing position descriptions and performance standards, team leaders select the best people and then orient, educate, train, coach, and motivate them. Each of these responsibilities is covered in more depth in other chapters.

Build the Team

This is similar to converting a group of musicians into an orchestra, the final product being an assemblage that can play a symphony.[13] Team building involves developing relationships, communicating, holding meetings, and interacting on a daily basis.

Leaders must create an ambiance that features support and rewards for risk-taking, creativity, openness, fairness, trust, mutual respect, and a commitment to safety and health. There must be opportunities for growth as well as security. Evaluate your team-building ability by taking the quiz shown in Exhibit 10–1.

Lead the Team

With the help of the team members, team leaders prepare mission statements, set goals, develop strategies and plans, design or improve work processes, provide resources, facilitate, coordinate, and troubleshoot. Here is an example of a simple departmental mission statement:

> The Department of Physical Therapy is committed to providing quality care at low cost to inpatients and outpatients without regard to their ability to pay. All staff members will maintain their expertise through continuing education and development.

Leaders must satisfy the affiliation needs of each team member. All employees want to be accepted by their colleagues. Leaders also encourage team members to train and coach each other. Here we are dealing with departmental culture. Ask yourself the questions listed in Exhibit 10–2.

Exhibit 10-1 Rate Yourself As a Team Builder

___ My teammates help each other and share advice.
___ My team functions well when I am not around.
___ I hire people who may be able to perform some tasks better than I can.
___ I do not try to hire people who are just like me
___ Each member of my team learns at least one new skill every year. Each one is working on a new skill now.
___ Each member of my team makes at least one suggestion every month.
___ I encourage differences of opinion and suggestions for improvement.
___ We resolve rather than avoid conflict and problems.
___ Every member of my team can name all our external and internal customers.
___ Every member of my team, in his or her own words, can state the mission of our organization.
___ Every member of my team can describe how our quality management program has affected our service.
___ Every member of my team follows safety procedures.
___ We prefer team over individual competition.
___ Every member of my team feels valued and accepted.
___ Our team has a "can do" attitude. We underpromise and overproduce.
___ Our team has a reputation for cooperating with other teams and individuals.
___ I would describe our team attitude as one of optimism and enthusiasm. Negativism and complaining are rare.

Exhibit 10-2 Ask Yourself These Questions about Your Departmental Culture

- Do I know the work and career goals of each of my employees?
- Do I know their first and last names, their spouses' names, and a little about their family?
- Are our lines of communication open? Do I really have an open-door policy?
- Can I list the top three priorities for each job?
- Are our dress code and conduct clearly documented and understood?
- Do we have a mission statement, and can each team member paraphrase it?
- Are my team members mutually supportive?
- Do I use a situational leadership style?
- Do we have a training program that supports our mission statement and satisfies the career aspirations of each team member?
- Do I delegate and empower effectively?
- Do I serve more as a facilitator than as a rule enforcer? Do I remove work barriers effectively?
- Do I spend more time listening to people than I do telling them?
- Am I a good role model?
- Do I welcome change and encourage risk taking?
- Does our team celebrate successes and learn from setbacks?
- Do I qualify as a change specialist?
- Am I efficient at streamlining paperwork and getting around bureaucratic procedures?

Coordinate

The team as a unit and individuals on the team often participate in cross-functional activities. Team leaders must coordinate these activities with people in other departments and services. They must also be ready to serve as followers in some of these interdepartmental task forces, committees, and focus groups. Typical topics relate to new services, safety, quality management, customer satisfaction, and employee morale.

LEADERSHIP STYLE

The ideal leadership style for team building is based on the perception that personal power is having power with, not over, people. Situational leadership fits that perception well. When new employees join a team, its leader uses a directive (paternalistic) style. He or she tells the employees what to do, shows them how to do it, explains why the work is important, and relates how it fits into the big picture.

Workers at this stage are frightened, insecure, and stressed, so that team leaders are patient and highly supportive at this time. Blanchard and Tager[14] warn against the "leave alone-zap" style, in which inexperienced workers are not given enough direction and then are zapped when they make mistakes.

As employees develop confidence in their ability, the leaders back off, give them more latitude, and encourage them to solve their own problems.

If supervisors fail to move on from the initial show and tell stage to one that expresses confidence in their employees, many employees will remain dependent on their leaders or be irritated by the spoon feeding. Parents encounter the same difficulty when they continue to treat adolescents as children.

Most employees can advance from the self-confidence level to a consultative stage, in which they participate actively in planning, decision making, and problem solving.

The delegative style, in which team members assume some or many supervisory responsibilities, is appropriate for some team members. In this participative paradigm, the team leader serves as a facilitator and moderator rather than as a manager.

In the case of autonomous (self-directed) teams, a democratic system is installed in which there are no supervisors or first-line managers. The team members select a group leader, or leadership is rotated.

CHARACTERISTICS OF GOOD TEAM LEADERS

Good team leaders use both the helicopter approach and the management by wandering around (MBWA) approach. Like helicopters, they hover above the work area, where they can view the total operation. When they spot trouble, they descend for a closer look or to get involved. MBWA is a proactive process. Instead of waiting for problems to be brought into their offices, team leaders make frequent visits to each work station to spot potential problems and to solicit suggestions from the service providers, vendors, and customers.

Some important features of good team leaders

- They provide a sense of direction and set high expectations and standards.
- They have both professional and team leadership skills.
- They are good role models. They cooperate with their counterparts in other departments, thus setting a good example.
- They provide feedback, both positive and negative.
- They criticize behavior, not people or personalities.
- They know their teammates individually.
- They are helpful and anticipate the needs and problems of their team members.
- They can answer most questions. When they cannot, they know where to get the answers.

- They really listen.
- They provide all the resources their team needs.
- They are willing to roll up their sleeves and help out when necessary.
- They do not play favorites, and their credibility is above reproach.
- They defend their people from outside harassment.
- They are quick to praise and to give credit.
- They accept responsibility for failures.
- They get rid of the deadwood.
- They treat people with respect, regardless of their position in the organization. They are never rude.
- They encourage creativity and risk taking.
- They reward cooperation as highly as they reward individual achievement (see Exhibits 10–3 and 10–4).

WHEN YOU INHERIT A TEAM

You may be reassigned to a lead a new team, be promoted to a leadership role, or be an outsider. If you have been a member of that team, you must make the adjustments discussed in Chapter 3. If you worked previously with the group in a

Exhibit 10-3 Rewards for Individual Effort

- Title
- Certificate of achievement
- Letter or memo of commendation
- Article in newsletter or other publication
- Name on desk or door
- Private office
- Status symbols such as business cards
- Merit pay increase
- Promotion or increased responsibility
- Flextime or choice of schedule
- Choice of assignment
- More training
- Approval of requests to attend seminars, workshops, or professional meetings
- Access to special places or people
- Opportunity to get more experience
- Praise
- Listening and asking for opinions

Exhibit 10-4 Rewards for Team Effort

- Special uniform, arm patches, or pins
- Parties, picnics, or cookouts
- Improved station furnishings
- New equipment, lounge, meeting room, or library
- Background music
- Better communication systems (intercom, computer, bulletin board, newsletter)
- Improved supply and inventory systems
- Meetings with guest speakers or audiovisual presentations
- More group training
- Merit pay for the group
- More responsibility (e.g., work and vacation scheduling; selection of new employees, vendors, or equipment; planning; and decision making)
- More access to information
- Reports forwarded to higher authorities

---

cross-functional activity, put aside old prejudices and stereotypes. Overlook previous areas of friction or irritation.

If you are new to the organization, get as much information as you can about the history, reputation, culture, and rituals of your new employer.

Check into the leadership style of the previous group leader. How had the group members responded? How effective was it? You can learn about this from your new boss and from interviews with team members.

Hold group meetings to discuss mission, strategy, plans, your leadership style, and your previous experience. Study the position descriptions and performance reviews of each employee, and hold individual meetings with team members. Find out as much as you can about their aspirations, complaints, and suggestions and about how you can make better use of their services. Prepare a skills inventory chart.

NOTES

1. R.S. Wellins, et al., *Empowered Teams: Creating Self-Directed Work Groups That Improve Quality, Productivity, and Participation* (San Francisco: Jossey-Bass, 1991).

2. J. Gilbert, Partnership: A new paradigm for health care, *Hospitals* 64 (1990): 72.

3. R.F. Littlejohn, *Crisis Management: A Team Approach* (New York: AMACOM, 1983).

4. B. Harper and A. Harper, *Succeeding as a Self-Directed Work Team: 20 Important Questions Answered* (Mohegan Lake, N.Y.: MW Corporation, 1992).

5. E.A. Kazemek, Ten criteria for effective team building, *Healthcare Financial Management* 45 (1991): 15.

6. L.R. Bittel, *What Every Supervisor Should Know,* 5th ed. (New York: McGraw-Hill, 1985).

7. P.P. Fay and A.G.K. Doyle, *Stages of Group Development. 1982 Annual for Facilitators, Trainers and Consultants* (New York: University Associates, 1982).

8. Fay and Doyle, *Stages of Group Development,* xx.

9. B.A. Fisher, *Small Group Decision Making,* 2d ed. (New York: McGraw-Hill, 1980), 165.

10. Fisher, *Small Group Decision Making,* 185.

11. Keye Productivity Center, *How To Build a Better Work Team,* 2d ed. (Kansas City, Mo.: Keye Productivity Center, 1991), 3.

12. M.M. Broadwell and R.S. House, *Supervising Technical and Professional People* (New York: Wiley, 1986).

13. W.J. Doyle and P.I. Doyle, *Gain Management: A Process for Building Teamwork, Productivity and Profitability Throughout Your Organization* (New York: AMACOM, 1992).

14. M. Blanchard and M.J. Tager, *Working Well: Managing for Health and High Performance* (New York: Simon & Schuster, 1985).

Chapter 11

Delegation and Empowerment

- why managers fail to delegate
- factors affecting willingness to delegate
- problems with delegation
- dumping
- upward (reverse) delegation
- hopscotch delegation
- selecting what and what not to delegate
- picking delegates, and getting their acceptance
- how to implement the delegative process
- when delegation falters
- horizontal delegation
- powerlessness and empowerment
- kinds of power
- the empowering process
- roles of executive staff and supervisors
- benefits and risks of empowerment
- reluctance to give or receive power

"After new supervisors settle in, the first test of leadership may center on how they delegate."[1(p.94)]

If we define supervision as getting things done through other people, then supervision is largely the process of delegation. If we did not delegate, we would have to do everything ourselves. It comes as no surprise, then, that the failure to delegate is often cited as one of the most frequent reasons why supervisors fail.[2]

WHY MANAGERS FAIL TO DELEGATE

- They are workaholics or perfectionists.
- They are insecure because:
  1. they are afraid that the delegate will fail

93

2. they are afraid that the delegate will do it better than they do

3. they are afraid that they will be accused of dumping

- They do not like to turn over what they enjoy doing.
- They do not think their staff are ready or willing.
- They have had unpleasant previous experiences with delegation.
- They don't know how to go about it.

Reluctant managers say things such as "I don't have the time," "Do you know what happened the last time I tried that?", "If you want it done right, do it yourself," "I can do it faster and better," or "When I try to delegate, they say it's not in their position description, or they ask what's in it for them."

The willingness of delegates is determined by the following:

- whether they think they are qualified
- whether previous efforts have succeeded or failed
- what their teammates may say or think
- whether they think they have the time
- whether they like what is delegated or see some reward in it
- whether they think they will have enough authority
- how much confidence they have that the delegator will support them
- whether they think they are being manipulated or dumped on

PROBLEMS WITH DELEGATION

Delegation is a two-edged sword. It can be the key to increased productivity, time management, and motivation, or it can be a wet blanket that squelches initiative and lowers morale.

Dumping

Dumping is when you load people with repetitive, mundane work that has little value to the organization or to the employees' growth.[3] Because dumping is often done on the spur of the moment, the recipient feels like an errand runner.

The bottom line is resentment on the part of the person selected. The perception of being dumped upon is just that: a perception. One person's meat is another person's poison. Delegation is likely to be perceived as dumping when delegates have a poor relationship with their bosses, when they have been dumped on in the past, when they know that others have refused to do the same task, when they fail to see any personal advantage in carrying out the assignment, when they have not been told that occasionally they will be asked to do things that are not in their position descriptions, and when they see the delegator wasting time while the delegates are doing all the work.

If you have good rapport with a subordinate and rarely take advantage of your authority, the subordinate will not mind some dumped work.[4] When a task is being discussed with one employee and another employee asks "How come she never asks me?", that is delegation. When an employee says "How come she always asks me?", that is probably dumping.

Upward (Reverse) Delegation

Upward delegation is the art of passing along to superiors what employees do not want to do. They are often successful because their bosses just cannot say no. Managers who seldom delegate are especially susceptible to upward delegation. As Drucker and Flower write[5:(p.52)]:

> Every subordinate is good at delegating upstairs. It's hard to resist because it's very flattering. They imply "You know so much better than I do, how to do my job" . . . and you do. You must learn to say "no."

Reverse delegation often follows attempts by a manager to delegate. The delegate reluctantly accepts a task, and then at the first obstacle he or she throws up his or her hands and tries to pass the buck back to the manager, who then becomes the reluctant delegate.

Sometimes upward delegation is necessary. For example, a person may be so overloaded with delegated assignments that he or she cannot get routine work finished. It is then up to the delegator to take back some of the work, to establish priorities, or to permit the delegate to transfer work to another person.

Hopscotch Delegation

Hopscotch delegation is when your boss bypasses you and gives assignments directly to your subordinates. To correct this, it helps to have good rapport with your superior. If you confront your superior when he or she is in a belligerent mood, you may get something such as "Well, you're never around when something has to be done." If this shunting of authority only happens infrequently or under special circumstances, it is probably best to ignore it.

When you feel that a confrontation is necessary, take a positive approach by downplaying the issue of authority and focusing on the advantages of your knowing what the boss wants done and on how your staff get confused and frustrated when they get conflicting or multiple orders.

If you cannot get action through your boss, or if you want to avoid a confrontation, try acting through your staff. Instruct them to hold up action on nonurgent orders from other people until they have checked with you. Another strategy is to have your associates politely ask your boss to make the request directly to you because they are working on a priority item of yours.

Inept Delegation

Failure to delegate authority or instructions results in the delegate constantly running into the delegator's office with problems.

HOW TO DELEGATE

Four Simple Ways To Pick What To Delegate

1. As you go about your daily routine, just before you tackle a task ask yourself whether this is something that someone else could do.
2. When you return from a vacation, list your duties that subordinates took care of while you were away. Some of these temporary assignments could become permanent.
3. At performance reviews, when you discuss future career plans for your associates ask them whether they would like to take over any of your responsibilities.
4. Select tasks from those listed in your position description (see below).

How To Delegate Using Your Position Description

1. List ten or more of your tasks, excluding any that may not or should not be delegated.
2. Indicate which of these could be assumed by someone else right now and which could be taught to a member of your team.
3. Prioritize each task according to:
   - how much time you would save by delegating the task
   - how significantly it would benefit or be acceptable to the delegate
   - the degree of difficulty (usually you should start with simple tasks, ones that relate directly to the delegate's current assignments,[6] or ones that are segments of a complex task)

What May Not Be Delegated

- *Accountability:* Delegators are still accountable to higher authorities for work that has been transferred.
- *Powers other than authority:* Only formal power, or authority, can be delegated (see Exhibit 11–1)
- *Functions forbidden by law, regulation, or policy* (licensure, certification, special training, qualification, or education is required for some duties)

What Should Not Be Delegated or Is Done with Caution

- sensitive or high-leverage activities dealing with people:
  - —interviewing, selecting, and orienting new employees
  - —approving new hires
  - —coaching, counseling, and disciplining
  - —evaluating employee performance
  - —recommending for promotion, special awards, or merit pay
  - —resolving personal conflicts, complaints, or grievances
- activities that involve too great a career risk for the delegator or the delegate
- activities that are perceived as dumping by the delegate
- special administrative responsibilities:
  - —formulation of mission statements, goals, objectives, strategies, and plans
  - —making, publicizing, explaining, and enforcing policies
  - —presiding over important meetings
  - —preparing or approving budgets and reviewing fiscal variances
- tasks assigned by your superiors to be done by you personally
- some functions that provide you with lots of pleasure

Exhibit 11-1 Kinds of Power

Authority—Delegated power: "You all now report to me."
Competency—Expertise: "See Louise, she's the specialist."
Knowledge—Information: "Ask Joe, he's on the committee."
Physical—Brute force: "If you want to stay healthy. . . ."
Connections—Whom they know: "His mother is on the board."
Fiscal—Who has the bucks: "He who gets grant money gets promoted."
Union—Selected by peers: "Nora will get action, she's the union rep."
Charisma—Persuasiveness: "He can talk you into anything."

Select the Delegates, and Get Their Acceptance

Select a delegate who has the necessary competence and willingness. The most qualified person for a particular assignment may not be the one who will benefit from it most, and often is not the most motivated person.[7]

Seek cooperation, not sullen compliance.[8] Consciously or unconsciously, delegates ask themselves, "What's in it for me?" If the answer is a negative one, the delegation is in trouble from the onset.

Be wary if you hear:

"Is that an order?"

"Do I have to?"

"That's not in my position description."

"Nobody told me I would have to do all that."

People are more willing to take risks if they know what is involved. Maybe in the past they took a small step, and Pandora's box opened. Tell them exactly what they are getting into, and give them possible outs.[9]

Start by telling them the following:

- why you have decided on the change
- why you picked them
- whether the change is voluntary
- what you expect
- what resources and authority are available
- what you are going to tell other stakeholders
- any modifications in their current assignments
- the check points and time table

When employees are reluctant because they do not think they have the time, agree to share some of the work, relieve them of other responsibilities, or promise to reverse the delegation with no loss of prestige to the delegate if time becomes a problem.

Employees also may be loath to accept responsibility and authority if it affects their peer relationships.

How To Implement the Delegative Process

- Select the right task and the right delegate.
- If this is a major change, get permission from your boss. Also discuss it with other stakeholders.

- Provide needed training, resources, and authority.
- Agree on a plan. Listen carefully to delegates' ideas about how to get it done.
- Set up check points. Pick these carefully. For example, if a large report is part of the task, have the delegate submit a preliminary rough draft to you before the final report is typed. Another advantage of establishing check points is that it gives you an opportunity to award some pats on the back.
- Monitor the progress of delegates.

Be patient and persuasive, not demanding. Avoid statements such as "Don't worry," "You should have . . . ," or "I wish you had. . . ." Help delegates when they get stuck and ask for help.

Every so often, stop by and ask how things are going, just as you do in your routine managing by walking around for the rest of your staff. Avoid constantly looking over delegates' shoulders or asking too many questions. Questions should reflect your interest in their approach rather than exhibit nervousness you may have about their ability to finish the job.

When Delegation Falters

Avoid the temptation to abandon ship when there are problems. Allowing people to make some mistakes is the best way to encourage meaningful growth.[10]

Although a delegator accepts responsibility for a failure, his or her confidence and trust in the delegate are not readily restored.[11]

When employees have done their best but failed, have them do a balance sheet for themselves. Ask them to identify what went well and what the shortcomings were. Always let them criticize themselves first.[12] Ask how you could have helped more, because when your delegate fails you too have failed.

Horizontal Delegation

The truly skilled delegator has the ability to delegate to people over whom he or she has no authority. These individuals may be colleagues or volunteers. Horizontal delegation increases in importance as health care institutions feature more cross-functional activities and make greater use of volunteers.

Success depends largely on factors such as persuasiveness, influence, interpersonal skills, rapport, degree of teamwork, past favors for the other person, the strength of one's network, available rewards (especially expressed appreciation), and past cooperation.

EMPOWERMENT

*"The wave of the future is empowerment of employ-
ees and maximization of their skills."[13(p.5)]*

Powerlessness

The issue of powerlessness of minorities has been addressed vigorously, whereas that of unprotected workers has largely been ignored. Unions focus primarily on reward systems and work environments, doing little to address the real power needs of their individual members.

When employees lack confidence in their ability or feel that external forces control them, their self-esteem plummets, and they feel powerless. Powerlessness reinforces feelings of low self-esteem and lack of control over one's work life. It is feeling like a puppet, with many people or other forces pulling the strings.

The need to empower people becomes critical when subordinates are overwhelmed by perceptions of powerlessness or lack of control over their daily work routines. The feeling of lack of control increases susceptibility to stress and burnout.

When powerlessness results in a victim mindset, the victims seek sympathy rather than power, and they divorce themselves from work-related responsibilities.

Those who suffer from a pervasive feeling of powerlessness are poor risk takers and often chronic complainers, pessimists, or negativists. Powerless people sometimes do not get angry, they get even. They slow things down and engage in subtle sabotage.[14]

What Is Empowerment?

Empowerment is a process of enhancing feelings of self-efficacy by removing conditions that foster powerlessness.[15] Bardwick notes that "empowerment means giving everyone—instead of just people with certain positions or certain job titles— the legitimate right to make judgments, form conclusions, reach decisions, and then act."[16(p.122)] Bardwick's comment also helps differentiate empowerment and delegation. Both involve the transfer of authority. Delegation, however, is a selective process and usually involves a limited number of employees. Empowerment is part of an organizational culture. Real empowerment means shifting power down the hierarchy to every employee who is willing to grab a handful ("Power to the people").

To empower is to move from autocracy and dependency to participative management. To feel empowered, one must feel competent and in control. Empowerment is not just the transfer of authority; it is also the removal of real and perceived feelings of powerlessness.

Exhibit 11–1 lists eight kinds of power. Management's capacity to empower employees is limited to the first three on that list: authority, competency, and knowledge.

When we hear "It's all politics around here" or "What do you expect in this bureaucratic organization," we are hearing statements that suggest lack of empowerment and convey feelings of powerlessness.

THE EMPOWERING PROCESS

Although empowerment requires the mindset of self-efficacy, this mental status cannot be acquired simply by employees listening to motivational speeches or reading inspirational messages about positive thinking. Neither can it be learned at seminars. It requires organizational changes that remove real and perceived feelings of powerlessness.[17]

Empowering requires the sharing of responsibility, authority, information, knowledge, skills, and decision making. Employees' self-esteem and feelings regarding their personal efficacy are strengthened when they know that:

- they are technically or professionally competent
- their performance is as good as or better than that of their colleagues
- they will receive positive feedback from superiors and associates

The Executive Component

Top management is responsible for strategies and actions to reduce powerlessness. These activities include the following:

- Remove layers of management to force individuals in the lower echelons to assume more responsibility and to be given more authority.
- Eliminate bureaucratic factors such as restrictive policies, rules, and procedures.
- Involve employees and employee groups in planning and implementing change.
- Provide the necessary facilities, equipment, and supplies.
- Encourage and reward innovation and entrepreneurship.
- Assign job titles that add to prestige and self-esteem.
- Provide education and training to enable employees to increase their self-efficacy and to assume more power.

The Supervisory Component

- Clarify jobs and performance expectations.
- Encourage employees to solve their own problems and to become more self-reliant.
- Assign them progressively more difficult tasks, starting with ones that ensure success.
- Encourage assertiveness. Provide training in that skill if necessary.
- Delegate as much as possible.
- Make employees responsible for complete, not fragmented, tasks.
- Change your role of manager to that of coach, teacher, supporter, resource person, and facilitator.
- Let employees fail forward (i.e., turn failures into learning opportunities).
- Provide the help employees need, but not more than that.
- Be the team cheerleader.
- Ask employees for advice, and take it.
- Reinforce the behavior you want through praise and recognition.
- Train, train, train.

The Benefits of Empowerment

Empowered organizations give employees the skills and authority they need to make decisions and solve problems. The rationale is that employees, being closer to the customer, can spot problems better and correct situations quicker when they have the authority to do so.

Empowerment can increase motivation, productivity, and quality. Teamwork and customer service are enhanced; full use is made of employees' expertise and potential. Leaders can mobilize stronger forces when responding to change and challenges.

Employees benefit, too. They enjoy their work more and take greater pride in their accomplishments. They correctly feel that they have more control over their work. This perception makes them more stress resistant and more willing to take career risks and to offer suggestions.

Not all companies have experienced success with the empowerment approach. Failures are more common than reported; employers do not like to broadcast their disasters.

The Risks of Empowerment

Empowerment does involve risks. Whenever there is a transfer of authority, there is risk. Some empowered employees erupt with streams of worthless ideas, and some do silly things. Managers must accept these and chalk them up to learning experiences.

Empowerment may also lead to overconfidence and misjudgment. Some empowered individuals abuse their prerogatives or have difficulty defining the limits of their authority; these are the loose cannons.

Not everyone wants to be empowered. Because there is always some risk involved, some subordinates shun the increased responsibility incurred. It is difficult to empower nonassertive introverts or people who cannot accept any guilt. Blame avoidance is also characteristic of the bureaucratic or victim mindset.

Employees who have seen leadership waves come and go are inclined to regard empowerment as just another transient management fad. They do not want to put a lot of energy into the change, only to watch it be replaced quickly by another gimmick while their new power flows back upstairs. Alternatively, their past experience leads them to believe that the change will not be handled effectively and that they will only end up with additional unrewarding work.

Reluctance To Empower

Many employers and managers do not want empowered workers. Their reasons are similar to those that managers have for not delegating, as noted earlier in this chapter. Some managers will come right out and admit that they feel that they have worked hard to earn the power they have and that they are reluctant to give up any part of it. In fact, some institutions find it necessary to replace managers who are unwilling or unable to make the necessary adjustments.

NOTES

1. H.M. Engel, *How To Delegate* (Houston: Gulf, 1983), 94.
2. W. Umiker, Five pitfalls of delegation for new supervisors, *Medical Laboratory Observer* 22 (1990): 31–33.
3. W.B. Werther, Jr., *Dear Boss* (New York: Meadowbrook, 1989), 162.
4. Werther, *Dear Boss,* 162.
5. P. Drucker and J. Flower, Being effective, *Healthcare Forum Journal* 34 (1991): 52.
6. Engel, *How To Delegate,* 152.
7. M. Yate, *Keeping the Best* (Holbrook, Mass.: Bob Adams, 1991).
8. Engel, *How To Delegate,* 99.
9. T. Kirby, *The Can-Do Manager* (New York: AMACOM, 1989).
10. Yate, *Keeping the Best,* 200.
11. Engel, *How To Delegate,* 37.
12. Kirby, *The Can-Do Manager,* 43.

104   MANAGEMENT SKILLS FOR THE NEW HEALTH CARE SUPERVISOR

13. Kirby, *The Can-Do Manager,* 5.
14. R.M. Kanter, *The Change Masters* (New York: Simon & Schuster, 1983).
15. J.A. Conger and R.N. Kanungo, The empowerment process: Integrating theory and practice, *Academy of Management Review* 13 (1988): 471–482.
16. J. Bardwick, *Danger in the Comfort Zone* (New York: AMACOM, 1991), 122.
17. P. Kizilos, Crazy about empowerment? *Training* 27 (1992): 47–56.

Part IV
Controlling

Chapter 12

Leaders and Managers

- responsibilities of leaders
- organizational culture
- managers versus leaders
- basic leadership styles
- special leadership strategies
- contemporary leadership activities
- characteristics of effective leaders
- six principles of leadership ethics
- tips for better leadership

Always remember that if you are a full-time manager you are rewarded for what your employees do, not for what you do.

Leaders and managers provide mission statements (why we are here), visions (where we are going), goals (how we will know when we have arrived), strategies (the journey of getting there), and a set of values (how we behave on the way).

Leaders must be walking mission statements who make their visions come alive by communicating them with enthusiasm and conviction. More important, they must express them in attitudes and action more than in words.

Leadership is not learned in seminars. It is either intuitive or gained through experience. The best leaders strive to develop the leadership skills of their team-mates so that the team's success does not depend on one person. Many organizations have failed because charismatic leaders failed to do this, and when they were no longer around, their back-ups were unable to cope.

Leaders must have the ability to motivate people over whom they have no authority. This is called horizontal management and is the mark of a true leader. To meet today's interdepartmental needs for coordination and cooperation, health care managers must possess leadership ability.

ORGANIZATIONAL CULTURE

Leaders shape the culture of their organizations. Organizational culture can be defined as "a pattern of basic assumptions that has worked well enough to be considered valid and to be taught to new members as the correct way to perceive, think and feel in relation to coping with problems."[1(p.109)] In other words, culture is simply the perception of the way things are done at work.

Today's health care culture demands pervasive and honest communication, that is, openness and authentic interaction in all operations. This translates into the sharing of knowledge, skills, news, experiences, problems, and setbacks. The result is learning at all levels.

To foster a service-oriented culture, supervisors communicate the values that represent spin-offs from the mission statement. They start putting values into action by treating employees as they want their customers to be treated. They get personally involved in service activities, often using periodic meetings of work groups to inspire and to solve problems.[2]

Leadership style plays an important role in a culture: "A culture in which the manager's leadership style features coercion and other direct power plays is less effective than those characterized by collaboration and participation."[3(p.44)]

LEADERS VERSUS MANAGERS

The United States has an oversupply of good managers but a severe shortage of good leaders. Business schools develop managers, not leaders. Here are some differences between leaders and managers:

- People obey managers because they must, people follow leaders because they want to.
- Leaders envision (Martin Luther King's "I have a dream"); managers marshal the resources to achieve visions.
- Leaders rely largely on intuition; managers rely on computer printouts, objectivity, and rationality.
- Managers stress conformity; leaders encourage creativity.
- Managers strive to satisfy the needs and wants of their customers; leaders astonish customers with new products or services.
- Leaders have more confidence and are more willing to take risks than managers.
- After leaders have reached goals, managers often take over.
- Managers' goals usually arise from necessity rather than desire.
- Managers are more like scientists; leaders are more like artists.
- Managers say, "I will support you"; leaders say, "Follow me."
- Managers are concerned with how; leaders are concerned with what.
- Managers control; leaders empower.
- Managers' proactivity is directed toward preventing problems; leaders' proactivity is directed toward entrepreneurship.

- Managers like big offices and desks; leaders seek new challenges.
- Managers find out how successful people do things; leaders explore new paths.
- Managers investigate better computer systems; leaders are interested in team building.

BASIC LEADERSHIP STYLES

Clusters of leadership characteristics have been identified as leadership styles. Like clothing styles, these fluctuate in popularity and vary according to the situation and the kinds of followers.

Authoritarian

> *Synonyms for this style are task oriented, telling, tight ship, theory X, top-down, paternalistic, autocratic, directive, and "I" management.*

Authoritarian leaders think people must be controlled closely and given external motivation (e.g., pay, benefits, and working conditions). They are task oriented rather than employee oriented. They tell subordinates what they want, but not why. They do not invite input from their people. Autocratic leaders encourage dependency. Most employees who work for these leaders exhibit apathy or hostility.

A subset of the authoritarian style is the paternalistic approach. Paternalistic managers exhibit either the features of a kind, nurturing parent or those of a critical, oppressive parent (benevolent dictator or tyrant). A paternalistic approach may be appropriate when one is dealing with:

- emergency situations (e.g., fire or disaster)
- inexperienced or insecure employees
- aggressive, hostile subordinates
- challenges to authority

Participative

> *Synonyms for this style include people oriented, theory Y, bottom-up, happy ship, and "we" management.*

Participative leaders believe that people want to work and assume responsibility. In addition, they believe that, if treated properly, people can be trusted and will put out their best effort. Such leaders motivate by means of internal factors (e.g., task satisfaction, self-esteem, recognition, and praise). They explain why things must be done, listen to what employees have to say, and respect their opinions. They are good delegators.

There are several subsets of this style. When in the consultative mode, leaders seek input from their followers before making important decisions. When in the delegative mode, leaders share responsibility with their colleagues.

One simple way to determine whether participative management is in place is to find out the average number of suggestions each employee makes annually. In many Japanese companies, where participative management flourishes, each employee submits dozens of ideas each year. Equally important is how many of the suggestions are acted on by management.

Participative managers know two magic phrases: "What do you think?" and "I need your help."

Theory Z

Unrelated to theory X and theory Y, theory Z was named Z to distinguish it from A (authoritarian). Adapted by the Japanese, theory Z is characterized by employee participation and egalitarianism. It features guaranteed employment, maximum employee input, and quality circles.

Bureaucratic

Synonyms for this style are rules oriented, by the book, and "they" management.

These managers act as monitors or police, enforcing policies, rules, procedures, and orders from upper management. These buck-passers take little or no responsibility for directives. Real leadership is incompatible with bureaucracy.

Bureaucrats play negative, self-serving political games. They advance in stable or static organizations by not making mistakes, minimizing risk taking, and blaming others. Government agencies and military services are loaded with these people.

A bureaucratic approach may be suitable for operations in which tasks must be performed in exactly the same way at all times (e.g., sorting mail or typing reports).

Situational

Synonyms for this style include contingency based, flexible, adaptive, and different strokes for different folks management.

Flexible leaders adapt their style to specific situations and to specific needs of different members of their team. As employees gain experience and confidence, leadership style changes from highly directive to supportive (task related to people related).

A practical guideline is to use a consultative or delegative style in areas of expertise and to provide direction in areas of weakness. Some managers, in an effort always to be participative, fail to be directive when direction is needed.

For example, two new employees may start work on the same date. If one has had previous experience and the other has had none, different styles are needed. A show-and-tell approach is needed by the latter employee but may not be appropriate for the former.

Laissez Faire

Synonyms include hands off, catch 22, fence-rider, absent, and "not me" management.

These managers avoid giving orders, solving problems, or making decisions. They are evasive physically and verbally, often being masters of double talk.

A positive form of laissez faire leadership is the democratic style. Now very popular, it features self-directed (autonomous) teams in which leadership is delegated to specially trained work groups. The members of these teams know more about the organization and are better trained, more motivated, and more productive. They solve problems, redesign work processes, set standards and goals, select and monitor new employees, and evaluate team and individual performance.

SPECIAL LEADERSHIP STRATEGIES

Manipulation

Manipulators get people to do their bidding by intimidating, engaging in emotional scenes (anger, tears, yelling, or seeking sympathy), making people feel guilty, or implying that they are owed something for favors rendered.

Manipulators are name-droppers. They also constantly say things that they do not mean, such as "I have confidence in you," "I don't want to upset you, but . . . ," or "We need to study that more."

Management by Crisis

You can always spot these people. Every day is a series of major or minor crises for them. They complain that they cannot get things done because they are too busy putting out fires. They react rather than anticipate. They solve problems instead of preventing them. They are surrounded by noise, confusion, and emotional upheavals.

Management by Exception

These leaders act as facilitators, supporters, and resource people. Their message is, "I don't interfere. Come to me with problems you can't solve or when I can help in some way. And please keep me informed."

Management by exception is appropriate for certain categories of professionals.

Management by Objectives

Although this approach has lost much of its popularity, some of its basic features remain useful. For example, when you are sitting down with employees at perform-ance appraisal time, focusing on the future can be done best by discussing future performance and educational objectives.

Management by Wandering Around

This important strategy is discussed in the next chapter.

CONTEMPORARY LEADERSHIP ACTIVITIES

Today's leaders are concerned with employee stress control. They are flocking to seminars about how to preserve the fragile self-esteem of their employees and how to replace victim mindsets with feelings of being in control of work and life. They keep tickler files of their employees' birthdays and the names of spouses and children. They provide each employee with a set of business cards.

Contemporary leaders are deeply involved in the following activities:

- team building and group problem solving
- cross-training
- empowering
- improved quality and customer service
- cost cutting
- managing change (new services, products, or facilities)
- staff reductions or shuffling

- decentralizing or establishing satellite activities
- worker safety and health
- environmental preservation
- patient home care
- point of care (e.g., expanded bedside services)

CHARACTERISTICS OF EFFECTIVE LEADERS

They are competent:

- People look up to them and respect their expertise.
- Their opinions and advice are sought after by associates within and outside their departments.
- They are asked to serve on important committees.
- They constantly improve their professional and leadership capabilities.

They are emotionally stable:

- They have a relaxed leadership style.
- They are cool and calm most of the time.
- They handle stress well.
- When they get upset with people, they focus on behavior, not on personalities or traits.

They get the job done:

- They expect and demand good performance.
- They are well organized and always seem prepared.
- They are proactive. They anticipate and prepare for change.
- They focus on important things. They do not nitpick.
- They match people with the right jobs.
- They do not waste their time or that of their followers.
- They stimulate innovativeness and invite ideas.

They are good communicators:

- They use memos, meetings, and other communication channels effectively.
- They give clear instructions and get feedback to make sure that their directions are understood.
- They are articulate and persuasive, but they do not manipulate.
- They are excellent listeners and are easy to talk to.

- They share information, but not gossip.
- They do not withhold bad news.
- They are good teachers.
- They praise in public and criticize in private.
- They acknowledge their own mistakes.
- They always seem to know what is going on.

They develop committed followers:

- They care about their followers and show it.
- They go to bat for their people.
- They empower and encourage autonomy and self-reliance.
- They get their people whatever they need to get the job done.
- They permit much freedom in how people do their work, but they insist on good results.
- They do not play favorites.
- They are just as attentive to people below them as to those above them in the organization.
- They invite and respect the opinions and suggestions of all their employees.
- They provide opportunities for employees to use newly learned skills or previously untapped skills.

They are unafraid:

- They thrive on responsibility.
- They take risks and bend rules.
- They are innovative and flexible.
- They chalk up failures to experience.

They are credible:

- They almost always tell the truth.
- They carry out their promises and commitments.
- They admit their mistakes.
- They do not take credit for the ideas of others.

SIX PRINCIPLES OF LEADERSHIP ETHICS

1. Use your mission statement and values when making ethical decisions.
2. Use the same standards of behavior for every employee, and follow them yourself.

3. Set your standards above those required by law.
4. Show the same consideration for employees as you do for your external customers.
5. Balance high tech with high touch.
6. Do not let the profit motive drive your strategy.

TIPS FOR BETTER LEADERSHIP

Remember the self-fulfilling prophesy. The self-fulfilling prophesy holds that strong expectations often lead to fulfillment of those expectations. If you expect your employees, including the underperformers, to perform well and you back up these expectations with conviction, these people will usually do better work.

These convictions, bolstered by praise, appreciation, respect, escalating delegation, and monetary rewards, do wonders for employees' feelings of self-worth, and they make vigorous efforts to live up to your expectations.

TIPS

* When you goof, take responsibility, correct the mistake, explain briefly what happened, and move on.
* Express feelings and frustrations without defensiveness and without inducing defensiveness.
* Increase your ratio of praise to criticism.
* Show that you care about others and accept them.
* Do not expect perfection of yourself or others.

NOTES

1. E. Schein, Organizational culture, *American Psychologist* 45 (1990): 109.
2. W.H. Davidow and B. Uttal, *Total Customer Service: The Ultimate Weapon* (New York: Harper & Row, 1989).
3. J.A. Young and B. Smith, Organizational change and the HR professional, *Personnel* 65 (1988): 44.

Chapter 13

Coaching and Mentoring

- definition and objectives of coaching
- an employees' bill of rights
- poor performance and the coaching process
- coaching starts during the orientation process
- management by wandering around
- enhance employee self-sufficiency
- completed staff work
- defend, facilitate, empower, and support
- positive and negative feedback
- how to praise and criticize
- mentoring
- mentors and mentees
- sponsors

COACHING

Coaching, a supervisor's most important function, is face-to-face, day-to-day leadership. When subordinates perform well, coaches provide reinforcement. When deficiencies are noted, coaches search for the cause and take appropriate action.

Good coaches are dedicated, enthusiastic leaders who are technically or professionally competent. They push or pull people to their level of capability, but not to a level of discouragement.

OBJECTIVES OF COACHING

The immediate objective of coaching is to get the daily work finished on schedule and to ensure its quality. Intermediate targets are building better teams, cross-training, empowering, delegating, and improving systems, techniques, and procedures. Long range objectives include employee career development and preparing people to handle key areas of responsibility.[1] Objectives directly related to individual team members include:

- to improve performance
- to help employees reach their full potential (self-actualization)
- to express confidence, to reassure, and to support
- to develop skills and expertise
- to help employees get their work done faster and better

Coaching goes far beyond the activities of instruction. Coaches deal not only with task performance but with attitudes, morale, discipline, ethics, and career development. Good coaches possess the ability to get average people to do superior work.

The effective coach functions as an instructor, facilitator, supporter, cheerleader, counselor, disciplinarian, evaluator, consultant, resource person, coordinator, problem solver, and troubleshooter. He or she shapes values, removes obstacles, builds on employees' strengths, stretches their skills, and builds personal relationships.

These coaches are almost always good storytellers.[2] They spin interesting yarns about work-related situations in which there are heros and heroines.

The conscientious coach honors an unwritten bill of rights that includes the following:

- fair and equal treatment
- basic dignity and respect
- preservation and enhancement of self-esteem
- performance feedback
- input into decisions that relate to employees' work
- collaboration in setting work goals and standards
- opportunity to develop skills to meet new challenges
- bidirectional (vertical and horizontal) communication

POOR PERFORMANCE AND THE COACHING PROCESS

The Principal Reasons for Poor Performance

- Employees do not know what is expected of them (coaches tell them).
- Employees do not know how to do what is expected (coaches show them).
- Employees do not know that their performance is poor (coaches inform them).
- Employees could do better if they tried harder (coaches motivate them).
- Employees face obstacles that prevent good performance (coaches remove the obstacles).

- Employees get discouraged (coaches support and encourage them).
- Employees feel that their work goes unnoticed or unappreciated (coaches lead the cheers).

COACHING STARTS WITH EMPLOYMENT

The initial phase of coaching consists largely of orienting and providing on-the-job training (see Chapter 9).

Do not abandon new employees after they have completed their indoctrination. Too often they are thrown into the work pool to sink or swim.

MANAGEMENT BY WANDERING AROUND

One of Tom Peters' major contributions is his concept of management by wandering around (MBWA). The wandering he espouses includes frequent contacts with people outside one's department, such as customers and suppliers, but we will limit our discussion to work site wandering.

Peters recommends that managers augment their open-door policy by getting out of their offices and into the action arena, where the customer interaction is taking place. Here are some principles of MBWA offered by Peters and Austin.[3]

- MBWA is meeting people in their offices or work areas rather than in yours.
- MBWA is not rambling around smiling and waving or saying "How are you doing?"
- MBWA is not being a nitpicker, work interrupter, or gossip monger.
- MBWA is listening more than telling.
- MBWA is asking whether employees have any problems and how you can help.
- MBWA is asking for advice and opinions.
- MBWA is catching people doing something right, not catching them doing something wrong.
- MBWA is carrying a little black book to write down employee suggestions for improving customer service and to note meritorious performance.
- MBWA is calling employees by their names and asking about their families or special interests.
- MBWA, when successful, results in a lot fewer memos.

Note that MBWA can backfire if the wanderers are perceived by their staffs as inspectors, critics, or interrupters. Like all management strategies, it has to be done right.

ENHANCE EMPLOYEE SELF-SUFFICIENCY

Go easy on advising or overdoing the helping hand bit. For example, a laboratory technician may be having a problem with an automated instrument. The technician, instead of watching how the supervisor makes the necessary adjustment, skips off for coffee.

Do not let employees transfer all their little problems to you. New supervisors must learn when and when not to solve other people's problems. You do not want to be a Teflon manager and slough off all the cries for help, but on the other hand you do not want to be a Velcro manager and let all the problems of other people stick to you.

Insist on completed staff work. This military term simply means that, when employees come to you with a problem, they must also have one or more suggestions for solving the problem. Once they become aware of this expectation, they will bring you fewer problems, and you will be assisted in making a decision by the suggestions that accompany those that they do bring.

Do not overdo advising. Try asking first. When someone wants an opinion, respond with "What do you think?" instead of "Here's what I would do."

Encourage people to take small risks. When they make bad decisions (we all do!) or fail to pick the best solution, do not punish their mistakes. Regard them as learning experiences. Do not tolerate repeats of the same mistake.

Insist that they do what they say they will. Ask for definite commitments, set deadlines, and, when appropriate, get them in writing.

Regard all subordinates as winners or potential winners, never as losers. Remember the self-fulfilling prophesy theory mentioned in the last chapter.

DEFEND, FACILITATE, EMPOWER, AND SUPPORT

Employees of effective leaders see their coaches as defenders who protect them from outside harassment. A major source of frustration is to be attacked by people against whom one is powerless. Coaches are the defenders against such hostility. Baseball managers know the importance of this. To prevent their players from getting thrown out of the game, they rush out on the field and protest an umpire's call, even when they know that the call was correct.

Coaches are facilitators who get their team the personnel, time, and other resources needed to function effectively. At times, supervisors must go on the warpath with suppliers or people in other departments and demand that some action be taken.

Coaches empower their staffs and strip away red tape to enable them to make decisions and solve customer or operational problems. Just being able and authorized to answer customers' questions is appreciated by frontline employees.

Coaches should not be adverse to rolling up their sleeves and pitching in to help once in a while. Support also involves providing user-friendly policies, instruments, and procedures and showing respect, fairness, and trust. It is giving a lot as well as expecting a lot. It is being available and visible. It is ensuring employee safety and wellness and fighting for their rights, benefits, and rewards.

POSITIVE AND NEGATIVE FEEDBACK

According to the contingency theory of reinforcement, behavior that is reinforced by positive consequences tends to improve. That which begets negative consequences or is ignored tends to decrease. We violate this every time we overload our reliable performers and reduce the workload of our goof-offs. We neglect this theory when we fail to give positive and negative feedback.

Not to give deserved praise is to overlook one of our most powerful motivators. A simple comment, such as "I knew you could do a bang-up job on that important project—and I was right," makes even an experienced veteran happy and proud.

To give undeserved praise consistently is to reduce the power of positive feedback and to make the recipients feel that they are being manipulated.

What You Should Praise

- performance that is beyond the call of duty; the person:
    —works extra long hours
    —substitutes for an absent colleague
    —returns to work after hours
    —submits a report ahead of schedule or a rush report on time
    —reports a problem and suggests several good solutions
    —handles a ticklish situation diplomatically
    —earns accolades for his or her work unit
    —receives special awards, achieves an outstanding educational record, or earns an advanced degree
- performance that is not outstanding but is consistently good; the person:
    —can always be relied on

—has a good attendance record and is rarely late

—is flexible and willing to adjust to change

—consistently meets job standards and work objectives

- substandard performance that shows improvement even though it is not yet up to your expectations
- an innovative idea that is suggested

What always amazes me at seminars is when attendees say that they seldom praise because their people only do what they are supposed to do. These are the same people who complain about their low employee retention rate.

When Not To Praise

- when the praise is insincere or only represents flattery (how about at the last cocktail party?)
- when it is not earned
- when it would embarrass you, the recipient, or others
- before you are certain who earned the praise

Why Praise Should Not Be Delayed

- You may forget to deliver it.
- The recipient is more likely to think that it is not important.
- The recipient may be confused as to what behavior is being rewarded.

Why Praise Should Be Specific

- Recipients should know exactly what it was they did that was appreciated. Misunderstandings are prevented.
- The praise is more believable.
- You avoid giving the impression that you like everything they do.
- They know that you know what is going on.

Example: **Poor**—"You did a great job last night."
                Specific—"You deserve a lot of credit for getting that emotional parent to calm down last night."

How To Praise

We have already mentioned that praise should be delivered as soon as possible after the deed, that it should be specific, and that the right person or persons should get it. The famous one-minute praisings of Blanchard and Johnson[4] enhance praise by including comments about how the praiseworthy event made you, the coach, feel. These authors also advise you to pause a moment after delivering the praise (to emphasize its importance) and to shake hands or to touch the praised person in a way that shows your support.

Phraseology such as "Great job" or "Wow" is important, but voice tone, facial expression, and body language are even more important.

There are exceptions to the old rule praise in public, criticize in private. Some people are embarrassed when praised in front of their peers. They may be subjected to harassment from some co-workers, and you may be deemed guilty of showing favoritism. Praise these people privately or in writing.

Some supervisors write brief thank-you notes on Post-Its and stick them to the outside of people's doors. Those who have adopted this practice have observed that the recipients leave those notes on their doors for several days.

There are also exceptions to the second part of that old rule. There are times when criticism should be given in front of others. Glib chronic offenders may come out of your office after receiving a reprimand and boast to co-workers that they were in your office helping you out of a jam. Chewing out these people in public puts a quick stop to that practice.

There are also times when witnesses are needed. If you are being subjected to sexual harassment, for example, voicing your objections to the behavior in public is the intelligent thing to do.

A thank-you note or memo with copies to the personnel department and/or to upper management amplifies the effects of a verbal compliment. In selected instances, get your boss to send a congratulatory note to the person or to make a special visit to your unit to thank that person personally.

Consider submitting a report to the editor of your organization's newsletter or local newspaper. Put a notice on the bulletin board.

How People React to Negative Feedback

None of us likes to receive criticism—constructive or not—because it attacks our self-esteem. How we react depends on who is delivering it, how legitimate it is, who else hears it, how fragile our sense of self-worth is, and what our stress level happens to be at the moment.

People may react defensively, counterattack, flee, or become emotional. They may look for shortcomings in the critic or weakness in the charge, or they may reluctantly accept the reprimand and promise to improve. They may try to blame others or strive to change the subject.

How To Criticize while Preserving the Employee's Self-Esteem

When supervisors find mistakes, they usually respond in one of four ways.[5] (1) They ignore the situation and hope that someone else will correct it or that the subordinate will do it on his or her own. (2) They call the subordinate's attention to the mistake and ask him or her to correct it. (3) They use an indirect approach by asking how things are going, hoping that the employee will admit to making the error. If not, they then call attention to it. (4) They use the enhancing value or the sandwich technique.

The enhancing value technique starts with saying something nice about what the person does and then making specific suggestions for improvement. The basis for this approach is to make the person feel that you are there to help, not to judge or demean. The following is a good example: "Ruth, your report is always on time. I appreciate that. Now, let's try to eliminate all those typos, OK?"

If you follow the above scenario with another positive statement, such as "I know that I can rely on you to take care of this" or "You are too good an employee to make mistakes like this," you have used the sandwich technique: two slices of goodies with a reprimand in between.

A caveat: *Do not use either of these last two techniques if the only time you give out bits of praise is when they are followed by negative comments. If you do, these approaches will backfire.*

Tips for Giving Better Negative Feedback

- Maintain a high ratio of praise to criticism. Aim for a four-to-one ratio because it takes at least four positive strokes to neutralize one negative one.
- Attack behavior, not personality or traits. Instead of saying "You are too careless," describe what the person is doing or not doing that provoked your remark.
- Use "I," not "you," language. Instead of saying "You have a bad habit of . . . ," say "I get upset when people. . . ." This is less traumatic to one's ego and evokes less defensiveness.
- Avoid subjective terms such as *attitude, work ethic,* and *professionalism.* If you feel that you must use such words, make sure that you follow with specific behavioral descriptions or examples.

- Avoid absolute terms such as *always* or *never* (e.g., "You are always late for my meetings").
- Do not try to diagnose or read minds. When you say "The trouble with you is . . . ," you are diagnosing. When you say "You think that what you do is clever," you are trying to get into their heads.
- Know when you should be tentative (usually when you are not sure of what happened or who the guilty party is). For example: "I've been told that someone in your unit has been making very critical remarks in the dining room about upper management. Can you shed some light on this?"
- Other helpful phraseology includes "What concerns me," "I'm worried about," or "Perhaps we have a problem with. . . ."
- Always give the person a chance to respond without interruption.
- Avoid being overly critical or coming down too hard on your people. If you are, they will react by devising ways to keep their mistakes hidden from you rather than trying not to make the mistakes.

Coaching Pitfalls

- overdoing the practice of management by exception (see Chapter 12 on leadership)
- thinking that you must have all the answers
- neglecting people because you think that you do not have the time
- labeling workers as average, losers, underachievers, or people with attitude problems
- not permitting some loose reins in how things are accomplished
- paying too much attention to the bottom line and not enough to your employees
- overuse or unskillful use of criticism
- underuse, overuse, or abuse of praise
- giving too much unsolicited advice

MENTORING

Mentoring is when a more experienced or a more powerful person guides and nurtures a less experienced or a less powerful person. It has a paternalistic aspect.[6] It teaches mentees how to survive, thrive, and advance within an organization or a profession.

Mentoring may begin shortly after a new employee comes on board. New hires, during orientation, have an excellent opportunity to find a manager, senior team member, or trainer whom they would like to have as a mentor. In some organizations, each new hire is matched with a mentor through a formal program, but usually mentors and mentees just find each other.

THE MENTOR

The mentor is a person, usually older than his or her mentee (and certainly more experienced), who is willing to select an individual and shape that person's career by teaching, sponsoring, advising, coaching, counseling, hosting, guiding, motivating, critiquing, removing obstacles, helping create a career development strategy, or serving as a role model.

A mentor can be someone in the same department, someone in another department, a retiree, or an outsider. He or she may be a senior manager or an expert in the same field. An employee's immediate supervisor is not the ideal mentor because the mentee will be more reluctant to ask questions for fear of appearing ignorant or irritating the supervisor.

Mentors teach what textbooks and teachers cannot, namely how to be successful in that particular organization or profession. They may suggest ways to cut bureaucratic red tape or to avoid troublesome people, policies, or practices. They show how organizations function and how to recognize and use power. They point out the cultural sand traps and the rituals that must be followed. Mentors teach things such as who has the clout, how decisions are made, and why one should not leave work until the chief does.[7]

Mentors share visions of their protegees' future, perceive their potential, and challenge them when they are not living up to this potential. They note real and potential handicaps of their mentees and recommend ways to eliminate or reduce these.

Mentors regard mentees as extensions of themselves. The actions of their protegees reflect on their careers.[8] They provide affirmation and offer feedback in a fashion that promotes the mentee's feelings of self-worth and competence.[9]

Mentors take an active interest in the employee's readings, work, and continuing education program. Readily available for questions, they are open, authentic, and receptive.

THE MENTEE

Accepting someone as a mentor means accepting that he or she is dominant. Mentees must respect their mentors and show some deference. They may send them birthday cards or call them occasionally.[10]

Mentees must have a sincere desire to assimilate information and to reconceptualize ideas. When they fail to take the advice of their mentors, they should apologize or explain, not avoid the mentors.

MENTOR-MENTEE RELATIONSHIPS

The relationship is similar to physician-patient or attorney-client relationships. If there are sexual feelings, they must not be acted on. Most pairs are of the same sex.

Mentor and mentee struggle with feelings of wanting to be autonomous and yet connected at the same time. Altering the relationship may prove stressful for both parties.[11] The relationship may quickly or gradually end, or the mentor and mentee may become peers or permanent friends.

SPONSORING

A sponsor is someone who takes responsibility for someone else's expertise, acceptance, or advancement. Sponsorship is usually a one-time event, such as sponsoring an applicant for admission to a professional society or social club. It may involve serving as a reference for a job hunter or recommending an employee for promotion.

In the next chapter we will discuss motivation and how coaches reward good performance.

NOTES

1. D.L. Kirkpatrick, *How To Improve Performance through Appraisal and Coaching* (New York: AMACOM, 1982).
2. T. Peters and N. Austin, *A Passion for Excellence* (New York: Random House, 1985).
3. Peters and Austin, *A Passion for Excellence,* 9.
4. K. Blanchard and S. Johnson, *The One-Minute Manager* (New York: Berkley, 1982).
5. Kirkpatrick, *How To Improve Performance,* 83.
6. J.G. Liebler, et al., *Management Principles for Health Professionals,* 2d ed. (Gaithersburg, Md.: Aspen, 1992).
7. A.J. Bernstein and S.C. Rozen, *Dinosaur Brains* (New York: Wiley, 1989).
8. Bernstein and Rozen, *Dinosaur Brains,* 174.
9. Liebler, et al., *Management Principles,* 287.
10. Bernstein and Rozen, *Dinosaur Brains,* 177.
11. Liebler, et al., *Management Principles,* 287.

Chapter 14
Morale and Motivation

- morale versus motivation
- signs of morale problems
- major morale factors
- how employers can improve morale
- how supervisors can improve morale
- proactive motivational strategies
- reactive motivational strategies
- recognition modalities
- reward systems
- motivating the average worker

Employee surveys have shown a steady decline in job satisfaction during the 1970s and 1980s.[1] Maintaining job satisfaction is especially challenging during times of recession, downsizing, reorganizing, mergers, budget cutting, and financial difficulties.

MORALE VERSUS MOTIVATION

Morale is a state of mind that is based largely on the perceptions of workers toward their work, their employer, their colleagues, and their supervisors. Favorable perceptions spread; unfavorable perceptions spread faster.

Morale must be differentiated from motivation. Morale concerns job satisfaction. If morale is high, people do not quit, complain, or give you a bad time. Morale factors are the things that unions fight for: pay, benefits, job security, and work environment (quality of work life). These factors represent the lower three levels of Maslow's hierarchy of needs: physiological needs (food, clothing, and shelter), safety (insurance, permanent job, and pension), and social (acceptance by fellow workers).[2]

Unfortunately, high morale does not mean increased motivation. Keeping employees smiling and dancing in the corridors does not equate to increased performance. The latter requires motivation.

Motivation is a cognitive drive that benefits the motivated person's employer. It occurs when Maslow's two higher need levels are met: self-esteem (ego), and self-actualization (achieving one's full potential).[3]

127

The acronym **RAGWAR** helps one remember Herzberg's famous list of motivating factors:[4]

> **R** = Recognition
> **A** = Achievement
> **G** = Growth (career)
> **W** = Work itself
> **A** = Advancement
> **R** = Responsibility

Although high morale does not motivate, motivation cannot be achieved until morale deficiencies (Herzberg called these factors dissatisfiers or hygienes[5]) have been eliminated.

SIGNS OF MORALE PROBLEM

Severe morale problems are easy to spot, milder forms are more subtle. Detection of discontent in the early stage is as important as the early detection of cancer. The longer it is permitted to continue unabated, the more difficult it is to reverse.

Productivity declines. Apathetic or rebellious employees may work the minimum required to keep their jobs.

Employees complain about the amount of work, working conditions, parking, safety, pay and benefits, their employer and managers, and their assignments. They may voice these complaints in the presence of patients and other customers.

They become resistant to change, rarely volunteer, and seldom pitch in and help. Absenteeism, tardiness, grievances, and turnover skyrocket.

They do not participate at meetings, except to voice complaints as they sit in the back of the room scowling with arms folded. They eschew making suggestions or approving the ideas of others. They fall silent or walk away when managers approach. Cynicism, sarcasm, and belittling flourish.

Conversations and energy are directed away from productive work. They talk about retiring, changing employers, or leaving their field. They talk about how their friends have better jobs. The more qualified ones often do leave, but the deadwood stays on board: They quit but stay. You often hear things such as "Thank God it's Friday," "Only 2 more years to go," "Don't ask me, I only work here," "We need a union," or "There's no point in knocking yourself out."

Whenever a morale slippage is suspected, management should circulate an attitude survey and share the findings with all managers. Alert supervisors who enjoy good rapport with their employees but whose observations are not solicited by upper management become aware of such problems long before management gets into the act.

MAJOR FACTORS THAT AFFECT MORALE

Employee Factors

1. basic personality type, especially optimism or pessimism
2. family and other outside situations
3. ability to adjust to job and fellow workers
4. ease and safety in getting to work and finding a parking space
5. employee-job match

Nature of Job and Job Ambiance

1. work that is stimulating or monotonous, fulfilling or unrewarding
2. prestige
3. opportunity for promotion or growth
4. job security
5. financial status of organization, economic conditions, and threats of competitors
6. amount of stress
7. quality and ease of communication

Attitude and Behavior of Employer and Management

1. how rewards are shared (e.g., upper managers get huge raises or bonuses while employees are laid off or asked to take salary cuts)
2. frequency of promotions from within
3. how management adjusts to financial crunches

Qualities of Supervision (see previous chapters)

HOW EMPLOYERS CAN IMPROVE MORALE

- Use and react quickly to employee attitude surveys.
- Establish a problem-solving culture.
- Control rumors.
- Insist on fair and equitable treatment of employees.
- Personally monitor employee morale.
- Know what competitors pay their employees, and try to offer competitive packages.

- Hire competent managers.
- Provide extensive supervisory training.

HOW SUPERVISORS CAN IMPROVE MORALE

- Treat people as winners or potential winners.
- Provide appropriate rewards and recognition.
- Ensure social acceptance, and instill pride through better orientation of new employees.
- Increase employees' comfort level by ensuring that they know how to do their jobs.
- Maintain a mindset of optimism and success.
- Assign discouraged workers to teams of go-getters.
- Permit more flexibility of work schedules.
- Keep all people informed.
- Become a change master.
- Involve people in decision making and planning to help them satisfy their social needs.
- Help them get raises:
  —Rewrite position descriptions. Document the degree of difficulty of their tasks, teaching and administrative responsibilities, the consequences of any errors on their part, and anything else that is truthful and justifies raising the salary level of the position.
  —Revise responsibilities and assignments to justify "in-grade" promotions.
  —Increase eligibility for promotion or merit pay by active mentoring.
  —Never resort to downgrading the performance of valued assistants to prevent their loss through promotion or transfer.

MOTIVATION

All motivation is self-motivation. Managers cannot motivate. What they can do is change the work ambiance in ways that affect motivation favorably.

All employees are motivated, but often that motivation is not directed at their jobs. For example, Steve, who shows little interest in his job, is an enthusiastic bowler, or a talented musician, or a leader in a professional organization; he has lots of motivation.

Efforts to affect motivation are either proactive or reactive. Proactive or anticipative measures precede performance; reactive activities follow performance and are principally techniques for reinforcing desired behavior or results.

Proactive Strategies

- Change job titles and rewrite position descriptions to make jobs more important (or appear so; see Chapter 4).
- Recruit and select motivated people (see Chapter 8).
- Upgrade orientation programs to preserve the new employees' initial enthusiasm (see Chapter 9).
- Increase employees' opportunities for education and training (Exhibit 14–1).
- Improve the job.

The most lasting motivation comes from the job itself, or more correctly from one's perception of the job and its importance. When people like their work but hate their job, watch out!

Exhibit 14-1 How Many of These Questions about Your Educational Program Can You Answer in the Affirmative?

1. Do you have a formal in-house education program?
2. Is this program available to each and every member of your staff?
3. Do you provide sufficient uninterrupted time for your employees to attend the in-house programs?
4. Does each employee have individualized career goals and plans? Are these discussed at annual performance review meetings?
5. Is there financial support for outside education courses? Do you modify work schedules or numbers of work hours to accommodate employees who enroll in these programs?
6. Do employees have the opportunity to cross-train or to learn new skills on the job?
7. Does each of your employees learn at least one new skill each year?
8. Are there real incentives for learning new skills?
9. When your employees attend seminars or workshops, do you discuss the practical value to your unit and to the employee before the meeting?
10. When your employees return from seminars and workshops, do you discuss what they learned and help them put that new knowledge and skill to use?
11. When you attend professional or technical meetings, do you share what you learned with others? Do you encourage your staff to do likewise?
12. Do you include educational topics in your routine staff meetings?
13. Do all your educational efforts focus on improved customer service?

The meaningfulness of work is based on how much it affects the worker, other people, and the bottom line of the work unit and the organization; the degree to which a job requires a variety of different activities and skills; and its holistic nature, or the degree to which the job requires completion of a whole, identifiable piece of work.

Interesting work and opportunities to develop skills and abilities, to be creative, and to be challenged are powerful motivators.

A high degree of control over one's work provides a healthy mindset. Lack of autonomy leads to frustration and stress. Having control translates into discretionary freedom of scheduling, prioritizing, and selecting methods. Here are some practical tips for increasing the motivational value of the work itself.

- Provide a diversity of experience by giving new assignments, cross-training, or rotating work stations.
- Swap assignments. You must know what each person likes and dislikes.
- Assign monotonous tasks or those requiring less expertise to less qualified employees, and make two people happy.
- Allow a little time for practical research, special projects, or service on committees, quality circles, or problem-solving groups.
- Permit a few fun tasks.
- Stimulate creativity by talking about new services, products, equipment, or procedures; sharing publications and handouts from seminars; and assigning problems.
- Provide holistic tasks, where employees can see the results of their efforts.

To move up a motivational notch, switch from a directive style to a participative style. To help with this, Leeds recommends asking your employees the following questions[6]:

- What do you like about what you do?
- How can I help you use more of your skills?
- What do you think you (or we) should do differently?
- How can we implement your ideas?
- What help do you need from me or from others?

Get them involved in decisions about their assignments. Consider differences in their motivational needs. Some people have a strong need for control or leadership, others for task achievement, and still others for socializing. For example, Sue gets her kicks when she chairs a committee, Joe is energized when presented with a balky instrument, and Jan is happiest when she can meet new people or work with a group of her friends.

Encourage team building (see Chapter 10).

Delegate and empower. Giving ambitious people more responsibility plus the authority they need to discharge that responsibility is empowering and has proven to be a strong motivator. Most people like to be in charge of something, even when that something is a minor activity (see Chapter 11).

Assign holistic tasks.

Reactive Strategies

Provide Recognition

When money is scarce for rewarding good service or is no longer the motivator it used to be, recognition and praise become more important. These factors elevate self-esteem, improve morale, and really motivate if applied skillfully.

A frequent complaint of health care workers is that they do not get the recognition and respect that they are due. Supervisors often misinterpret this to mean that upper management is at fault. Recognition, however, is a lot more than formal ceremonies where accolades, plaques, and certificates are handed out. Such events are too infrequent and too impersonal to have a major impact. Of much greater significance is the day-to-day, person-to-person dialog in which supervisors express their appreciation in ways that convince employees that they are important. This is what really satisfies the employee's ego needs.

Your messages, verbal or written, tell employees whether you truly believe in the value of their efforts and their worth. What gets rewarded informs people of what kind of performance is valued most. Make sure that the recognition is perceived as fair.

In the last chapter we discussed the use of praise. Here are some other modalities for providing recognition:

- Thank subordinates, colleagues, superiors—anyone in your network—on a daily basis. Say "Thanks" more often. Keep a box of thank-you notes in a desk drawer. Send out at least one every day.
- A pat on the back substitutes nicely for a verbal positive stroke.
- Ask someone whether he or she would be willing to serve as a mentor for a member of your team, or for you.
- Change an employee's title.
- Give team recognition by bringing in a treat (maybe sponsor a party or a dinner).
- Attend a committee meeting to thank the group.

Provide Rewards

Mention has already been made that money is a dissatisfier, not a motivator. Take it away and performance falls, but increasing it does not motivate. Employees think that they have it coming. Any motivational effect is transient.

Take with a grain of salt, however, those reports that people are motivated more by their work than by rewards. That is trickle-down thinking. Let us face the fact that, except for volunteers and some independently wealthy people, most employees get their biggest bang from the rewards of their efforts, not from the work itself.

Employers can keep telling their employees how great they are, but if they fail to back this up with fatter paychecks even though the organization is not in financial difficulty, those employees soon realize that they are being manipulated.

The Japanese get the maximum mileage out of their bonus systems. Many Japanese workers receive 25 percent of their pay in the form of flexible bonuses; in the United States the average is less than 1 percent.

There are useful monetary rewards other than salary. The cost and importance of benefits has increased markedly. Medical insurance coverage, maternity plans, and day care for children and parents are getting much more attention in the 1990s. Other rewards that have significant monetary value include offices or expanded work space, services of typists or other assistants, and support for educational or professional advancement (see below).

Support Career Development

Provide more training, and support educational efforts. Training and education are among the most powerful motivators for the health care professional.

Enable your employees to attend in-house educational offerings. A common complaint in health care facilities is that it is difficult to attend educational sessions because the workload is so great and because the attendance is frequently interrupted (those dreadful beepers). Here are some other worthwhile activities:

- Encourage each person to become a specialist in some aspect of your unit's activities.
- Help employees develop goals, objectives, and plans.
- Provide subscriptions to professional or technical publications or a small personal library.
- Pay for employees' membership in professional societies.
- Approve tuition costs for educational programs
- Establish special research or investigation projects.
- Reimburse employees for attendance at professional meetings, workshops, or seminars.
- Give assignments that promote career development.

MOTIVATING THE STEADY BUT UNSPECTACULAR WORKER

Managers spend much time devising gimmicks for rewarding their star performers or coping with their problem people while neglecting their loyal supporters who show up every day, do not make waves, and live up to all the specifications of their position descriptions. I hope that most of your subordinates fall into this category.

In addition to providing some of the motivators already described, try holding periodic individual meetings with each of these employees in addition to the annual or semi-annual performance review.[7]

Before the meeting, review their records and your personal observations. Focus on some noteworthy behavior, such as excellent attendance or frequent volunteering to substitute for absent co-workers.

At the meeting, apologize for not spending more time with the person, and congratulate him or her for whatever it is you picked out. Use the opportunity to ask for suggestions for improving service or teamwork. Ask whether there is anything you can do to make his or her job more pleasant. Most employees are more relaxed and willing to talk frankly at these informal sessions than at the mandatory performance appraisal interviews.

NOTES

1. R.J. Doyle and P.I. Doyle, *Gain Management* (New York: AMACOM, 1992), 9.
2. A.H. Maslow, *Motivation and Personality* (New York: Harper & Row, 1954).
3. Maslow, *Motivation.*
4. F. Herzberg, *Work and the Nature of Man* (Cleveland: World, 1966).
5. Herzberg, *Work.*
6. D. Leeds, *Smart Questions* (New York: McGraw-Hill, 1987).
7. F.C. Nail and E.K. Singleton, A common sense survival strategy for nursing supervisors, *Health Care Supervisor* 4 (1986): 50–58.

Chapter 15

Counseling Employees

- the goal of counseling
- the three major kinds of problems
- is there a problem, and is counseling the answer?
- where managers go wrong
- why employees violate rules
- five important preparations for the interview
- the interview, step by step
- common defensive responses by employees
- the follow-up
- subsequent meetings

There are two kinds of counseling: career counseling, when the counselor serves as an advisor or mentor (see Chapter 30), and remedial counseling, when a supervisor deals with employee performance that has strayed from established norms. This chapter focuses on the latter.

The goal of counseling is to correct deviant performance while preserving the self-esteem of the individual. A confrontation provides the confronted person with an opportunity to look at his or her behavior and to decide whether to change. The goal should never be to release anger or frustration or to punish the employee.

Unsuccessful counseling usually culminates in disciplinary measures.

THE THREE MAJOR KINDS OF PROBLEMS

1. Underperformance: unsatisfactory productivity or work quality
2. Bad work habits or violation of policies or rules
3. Inability to get along with others

IS THERE REALLY A PROBLEM?

When performance or behavior is borderline, you must decide whether action is needed and, if action is indicated, what it should be. In marginal instances, ask yourself "What if everyone did (or did not) do that?" or "If I do nothing, what adverse effects are likely to ensue?"

If you are blessed with a team of overachievers, you may feel that the work of a marginal performer is unsatisfactory because it compares unfavorably with that of the other employees. This trap can be avoided if performance is judged on the basis of established standards, not by comparing employee accomplishments.

IS COUNSELING THE ANSWER?

Counseling is not the remedy for all personnel problems. A useful flowchart is given in Figure 15–1.

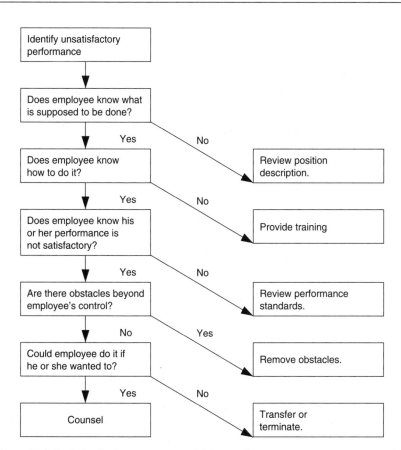

Figure 15–1 Analysis of and responses to unsatisfactory performance.

Note that in most instances counseling is not the best remedy. There are two additional situations in which counseling is not appropriate. One of these is when negative consequences to the employee follow good performance (e.g., if an employee is chided by co-workers when that employee exhibits extra efforts or if supervisors overload their good workers). The other is when positive consequences follow poor performance (e.g., if a complainer gets a lighter workload or if the only time an employee receives any attention is when he or she misbehaves). Obviously the proper action in these situations is to change the reward and recognition system.

WHERE MANAGERS GO WRONG

- They don't take action because:
  —they are not aware of the problem
  —they ignore the problem
  —they postpone action until the next performance review (employees should not have to wait until performance appraisal time to learn that they are not performing up to expectations)
- They assume that the problem is one of poor attitude.
- They fail to monitor postmeeting behavior.
- They fail to escalate from counseling to disciplining when no improvement occurs or relapses continue.

WHY EMPLOYEES VIOLATE RULES

- They never learned, or they forgot, the rules.
- They see the rules as meaningless or too restrictive.
- They note that the rules are rarely or unevenly enforced.
- They are influenced by others.
- They find that the rewards of misbehavior are higher than the risks or the penalties.
- They are misfits or malcontents.

PREPARING FOR THE COUNSELING INTERVIEW

Get the facts. What have you or others observed? What have you documented? Is this a relapse? If so, what was agreed upon at previous confrontations? Review the employee's record, especially any written reprimands, customer complaints, and the last formal performance appraisal report.

Be certain of the content and context of any policy or rule that has been violated. Study the document yourself, word for word.

Look for patterns. For example, in the case of absenteeism, individuals may be calling in sick only on Mondays or Fridays or on days when they are scheduled to perform unpleasant chores.

Explore the perceived benefit-risk ratio of the behavior from the employee's viewpoint. For example, when an employee goes shopping on sick days or takes long breaks and is never called on it, the benefit-risk ratio is very high. There is no incentive to reform.

If you are inexperienced in these matters, consult with a member of the human resources department. If the problem is a serious one, discuss it with your boss.

Schedule a place, date, and time. The location should be one where there will be no interruptions (your office may not be the ideal location).

Hold the meeting in the morning so that you have the rest of the day to show the person by your words and behavior that you do not bear a grudge toward him or her, only toward the behavior. You will smile and chat just as you would if there had not been a problem discussed.

Do not procrastinate. Think of the damage that is taking place while you hesitate. Also, the more you delay, the harder it will be to convince the person that the matter is important.

Mentally rehearse these aspects of the upcoming meeting:

- your exact opening remarks
- statements you will use to boost the employee's self-esteem
- the solution you hope to lead to
- how you will respond to rebuttals, defensive reactions, anger, tears, or threats

THE TEN-STEP COUNSELING INTERVIEW

Step 1

Greet the person with a smile; you are going to help, not punish, this employee. Thank the person for coming. The theme of the initial session should be helpfulness.

Never apologize for calling the meeting. You weaken your position when you start with something such as "Joyce I hate to bring this up, but. . . . " Equally bad is hitting the person with an intimidating statement such as "We've got to talk about your unsatisfactory performance."

Assume that the person wants to do a good job, and say so. Address self-esteem by articulating some specific attribute (for example, "Joyce, I receive many compliments from our medical staff about your caring attitude toward patients").

Continue with something such as "Joyce, I have a problem that I need your help with." (This is true. It really is your problem!)

Step 2

Describe the situation in specific, nonjudgmental terms. Select your words carefully to focus on the behavior rather than on the person.

Remember that you want to find out whether Joyce is aware of the problem, especially if a policy or rule is being violated. So, be tentative. This is even more important if there is some question as to the validity of the alleged behavior. Empathize by admitting that her job is not an easy one.

Step 3

Explain how the behavior affects your department, other people, or you.

Avoid absolute words such as *always* and *never*. These words are almost always inaccurate and invite contradiction (e.g., "You're never on time" is countered with "I'm usually on time"). Avoid sarcasm, kidding, or other put-downs. These elicit resentment and serve no useful purpose.

Avoid quotations from policy manuals unless the employee challenges the authenticity of your charge. Taking refuge in a handbook makes you appear weak. For the same reason, do not say, "Management expects. . . . " Do say, "I expect. . . . "

To convince the person that this is important, emphasize how the behavior affects you (e.g., "When I see———, I get so upset that I take it out on my family").

Step 4

Give them time to respond, until they run out of gas. Do not interrupt, even if they utter untruths or make countercharges. Do not become defensive or lose your cool.

Use your best listening skills. Instead of judgmental responses ("You don't try hard enough") or defensive responses ("That's not true and you know it"), use responses that are empathic ("I can understand why you . . . "), probing (when, where, who, why, and how), paraphrasing ("I hear you saying . . . "), or summarizing ("Can we conclude that . . . ?").

Jot down the key points they make, you may need to refer to these later.

Step 5

Get them to admit that there is a problem and that they are part of it. This is often difficult, especially if the behavior has been tolerated for some time. They may respond sarcastically with "Big deal" or something similar.

Ask them what they think the effects of this continued behavior could be (e.g., on their next performance appraisal). This forces them to think about consequences that are not in their best interest.

Empathize with their frustration (e.g., "You say that you experience frustration when, despite your best efforts, things have a way of falling apart. I can appreciate that").

Step 6

State that the problem must be solved, that it is up to them to solve it, and that you are there to help. The solution should not be yours because:

- quick solutions by you make the person feel stupid
- solutions by you that do not work make you look stupid
- the employee may feel obliged to take your advice when he or she has a better solution
- an employee tries harder when it is his or her solution
- the employee becomes dependent on you for all solutions

If you cannot accept their first offering, keep asking for alternatives until they come up with one that you can live with. Discuss the pros and cons of each suggestion. Avoid directive phrases such as "If I were you . . . " or "Here's what you should do." Compliment them for coming up with solutions.

If the discussion stalls, ask some leading questions to guide the person to additional alternatives. Do not impose your solution unless absolutely necessary!

If it becomes obvious that despite your best efforts you are not getting near a solution, do not make it a matter of wills. Simply state your position and what you expect, and then end the meeting.

Step 7

Offer to help in the implementation (e.g., "Joyce, it's up to you to take care of this. However, I will cooperate. When I notice_____, I'll remind you").

Step 8

Summarize what is agreed upon. Repeat your expectations clearly and empathically. Insist on their commitment. Include a deadline for the solution to take effect.

Step 9

End on a positive note and with an affirmation. Thank the employee for cooperating, and express confidence in his or her ability to solve the problem. For example, "Joyce, I appreciate your cooperation. I knew that I could depend on you to take care of this problem. This past performance is way below what you are capable of."

It is often a good idea to set a date for a follow-up meeting.

Step 10

Document. A common and serious deficiency is the lack of documentation. All too often, counseling is not successful and must be repeated or ratcheted up to disciplinary action. When either of these becomes necessary, you will be grateful for having a record on hand.

Record the date, the problem, the employee's comments (exact words are best), the agreed upon resolution, any warning given by you, and the deadline for acceptable response.

I recommend that these notes not be placed in the employee's file. If you do that, you have given a written reprimand—the second step in disciplining—not a counseling session. You must also give the employee a copy. More significant, you have changed from counselor to disciplinarian, a change that erodes your relationship with that employee.

Maintain confidentiality. Keep your notes locked up, secure from prying eyes. Do not discuss the meeting with anyone other than your immediate superior and/or a member of the human resources department.

COMMON DEFENSIVE RESPONSES BY EMPLOYEES

Keep in mind that any unpleasant behavior demonstrated by the employee during the interview represents behavior that the individual has found effective in the past.

They Balk at Any Discussion

- They say they don't want to discuss the matter right now.
- They deny everything you say.
- They refuse to listen or keep interrupting.
- They talk louder and faster.
- They weep.

- They storm out of your office.
- They clam up and will not say anything.

Solutions: Insist on a dialog. Respond to loud, angry outcries with something such as "You're starting to yell, Joyce."

If Joyce runs out of your office, don't chase after her. Simply wait until later in the day, or the next day, and then send for her again. Start all over.

If they cry, hand them a box of tissues, and wait for the tears to stop.

A person who suddenly clams up may be trying to decide whether to say something of a sensitive nature. If you break the silence too soon, you may never know what that was. If the silence persists, say "Joyce, I thought we were having a conversation." Lean forward and look like you expect a response. If this is not effective, give a sigh and remark that it is obvious that you are both wasting time and that the meeting will have to be postponed. Reschedule, then send the person home or back to work.

They Try To Minimize the Problem
They retort sarcastically, "OK, I haven't been the employee of the month, I'll try to do better if that'll make you happy."
Solution: Never accept this. Say that you are glad that they recognize that there is a problem but that you must emphasize that this is an important issue and that something definite must be done about it.
They challenge you with "The old boss never said anything about that."
Solution: Respond with "I'm not your old boss."
They say, "If this is so important, how is it that you never said anything about it before?"
Solution: Respond with, "I thought that you would take care of it without my direction," or admit that you should have acted sooner.
They claim that work is not affected (e.g., Joyce responds to the charge of wasting time with "I get my work done, don't I?").
Solution: Respond with, "Yes, but you interfere with the work of others and set a bad example for the new employees."

They Counterattack

- They threaten to go over your head.
- They threaten to quit.
- They accuse you of the same behavior (e.g., "You have your nerve accusing me of that. I have seen you doing the very same thing").

Solutions: If they threaten to quit, to go over your head, or to expose something damaging about you, reply that they may do whatever they choose but that you recommend that they give long and serious thought to such a drastic move and to the impact it can have on their future.

They Try To Sidetrack the Discussion

- They blame others (e.g., "Helen does the same thing. How is it you never say anything to her?").
- They blame a myriad of personal problems at home.

Solutions: If they try to sidetrack the discussion, respond that nothing will be accomplished by accusing others. If the person blames problems at home, channel the discussion back to the work situation. If signs and symptoms suggest a serious personal problem, however, such as drug or alcohol abuse or financial distress, recommend professional help. In most instances a good comment is "Joyce, I'm not qualified to help you with those kinds of problems. I can recommend a professional counselor if you like, but for now let's get back to the problem at hand."

THE FOLLOW-UP

The counseling process does not end with the interview. Managers often dismiss the subject from their minds because they are so relieved that the confrontation is over and that the employees have promised to solve the problems.

The follow-up consists of monitoring performance and reinforcing desired behavior. Positive strokes motivate, negative strokes or the absence of feedback demotivate. Support improvements with smiles and pats on the back. Do not wait until perfection has been achieved. Reinforce each small step with something such as "I know that you are making a special effort, Joyce, and I appreciate that."

Identify and address specific concerns that call for exploration or reassurance.

THE COMMENDATORY MEETING

When the problem appears to have been solved, hold a commendatory meeting at which you:

- describe the improvement you have noted
- encourage the person to relate how the improvement was achieved
- offer to help with any unanticipated roadblocks
- close with expressions of appreciation and an affirmation

WHEN REPEAT SESSIONS ARE NEEDED

If the undesired behaviors or results persist, you are faced with several choices. You can extend the deadline if there has been some progress, you can institute disciplinary actions, or you can counsel again. Most often you will choose to repeat the counseling session. Now, however, you have two problems: the initial one, and the new one of the employee failing to deliver on his or her commitment.

Your objectives in the repeat session are to let the employee know that you are aware of the continued problem, to inform the employee of the risk he or she is taking, and to give the employee one more chance before disciplinary action is taken.

To emphasize the importance of the subject, ask your boss or a representative of the human resources department to sit in on the meeting to add gravity to the situation from the perspective of the employee and to give you support.

At this session, manifest less patience, and skip the smiles and affirmations. On the other hand, avoid accusatory expressions (which are usually the ones that start with "You didn't try very hard" or "Why did you . . . ?").

Probe for possible roadblocks beyond the employee's control. Most important, insist that the employee come up with a new solution (or resolution), and state what the consequences will be of another failure.

Make certain that you set a target date.

Here are the seven key points to be covered in the repeat session:
1. Review the agreements reached at the previous session.
2. State what you have observed or learned that indicates that the agreement has been broached.
3. Ask for an explanation.
4. Insist on a new solution or effort.
5. Indicate the consequences of continued noncompliance. Avoid making a threat that you do not intend to carry out.
6. Agree on the new action to be taken and a new follow-up date.
7. Indicate your reluctance to give up on the employee and your belief that he or she can correct the situation.

SUMMARY OF PRINCIPLES THAT ENSURE SUCCESSFUL INTERVENTIONS:

- Initially confront as a friend, not as an antagonist.
- Be direct and honest.

- Listen more than you talk.
- Say how you feel. Ask them how they feel.
- Select the best time and place for confrontations.
- Don't nitpick.
- Make them come up with solutions.
- Go for win-win solutions.
- Be willing to compromise.
- Work with facts, not assumptions.
- Be optimistic. Expect positive results.
- Preserve their self-esteem.
- Don't pontificate or be condescending.
- Don't expect the impossible.
- Look for the good in the person.
- Catch them doing something right, and reward it.
- Monitor and reinforce.

In a subsequent chapter we will discuss specific employee problems.

Chapter 16

Performance Review and Planning Interviews

- the importance of employee feedback
- the important perception of being a winner
- potential flaws in appraisal interviews
- essentials of performance reviews
- preparations for interviews
- why salary should not be discussed
- getting the interview off to a good start
- review of the position description
- discussion of past performance
- discussion of future performance
- the planning process
- the all important objectives
- ending the interview
- postinterview activities
- bottom-up and peer performance appraisals

In this chapter the discussion is limited to performance appraisal interviews, which I prefer to call performance review and planning interviews. We will not discuss performance rating systems because supervisors seldom have input into the construction of these documents, and practically every organization has its form. A good reference for rating systems is Henderson's *Performance Appraisals.*[1]

Appraising performance in the 1990s has encountered numerous possible legal pitfalls. If the recommendations in this chapter are followed, so that employee performance is objectively and regularly documented, legal liabilities will be minimal. For readers who want more on the legal aspects, I recommend the Alexander Hamilton Institute's *Performance Appraisals: The Latest Legal Nightmare.*[2]

FEEDBACK TO EMPLOYEES

> *"The type of recognition that inspires or discour-*
> *ages high performance is the feedback you give on an*
> *ongoing basis . . . "[3(p.139)]*

The most powerful feedback is derived from day-to-day coaching. Relying entirely on an annual or semiannual performance review is equivalent to using a single examination to determine whether a student passes or fails.

Fair administration of any reward system depends largely on results-oriented, behavior-referenced, and equitable performance appraisals. Of much greater value is using these sessions to provide recognition for past service, to help employees improve their expertise, and to assist them in developing their careers. The employees' supervisors and employers benefit by having more competent and confident workers.

The effect of these meetings on self-esteem can be positive or negative. A good performance review and planning session results in both parties feeling that they have gained something. To boost morale and confidence, we must make every one of our workers feel like a winner.

THE IMPORTANCE OF PERCEIVING ONESELF AS A WINNER

Success breeds success. A little of it makes us want to do even better. Expressions of appreciation and commendations are more effective than criticism, however constructive and well intentioned the criticism may be. Studies have shown that performance usually decreases after criticism. Therefore, it makes sense to spend more time delivering positive strokes than we spend harping on deficiencies.

Use prior counseling sessions to deal with performance problems, and use performance reviews to express appreciation, to boost morale, and to envision a better future.

POTENTIAL FLAWS IN APPRAISAL INTERVIEWS

> *"Leading a performance appraisal can be either*
> *difficult and depressing, or dynamic and positive.*
> *The attitude, planning, and approach of the person*
> *conducting the review will make the difference."[4(p.i)]*

Any of the following can detract from the value of these meetings:

- The process is not taken seriously by either party. This is manifested when there is inadequate preparation by the manager or the employee, when the meeting is repeatedly postponed or left until the last minute and then done hurriedly, and when the interviewer permits frequent interruptions during the meeting.

- The manager has only superficial knowledge of the employee's performance.
- The review is used to distribute salary increases instead of to improve performance.
- There are no documented, updated, specific work standards or objectives.
- The meeting is conducted as a lecture rather than as an interview. The supervisor does all the talking.
- The evaluation is highly subjective or lacks honesty.
- There is too much judging and too little listening.
- There is insufficient positive feedback or care for the interviewee's self-esteem.
- Reprimands or criticism were not previously discussed and catch the interviewee by surprise.
- Emphasis is on the past rather than on the future.
- The interview consists of little more than "You're doing just fine," handing out reports without comment, or only inviting questions about the report.
- The same rating form is used for managers and nonmanagers, resulting in insufficient evaluation of supervisory competencies.

SELF: THE ESSENTIALS OF PERFORMANCE REVIEWS

> **S =** **Standards,** results, or expectations. These provide the criteria for evaluations.
>
> **E =** **Evaluate** past performance objectively and fairly while preserving or boosting self-esteem.
>
> **L =** **Listen,** which is key to all successful interviews. Great listeners have great interviews.
>
> **F =** **Future.** Planning for the future is the most important part of the interview.

A performance review should be an exchange of information and ideas, not a report card. As Maddux writes, the effective interviewer ". . . helps employees evaluate the usefulness of their ideas, recognize their weaknesses, and exploit their strengths. The leader acts as a resource and enabler, rather than as a judge."[5(p.19)]

A good review combines the features of recognition, self-appraisal, joint problem solving, and management by objectives. Emphasis is on the future rather than on the past. The past is mainly a prelude to a discussion of how the employee can do better in the future.

PREPARATIONS FOR PERFORMANCE REVIEW INTERVIEWS

As for any meeting, advance planning is the key to success. The meeting has two components: the process and the content. The process consists of the format and the interviewer's skill. The content is what transpires during the meeting.

Employees are given copies of the following:

- their position descriptions, including performance standards
- the evaluation form used to report the review
- the report of their last formal review
- new departmental objectives
- their continuing education record
- instructions about how to prepare for the meeting (Exhibit 16–1)

In addition to the preparations listed in Exhibit 16–1, employees may be asked to fill in the evaluation form and give it to the interviewer before the meeting; this constitutes a form of self-appraisal.

KEY PREPARATIONS BY THE SUPERVISOR

Record performance on a regular basis. To assist in this documentation of performance, keep a critical incident file. In this file, record specific examples of superior or below-standard performance by each employee, and use this data for counseling or for the next formal performance review.[6]

Exhibit 16-1 Employee Preparation Instructions

1. Review your position description. List any changes since your last review. Pencil in any changes you would like.
2. Scan your last review. Be prepared to discuss the objectives you achieved and those that were not achieved.
3. Prepare a new list of objectives.
4. Review your current continuing education record.
5. Jot down or be prepared to discuss:
   - how you feel about your performance since the last meeting
   - what you consider your most valuable contribution to the organization since your last review and what gave you the most satisfaction
   - what changes in systems, procedures, equipment, service, cost containment, or quality improvement you suggest we consider
   - anything that is preventing you from reaching your full potential
   - what frustrates you most at present
   - what we can do to help

Review the employee's personnel file. Scrutinize the following:

* the position description and standards of performance (all too often this document has been filed away and has not been updated despite numerous changes in duties and responsibilities)
* continuing education and attendance records
* commendations, special recognition, and awards
* incident reports, records of counseling, and any disciplinary actions
* the report of the last review

Review new departmental objectives or anticipated activities that may affect the employee. You want to synchronize the employee's objectives with those of your department with new emphasis on quality improvement, team building, safety, or customer satisfaction.

Discuss the employee's performance with other observers. The latter may include other managers for whom the person works or individuals involved in the work flow of the interviewee.

Prepare an agenda. Set a date, time, and place. Give employees sufficient time to prepare for the meeting. Set aside at least an hour for the interview.

Formulate key remarks. Select the exact words to use for introductory statements, to criticize, and to confront defensiveness. Expunge the word *average;* everyone thinks he or she is above average.

Anticipate problems. Be ready to cite specific examples to illustrate your points.

Make necessary changes in your interview procedure. Appraisal forms usually may not be altered, but you can add items. If your organization still uses rating forms based exclusively on traits and nonspecific behaviors (honesty, loyalty, quantity and quality of work, and the like), add behavior-anchored criteria that relate directly to duties and responsibilities documented in position descriptions. There should be indicators relating to quality improvement and customer satisfaction.

Many organizations use the same form for all categories of employees and for all hierarchical levels. These forms often lack criteria pertaining to administrative and supervisory responsibilities. If you evaluate individuals who serve in leadership roles, add these factors (Exhibit 16–2).

Another appropriate evaluation item is the employee's degree of success in achieving objectives formulated at previous performance reviews.

WHY SALARY SHOULD NOT BE DISCUSSED

Once salary talk is introduced, it dominates and distorts the discussion. Even worse, it invites an adversarial relationship. Instead of accepting higher work standards or more challenging objectives, employees argue for lower ones.

Exhibit 16-2 Managerial Competencies

Maintains contemporary professional knowledge and skills
- Keeps up to date in both professional and managerial fields.
- Regularly attends seminars and other meetings.
- Meets all continuing education standards.

Demonstrates initiative and flexibility
- Identifies needs for innovation and change, and effectively implements changes.
- Solves problems quickly and skillfully.

Maximizes the use of personnel and material resources
- Keeps within budgetary limits.
- Manages time of self and subordinates effectively.
- Evaluates, selects, and maintains equipment and supplies skillfully.

Communicates effectively
- Keeps vertical and horizontal channels of communication open and active.
- Enjoys good rapport with other team members.
- Makes efficient use of meetings and other information systems; has mastered our computer system.
- Is skilled in interviewing techniques.
- Possesses good writing ability.

Shows other leadership abilities
- Coaches, counsels, and evaluates performance well.
- Maintains high morale, enthusiasm, and motivation.
- Is skilled in selecting, orienting, and training new hires.
- Deals promptly and effectively with personnel problems.
- Coordinates and cooperates well with other work units.
- Delegates and empowers effectively.
- Organizes, assigns, and schedules skillfully.
- Recognized as a good team builder
- Accomplishes assignments and challenges on time and to the satisfaction of superiors.

If the person is told that no monetary reward is forthcoming, the resulting resentment prevents a free-wheeling discussion of new objectives and plans.

When employees press for a discussion of salary adjustments, reply that, although performance ratings are important, other factors affect salary. These factors may include the employee's new objectives, the availability and market value of certain specialists, what competitors are paying, and budget constraints.

Tell the employee that he or she will be informed later when the information is available. Discuss this at a subsequent brief meeting (see Chapter 27).

If it's absolutely necessary to discuss salary at the performance review, save that discussion for last.

THE FOUR SEGMENTS OF A PERFORMANCE REVIEW AND PLANNING INTERVIEW

1. Get off to a good start.
2. Update the position description.
3. Discuss past performance, and complete the appraisal form.
4. Obtain a commitment for future performance.

Get off to a Good Start

Begin the interview by making the employee feel at ease and thanking the person for his or her support. If you dislike these meetings, do your best to conceal that fact. You owe your reports at least 1 hour of quality time annually.

Instead of an introduction such as "Well, it's that time again, let's get it over with," say "It's good to be able to sit down and review the past 6 months with you, John. First of all, let me thank you for all your efforts and for putting up with me without complaining. We have all been under considerable stress, and at times I am not the easiest person to get along with."

This is a good time to discuss some of the questions posed in the preparation list (see Exhibit 16–1), especially those about what gave the employee the most satisfaction or about what he or she regarded as the most significant. This approach enables you to put your listening skills to immediate use and indicates your interest in the employee's accomplishments.

Update the Position Description

Position descriptions provide the underpinnings for effective performance appraisals. The segment of job descriptions that describes responsibilities or key result areas is important because it enables the interviewer to concentrate on performance as measured against mutually understood expectations. Add quality improvement and client satisfaction descriptors if this has not already been done.

The following questions are appropriate:

- Are you performing any duties not listed in your position description? What are they?
- What more would you like to be responsible for?
- What are you doing that you think should be done by someone else?
- What assignments do you find most enjoyable? Least enjoyable?

Review the standards of performance. Does the person understand and accept these? Should any be added or changed?

Consider the employee's range of authority. Has lack of authority been a barrier to performance? Has the right to more freedom of action been earned?

Discuss Past Performance and Complete the Appraisal Form

Follow the instructions of your human resources department, but do not limit yourself to these guidelines. Some experts recommend that this step be the last one in the interview.

Customer comments, commendatory or incident reports, and complaints should be given substantial weight in the rating process.

Make use of the concept of self-appraisal by asking employees to rate themselves before you do. This tells subordinates that their input is important, sets the stage for collaboration, minimizes defensiveness, gives you more information, and saves time because you can now focus on the few areas in which there is an honest difference of opinion.

About 90 percent of employees rate themselves the same as or below what their bosses do. Ten percent rate themselves higher. Of these, half accept the lower ratings, and only the remaining 5 percent balk at the differences.[7]

Employees are more likely to rate themselves higher when performance-based salary schemes are in place. When people dispute your rankings, listen carefully to their complaints. Don't become defensive. Permit them to write dissenting opinions.

The most common and serious error is to overrate marginal performers. Overrating often returns to haunt managers. Commendatory comments should include a description of the specific event or behavior, what beneficial effects accrued, and an expression of your appreciation.

Get a Commitment for Future Performance

More than half the interview should consist of a discussion of the future. Past performance provides the database for planning future activities.

There are two goals. The first targets activities needed to improve performance. The second deals with career development, or reaching one's full potential.

Goals are meaningless—like most New Year's resolutions—if there is no commitment. Don't accept "I'll try." This is a noisy way of doing nothing. When people say that, they are building excuses for failure. If they fail, they claim that they did what they said they would: try.[8]

PERFORMANCE IMPROVEMENT

There is little chance for improvement unless there is agreement that improvement is needed, is possible, and is arrived at after honest dialog.

Because this is the most sensitive part of the interview, tread lightly. Never surprise an interviewee with complaints that have not been discussed before this meeting. You should always be able to initiate criticism with "As we discussed before...." For specific tips on delivering negative strokes, see Chapter 15. Exhibit 16–3 lists some additional suggestions for discussing deficiencies.

Use a directive approach when you want to reinforce a particular kind of behavior (e.g., "Your monthly progress reports are outstanding. Don't change a thing!").

When developing new objectives or when dealing with a performance problem, use a nondirective approach, such as "What is the one thing you can do in the next 12 months that will really make a difference?"

Encourage the employee to identify as many reasons for variances as possible. Contribute some of your own.

THE PLANNING PROCESS

Employees who leave an appraisal session without new work plans are short-changed. The planning process consists of three steps: (1) the mutual selection and prioritizing of topics and the commitment of the employee to meet the objectives of these topics, (2) a written plan that includes a time and cost schedule, and (3) a time table for reviewing progress and a target date for reaching objectives.

Open this segment by enlightening employees about any departmental changes that may affect their objectives. When employees have difficulty in articulating new work activities, simply ask them what they think needs to be done. Another useful tactic is for the rater to state three things he or she would like to see improved and for the ratee to mention three things the rater could do, or stop doing, to help.

Exhibit 16-3 Suggestions for Discussing Performance Deficiencies

- Limit criticism to one or two major problems. If there are others, discuss them at another meeting.
- Offer your support.
- Save critical remarks for last.
- Before you criticize, encourage self-criticism.
- Use all your listening skills.
- Respond supportively:
  —Reinforce points of agreement
  —Handle disagreement diplomatically
  —Use joint problem-solving approaches
  —Avoid being defensive
- Avoid terms such as *attitude, work ethic, professionalism, weakness,* and *deficiency.*
- Do not use the global comment "needs more experience" when documenting improvement needs. Spell out the exact experience that is needed.

Kinds of activities that may warrant consideration include the following:

- improved performance in selected key results areas
- increased internal and external customer satisfaction
- special assignments or newly delegated responsibilities
- innovations or new projects
- service on committees, problem-solving groups, quality circles, or other teams
- continuing education and other career development measures
- development of new systems or procedures
- cost-control or quality improvement measures
- time management, including customer turnaround times
- succession planning (if manager)
- team development (if manager)

For each planned activity, have the interviewee answer these questions:

- What is to be accomplished? What must be done? What is needed?
- Why do I want to do this?
- How will I accomplish this?
- Which alternative courses are feasible?
- Whom must I get to help?
- When will I start, and when should I be finished?

SCRAM: CHARACTERISTICS OF GOOD OBJECTIVES

S = Specific
C = Challenging
R = Relevant
A = Achievable
M = Measurable

The objective "I'm going to be a better communicator" is commendable but is not specific and is questionably measurable. Changed to "Within 6 months my listening skills will elicit favorable comments from my mentor, my spouse, and my supervisor," the two criteria of specificity and measurability are achieved.

Objectives must be challenging and yet attainable. If a person has an 80 percent chance of achieving an objective, the objective will be challenging. If the chance is 50 percent or less, the objective will be incapacitating.

Relevance refers to congruence with goals. Developing computer programming skill may meet other criteria, but if that skill is not needed in the employee's current or foreseeable future it lacks relevance.

When there are serious obstacles, include a list of these obstacles and methods for overcoming them.

If there are multiple objectives, they should be prioritized. A time table with check points for when the employee must get back to the supervisor is important. The supervisor should have, and periodically refer to, a check-off list of major objectives for each of his or her reports. It is at these critical times when plans must be altered or when the supervisor provides moral or active support.

CLOSING THE DISCUSSION

End the interview by summarizing key points, reassuring, expressing confidence, and thanking the person for cooperating with the process as well as for past services. Schedule follow-up sessions, if necessary, for the following:

* salary discussion
* remedial or career counseling
* detailed planning for complex activities
* progress in meeting objectives (don't wait for the next formal review)

> **A caveat:** *Never add negative comments after the employee has signed off.*

POSTINTERVIEW ACTIONS

Make certain that the appraisal form is filled out completely and that the new objectives and action plans have been documented.

Employees must be given an opportunity to respond verbally and in writing to adverse comments and/or unfavorable performance ratings. Do not neglect to:

* remind employees about their plans
* congratulate and motivate them
* confirm promised support or offer more
* modify, replace, or cancel objectives
* document achievements

BOTTOM-UP (REVERSE) AND PEER APPRAISALS

It is a mistake to rely on complaints and grievances to detect supervisors and managers who are not performing up to par because only a small percentage of employees lodge official gripes.

Detection of the bad apples is often complicated by the fact that their numbers may look good over the short haul. By the time signs such as high turnover, absenteeism, and grievances surface, irreparable damage may have been inflicted.

Progressive organizations conduct opinion surveys among their employees, and these may be supplemented by formal bottom-up appraisals, in which subordinates anonymously rate their bosses. This is often a part of the development of an enabling culture.

Another strategy is peer reviews. To prevent hurt feelings and possible retaliation, these programs require intensive training and preparation.

NOTES

1. R.I. Henderson, *Performance Appraisals,* 2d ed. (Reston, Va.: Reston Publishing, 1984).

2. Alexander Hamilton Institute, *Performance Appraisals: The Latest Legal Nightmare* (New York: Modern Business Reports, 1986).

3. M. Blanchard and J. Tager, *Working Well: Managing for Health and High Performance.* (New York: Simon & Schuster, 1985), 139.

4. R.B. Maddux, *Effective Performance Appraisals,* rev. ed. (Los Altos, Calif.: Crisp, 1987), i.

5. Maddux, *Effective Performance Appraisals,* 19.

6. M. Yate, *Keeping the Best* (Holbrook, Mass.: Bob Adams, 1991).

7. A.H. Locher and K.S. Teel, Appraisal trends, *Personnel Journal* 67 (1988): 139–145.

8. W.B. Werther, Jr., *Dear Boss* (New York: Meadowbrook, 1989).

Chapter 17

Disciplining and Downsizing

- what is disciplining?
- quality of work life is important
- competent managers have fewer disciplinary problems
- counseling versus disciplining
- the reward/risk-penalty theory
- progressive discipline and other punitive measures
- employee reactions to being disciplined
- oral and written reprimands
- suspensions and discharges
- legal challenges
- the final meeting
- nonpunitive discipline
- termination for poor productivity or quality
- sound disciplinary principles
- reduction-in-force separations

THE GOAL OF DISCIPLINING

Disciplining is not punishing, at least not at first. Disciplining is an educational effort to nudge unsatisfactory performance up to an acceptable level while preserving employee perceptions of self-worth.

The initial goal is not greasing the slide to separation. It is providing traction for employees to climb back—to correct behavior and to salvage the employee.

Disciplining usually addresses behavioral deviations rather than uncomplicated underperformance, although both can result in termination of employment.

Discipline should be fair, firm, and fast. Delay only increases emotional stress, especially yours. If all you do is complain to others about an employee, you deserve what you get: continued problems and loss of respect of your followers and superiors.

Skilled discipline has been likened to a red-hot stove. It provides a warning (red or sizzling), does not discriminate; and is immediate, consistent, and effective.

QUALITY OF WORK LIFE IS IMPORTANT

When employers treat their employees as they would like to be treated, disciplinary problems are few; so are grievances, resignations, and union entry.

A high percentage of formal complaints or grievances are the direct result of disciplinary action. For a discussion of the factors that affect quality of work life (QWL), see Chapter 14.

Employers must also consider the QWL of their managers. This includes providing clear and reasonable policies and guidelines and supporting their managers in the implementation of disciplinary measures. Many supervisors delay or avoid taking action because they fear lack of support.

COMPETENT MANAGERS HAVE FEWER DISCIPLINARY PROBLEMS

Disciplinary measures are less frequently required when managers are skilled in selecting new employees, provide thorough orientation and training, use adaptive leadership styles, and function as competent coaches and counselors.

The best discipline—self discipline—is achieved when employees are treated as responsible adults. Some managers treat their employees as children and then are surprised when these employees behave as children.

Managers who practice management by intimidation spend much of their time trying to catch people doing something wrong. The employees respond not so much by cleaning up their act as by avoiding being caught.

COUNSELING VERSUS DISCIPLINING

Disciplining interlocks with counseling. In most organizations, counseling is accepted as the first step in disciplining, the so-called oral reprimand. Some experts believe that counseling moves into the arena of discipline only when the counseled employee is warned of the consequences of failure to perform up to expectations.

Others regard any counseling session as an oral reprimand if the supervisor can prove that a meeting was held and that the topic was on target. This can be important in progressive discipline. For example, most such policies mandate one or more oral reprimands for most offenses before more punitive measures may be administered.

Counseling or oral reprimands are not appropriate for more serious forms of misbehavior. Immediate suspensions or dismissals are indicated in these cases. Most hospitals provide managers with guidelines for responding to disciplinary infractions (Exhibit 17–1).

Exhibit 17–1 Guidelines for Disciplinary Action

Class I: Minor Infractions

Discipline

First offense—Oral warning
Second offense—Written warning
Third offense—1-Day suspension
Fourth offense—3-Day suspension

Typical Subjects

- Unsatisfactory quality or quantity of work
- Discourtesy to patient, staff member, or co-worker
- Lateness
- Absenteeism

Class II: More Serious Infractions

Discipline

First offence—Written warning
Second offense—3-Day suspension
Third offense—Discharge

Typical Subjects

- Unavailability when scheduled for work
- Performance of personal work on hospital time
- Violation of smoking, safety, fire, or emergency regulations
- Unauthorized absence

Class III: Still More Serious Infractions

Discipline

First offense—Written warning
Second offense—Discharge

Typical Subjects

- Insubordination
- Negligence
- Falsification of records, reports, or information
- Improper release of confidential or privileged information
- Sexual harassment

Class IV: Most Serious Infractions

Discipline

First offense—Discharge

Typical Subjects

- Absence without notice for three consecutive days
- Fighting on the job
- Theft or dishonesty
- Intoxication or use of alcohol or drugs on premises
- Willful damage to hospital property

THE REWARD/RISK-PENALTY THEORY

We often fail to appreciate the fact that most employees misbehave not because they are bad or want to harass their superiors. It is usually simply a matter of their deriving some benefit, sometimes an unconscious one, from what they are doing or not doing.

Consider the ratio of reward to risk or penalty. This plays out on our highways every day. Motorists drive a little over the speed limit because they get to their destination quicker (the reward), but most of them do not drive at breakneck speed because they know that this increases the likelihood of being pulled over by police or flirting with death (risk and penalty).

Managers must recognize the reward that the employee perceives and endeavor to reduce its value, to increase the penalty, or to affect both parts of the equation.

Failure to detect dysfunctional behavior or to take action means that the employees perceive no risk or penalty and therefore have no incentive to change.

PROGRESSIVE DISCIPLINE

This is called progressive because it implies that the disciplinary measures will become increasingly severe until there is a resolution of the problem. In its traditional form, progressive discipline consists of the following four steps:

1. the oral reprimand
2. the written reprimand
3. suspension
4. discharge

OTHER PUNITIVE MEASURES

There are, of course, other disciplinary actions. Innovative managers can come up with almost as many punitive measures as their employees can find ways to avoid them. Some of these measures include the following:

- withholding, or delaying, salary increases
- denying promotions
- lowering performance ratings
- placing on probation
- demoting or transferring

- denying requests for educational support or time off
- withdrawing special privileges or authority
- giving unpleasant assignments
- canceling special projects
- removing from teams, committees, or other work groups

EMPLOYEE REACTIONS TO BEING DISCIPLINED

- They quit and leave.
- They quit but stay because of vested time, unwillingness to change jobs or lifestyle, or lack of opportunities elsewhere.
- A significant percentage of employees who are disciplined resort to filing complaints or grievances. They seek redress via unions, courts, the Equal Employment Opportunity Commission, the Occupational Safety and Health Administration, or other governmental agencies.

THE ORAL REPRIMAND

Avoid gunnysacking. Gunnysacking is saving up all your complaints and then, one frustrating day, dumping the entire load on someone.

Deliver reprimands as soon as possible after the misbehavior, *but not until you have control of your emotions.*

Keep it confidential. If the person has an office, go there. It will arouse less interest than when you call the person into your office.

Do not be apologetic. Describe what is wrong and how you feel about it. Do not exaggerate. Attack the problem, not the person. Avoid starting sentences with *you* or using subjective words such as *attitude, work ethic,* and *professionalism* and absolute terms such as *always* and *never.*

Let the person respond, *but cut short a litany of lame excuses.* Anticipate remarks such as "You're not being fair" or "You can't say things like that to me."

Articulate exactly what you expect. End by expressing confidence in the employee's ability to change. Provide an affirmation that you still value him or her as member of your team.

If this is a repeat reprimand or has previously been addressed by coaching or counseling, use the counseling technique you learned in previous chapters. Be less empathic and more formal, however. The employee should get the impression that your patience is running out.

You may want to start with "Joyce, your previous attempt hasn't worked, and I can't tolerate any more of this behavior. It is way below what you are capable of, Joyce. In fact, I still have difficulty understanding it."

Now give Joyce air time, but cut it off when she starts to repeat or tries to divert your attention to something or someone else. Bring her back to the issue with "Joyce, we're here to discuss your problem. Let's stick to that."

Warn of future action. For example, "Joyce, if this is not corrected immediately, it will be necessary for me to_____" (specify what _____ is).

After the meeting, treat the person in a friendly fashion as you did after the counseling session. You and the employee have joined forces against a common enemy; you are allies in the endeavor.

If you have an employee who was hired by your boss or who was highly recruited and he or she is not measuring up to standards, make certain that you discuss this with your boss.[1]

When you must discipline an employee who is popular with his or her co-workers, you must rely on the support you have built up with your team. If they trust you and know that you are fair, they will support your decision.

THE WRITTEN REPRIMAND

In a large percentage of cases, the written reprimand ultimately leads to a separation, voluntary or otherwise, so proceed with caution. Your human resources department may have a special form that you must use for this purpose.

Discuss the problem with your boss or a member of the human resources department before you write up the report. Find out whether you have the authority to issue written reprimands.

A written warning must be crafted carefully. It is a legal document and may end up in court. Avoid any statements that you cannot prove. Provide observations and actual statements, not opinions or hearsay. A list of essentials is presented in Exhibit 17–2.

When you meet with Joyce, explain that a written reprimand constitutes a formal warning and will be documented in her personnel file. Review any previous counseling sessions or oral reprimands for the same problem. Be specific as to your expectations and the final date for compliance (e.g., "If within the next 60 days you are late for work one more time without an acceptable excuse, you will be sent home on a 1-day suspension without pay").

Tell Joyce that there is a statute of limitations, that after a period of time (e.g., 6 months) the record of the incident will be removed from her personnel file.

Insist that Joyce read and sign the report. Inform her of her right to attach a rebuttal or to confer with your superior.

SUSPENSIONS

Some offenses call for immediate suspension or discharge without any antecedent counseling or reprimands (see Exhibit 17–1). In many organizations, supervisors may only recommend such action; the actual order must come from a senior executive.

Exhibit 17–2 Essentials of a Written Disciplinary Report

Description of the problem
- State facts, not assumptions, hearsay, or opinions.
- Give dates when possible. Provide examples.
- Record names of witnesses and/or involved persons.

Record of previous warnings
- Give dates.
- Indicate what was said by you and by the employee.
- State what changes in conduct, if any, resulted.

Record of previous written reprimands or punitive actions
- Attach copies.
- Indicate what punitive measures were taken.
- State what changes in conduct, if any, resulted.

The employee's document of explanation, denial, or rebuttal
- If the employee chooses to do this, include a copy.
- If the employee chooses not to do this, describe what the employee stated as accurately as possible. Include the statement that the employee chose not to prepare such a document.

Record of punitive action now being decreed
- Include a statement that the punishment was explained to the employee.
- Include a statement that the employee understood what was to happen.

Description of expected performance
- Include the target date for achieving satisfactory performance.
- Describe what will or will not be tolerated.
- Provide your signature and that of the employee. If the employee refuses to sign, call in a witness and repeat the question, and if the employee still refuses to sign have the witness verify that.

If the employee has received oral and written warnings in the past, a formal meeting may not be needed. Your human resources department will provide the necessary form or instruct you on how to prepare the report.

When Joyce returns to work after a suspension, treat her as any other employee. Be businesslike, neither clubby nor aloof. She has already been punished.

DISCHARGES

Today's managers are reluctant to fire people. They cite all the roadblocks and potential legal backlashes that may result from such action. Townsend, however, in his best seller *Up the Organization,* states that purging bad performers is as good a tonic for the organization as rewarding the star performers.[2]

One surprising observation is that many fired people will subsequently say that it was one of the best things that ever happened to them.

Many managers feel that it is all but impossible to fire anyone. If specific work standards are in place and mandated procedures are followed, however, terminations are not that difficult. All too often supervisors create the problem by accepting unsatisfactory performance or behavior over a period of time and by rating performance as satisfactory when it is not.

The prescribed procedure for personnel separations, both process and content, must be adhered to carefully. Usually the actual termination is carried out by the human resources department.

Cautious employers insist that a personnel professional and an employment lawyer review and approve all discharges before employees are notified.[3] This is for good reason. A significant number of fired employees file wrongful dismissal suits, and these can be expensive and time consuming for the employer. Those who file such suits usually charge that they were fired without cause or for insufficient reason or that the termination violated a longstanding written or verbal agreement with the employer.

Employers protect themselves by providing employee handbooks that clearly state the organization's disciplinary policies and avoid mention of permanent employment or statements that employees can be terminated only for cause. They also insist on good position descriptions, performance standards, and performance appraisals. They warn their managers about the danger of rating people higher than they deserve.

To sustain a discharge against legal challenges, an employer must be able to prove the following:

- that there are specific work standards and policies and that employees are repeatedly reminded about these
- that what was alleged did take place, involved the employee, and warranted the discharge
- that such behavior has not been condoned in the past or that other workers have been discharged for similar offenses
- that the sequence of progressive discipline followed prescribed policies and procedures
- that the employee made no genuine effort to heed the previous warnings even though he or she had been informed as to the consequences
- that the firing was based on behavior or results, not on any of the following (wrongful discharge):
  —discrimination (gender, race, religion, age, or disability)
  —whistle blowing related to safety practices, illegal acts, sexual harassment, military or jury duty, or worker's compensation claims
  —violation of implied contract (the employee was promised a permanent job)

> **A caveat:** *Without standards and documentation, you and your employer will be in deep trouble.*

THE TERMINATION MEETING

Prepare yourself emotionally. Avoid taking responsibility for the termination. It is a business decision, not a personal one. You may want to discuss this with a trusted friend, but be careful to protect the employee's privacy.

A termination interview should never be initiated with a possibility of reconsideration in mind. All such possibilities should have been exhausted before the final meeting.

Ideally the meeting is held on a Friday afternoon after other employees have departed and shortly after the employee has received written notice from the human resources department.

Briefly describe why this action was necessary and that the action has been reviewed by management and is final. Say that you are sorry that things did not work out, and wish the person well. If the person gets angry or breaks into tears, stay calm. Do not get drawn into a debate or agree with any charges the person makes. Say that the human resources department will discuss terminal pay and benefits and will have the person's final check ready.

The supervisor's responsibility may include ensuring that the employee has returned keys, identification, and other items belonging to the organization.

NONPUNITIVE DISCIPLINE

Punishment breeds resistance, encourages subterfuge, and undermines employees' willingness to make future contributions to the organization. The nonpunitive or positive disciplinary approach has been successful in overcoming many of these adverse effects.[4]

The theme of the nonpunitive approach is building commitment instead of enforcing compliance. It is congruent with the principle of participative management in that it, too, is treating employees as adults, not children.

Encouragement replaces threats. Rules are referred to as employee responsibilities; verbal and written warnings are expressed as suggestions. Discussions are low key with emphasis on problem solving. For example, Joyce is told that her performance threatens the unit's success and her future.

When these discussions fail, the suggestion is made that there may be a poor employee-job fit and that a change in employment may be beneficial for all parties.

The most radical departure from the traditional disciplinary approach is the 1-day suspension with pay. The employee is given a day of decision. The supervisor says something such as the following:

> Joyce, our solutions have not worked. I have serious concerns about whether you want to continue here. Joyce, I don't want a commitment right now. Take the rest of the day [or tomorrow] to think over what you want to do, then let me know what you've decided. If you want to continue as a member of our team, fine. However, you'll have to give me a signed, firm commitment that you will fulfill all your responsibilities. If you don't, then we both have failed and your employment will end.
>
> Joyce, as a token of our faith in you, and as a sign that we want you to stay with us, you'll receive full pay for the day of decision.

This strategy has reduced the filing of grievances over terminations, decreased involuntary turnover, and improved morale. The only objections have been from employees' coworkers, who resent someone getting a day off with pay while they must do that employee's work.

TERMINATION FOR POOR PERFORMANCE

If a termination is the result of poor performance without any violations of rules and regulations, make certain that the employee has been given ample warning and an opportunity to shore up his or her performance. The work record must be adequately documented.

SOUND DISCIPLINARY PRINCIPLES

Know:
- exactly what the unacceptable behavior is and what policy or rule has been violated
- any mitigating circumstances
- the scope of your authority
- how similar offenses have been handled in the past

Assume that:
- employees want to do good work
- employees must perceive some benefit from their unacceptable behavior
- you or others may be partly to blame
- you have many punitive options

Act:
- quickly once you have the information you need
- after consulting with your superior or the human resources department
- consistently and fairly
- by using punishment only as a last resort
- by selecting penalties that are appropriate for the offenses
- by documenting, documenting, documenting
- by having the terminated employee leave the premises as soon as possible

Do not:
- let misbehavior develop into habits
- act before you get the facts
- be apologetic
- use words such as *loyalty, attitude, work ethic, professionalism,* and *maturity*
- say "Management expects . . ."; say "I expect . . ."
- trap yourself into a series of verbal warnings for the same problem with the same employee

DOWNSIZING

Restructuring, acquisitions, mergers, and financial reverses result in reductions in force (RIFs). Sometimes RIFs can be achieved by early retirements, attrition, hiring freezes, voluntary separations, or reduced work hours. These measures are often insufficient, however, thus necessitating involuntary separations.

If the mandate you receive is to reduce the payroll to a certain level, hold brainstorming sessions with your employees for ideas for reducing salary costs without laying off anyone. Some senior people may decide that this is a good time for them to end their careers. Some full-time employees may opt for part-time employment, and part-timers may be willing to reduce their hours, especially if they have greater schedule options.

A key decision for the chief executive officer is whether the selection of those who are to be furloughed is to be based on seniority or on value to the organization. If the latter, supervisors may play an important, and sometimes painful, role in the selection process.

Supervisors must face the anger of those who leave and the apprehension of those who remain.

HANDLING THOSE WHO LEAVE

The reaction of people who are laid off is much like that of patients being told that they have cancer. First there is disbelief, then anger or depression, and finally acceptance.

Be tolerant of their anger, bitterness, and hostility, and be empathic when the tears flow. Console yourself with the knowledge that most of these people will recover and find new and sometimes more satisfying positions.

Answer their questions honestly, and make sure that they get the information they need about benefits and eligibility for unemployment benefits. If outplacement services are available, encourage employees to take full advantage of them. These may include placement services, help with job applications and interview techniques, psychological testing, and training for new vocations.

Use your personal network to try to find new jobs for them, or at least to steer them in the right direction.

The likelihood of recalls is important, but refrain from giving false hopes. If the likelihood of rehire is high, keep in touch with them.

HANDLING THOSE WHO REMAIN

Layoff survivors often feel guilty and depressed as a result of losing friends and colleagues. They may experience a drop in self-esteem and morale. In the back of their mind is the fear of future layoffs.

Remain visible; do not hide in meetings or bury yourself in paperwork. Share their concern about their buddies who are being laid off.

Distance yourself from idle gossip. Keep yourself informed, and share that information. Explain the rationale for the changes. Answer questions honestly, and listen to expressions of frustration and fear. Do not wait for staff meetings or newsletters to keep your team informed. Call special meetings whenever you learn new things.

You and your staff must pick up the slack. Ask for your staff's input and cooperation in closing ranks and getting the job done with fewer people. Point out the increased need for teamwork and for everyone to make a special effort. Prepare a list of duties and responsibilities that must now be assumed by others. Announce assignment changes, and provide any additional training that may be needed.

Use your reward and recognition system to reward your team or individuals who make special efforts.

NOTES

1. M.M. Broadwell and R.S. House, *Supervising Technical and Professional People* (New York: Wilely, 1986).

2. R. Townsend, *Up the Organization* (New York: Fawcett World Library, 1971).

3. J. Greenan, Judged by the jury: Lessons from a wrongful termination lawsuit, *H.R. Focus* 3 (1992): 15.

4. J.R. Redeker, Discipline, part 2: The nonpunitive approach works by design, *Personnel* 62 (1985): 7–10.

Chapter 18

Managing Your Boss

- pick a good boss
- get to know your boss better
- communication is the key to success
- increase your responsibility and authority
- be loyal and show respect
- when you have more than one immediate superior
- general tips
- difficult bosses
- when you have serious, legitimate gripes

PICK A GOOD BOSS

It is not likely that you will be asked to select your boss. If you are job hunting and multiple employers are seeking your services, however, one of your considerations should be the person to whom you will report. Your opportunity for promotion is greater when that person is on the inside lane of the promotional track, is ready to retire, or is likely to resign. Managers whose careers are in ascendancy can also carry people up with them.

You also want to know about leadership style, morale, and turnover in that unit. The importance of this information cannot be overemphasized, if for no other reason than that for most employees their greatest stressor is their immediate supervisor.

This information is not found in any handout, but with some in-depth probing you can learn much, especially if you have the opportunity to talk to some of the personnel and to ask questions of several managers during your employment interviews. The person you are replacing is usually the best source.

GET TO KNOW YOUR BOSS BETTER

Let us assume that Ann Smith is your boss. Mention has already been made of leadership styles. Communication preferences are also important. Learn how Ann wants to receive data from you. Does she want to read it, like John Kennedy? If she is a listener type, like Harry Truman, you go in and talk to her.

Other considerations are Ann's likes and dislikes, her decision-making style, and any form of stereotyping or other hang-ups. Most important of all, what are Ann's expectations and priorities concerning your performance? If either you or Ann is new on the job, take time to review jointly your position description and work standards.

Watch out for the boss who thinks disagreement is insubordination or who steals credit for all your accomplishments.

COMMUNICATION IS THE KEY TO SUCCESS

Take the initiative for keeping Ann informed. Never hide problems. Do your homework, encapsulate the material, and be prepared to offer at least one solution. "It is easier to help your boss make up her mind than it is to persuade her to change it."[1(p.238)]

Do not waste her time with trivia or gossip. Learn when to speak up and when to remain silent. Avoid disagreements in public, and never embarrass her in front of others. Be assertive, but not aggressive or threatening.

Pick the right time and place for your one-on-one meetings. Some bosses want input first thing Monday morning so they can get a handle on operations. Others do not want to hear or see anyone until they get their desk cleared and their correspondence taken care of.

INCREASE YOUR RESPONSIBILITY AND AUTHORITY

When you have brought Ann certain problems and have learned what the usual solutions are, say "Ann, do you still want me to bother you with this kind of problem?"

Maintain good relationships with other work units (your internal customers). You want Ann to know that you are someone she can trust to represent her department.

Start by identifying three ways you can help your boss. For example, if you know that Ann hates to prepare reports and to talk to sales representatives, offer to prepare rough drafts of reports and to represent her when vendors appear.

Accept delegated responsibilities with enthusiasm. Better still, seek out additional responsibilities. For example, volunteer to chair a committee or to lead a focus group.

Remember that promotions are based not so much on what you have done as on what your superiors think you can do for them in the future.

Gain the respect of your colleagues. Become a resource person and troubleshooter. This goes a long way toward developing a power base. Do not shift blame or point fingers. Never take credit for something others have done. Instead, lead the cheers for their accomplishments.

Constantly expand your professional and social network. Do this more by getting people obligated to you than by asking favors.

BE LOYAL AND SHOW RESPECT

This does not mean brown-nosing, although a little of that helps too. It does mean making your boss look good. Loyalty can be expressed by standing up for Ann when she is being criticized, coming to her meetings on time, showing up at social functions of the organization, being willing to make the extra effort, and generally expressing enthusiasm.

Most important is a tone of respect in daily communications. Know when and how to dissent. Most managers accept disagreement if it is done tactfully. Learn how direct you can be, and be diplomatic. Remember that what you think is a bad decision by Ann may be one she has had imposed on her.

Share credit for your accomplishments with her.

WHEN YOU HAVE MORE THAN ONE IMMEDIATE SUPERIOR

An increasing number of employees report to two or more bosses. This can lead to conflicts of time sharing or priorities and even conflicting orders.

Meeting with both bosses to get scheduling conflicts solved may be effective, especially if you can offer compromises that will satisfy each of them. This does not always work, however. Sometimes when you get competing assignments, it is best to let the junior boss know you have other work for the senior one and to ask him or her to resolve the conflict with the other boss.

GENERAL TIPS

Do:

- look and act as a professional.
- acknowledge the support of others
- say nice things about your boss to other people (it will get back to him or her)
- act as a devil's advocate occasionally, then yield gracefully (bosses like to persuade people)

- develop a reputation as a problem solver
- be willing to risk your reputation by trying new things
- have the courage to stand up for what you think is right
- live up to your promises
- protect and defend the reputation of your organization and your boss, inside and outside the organization
- keep frustrations and negative thoughts to yourself
- prevent your boss from making a serious mistake
- if necessary, modify your behavioral style
- know when to opt for transfer or resignation

Do Not:
- do anything that would lead your boss to regard you as a threat
- say "That's not in my position description" or "I was not hired to do that"
- let pessimism or negativism creep into your attitude
- steal credit
- knock your boss, co-workers, or organization in public
- distort the truth
- develop an amorous relationship with your boss
- threaten to resign when you do not get your way
- sacrifice your professional and ethical values

DIFFICULT BOSSES

Look at the bright side. Sooner or later, most of us must deal with an unpleasant or incompetent boss. When you have one of these early in your career, you have a wonderful opportunity to fine tune your skill in getting along with a difficult person who has power over you. I shall always be grateful to my first commanding officer in the U.S. Navy. He was a real S.O.B., but I learned how to tolerate him, and from then on all my commanding officers seemed like pussycats.

If you feel that Ann is a dreadful boss, examine your own behavior. Are you doing anything that irritates her? Is your office a mess while hers is spotless? Do you show up at her meetings late and without excuses? Are you occasionally careless about your appearance while Ann is always impeccably dressed? Do you get a lot of personal phone calls or visits or have to drop things and run home? Do you routinely get to work after Ann has arrived or leave before she does? Have you been sensitive to things that you say or do that annoy her?

Procrastinators

These are usually agreeable, well-intentioned folks with perfectionist tendencies. They avoid or put off decisions for fear of making mistakes or offending others.

Try to find the reasons for their hesitancy and eliminate them. Give them positive strokes when they do make decisions.

Be reassuring and optimistic. When you need an approval, have all the data ready. Tell them that you have checked out your proposals carefully. Establish deadlines for their answers (e.g., "Ann, if I don't hear from you by Friday, I'll assume it's O.K. to go ahead, right?").

Instead of asking permission, send a memo stating what you intend to do unless you hear to the contrary. Make sure that you give her sufficient time to get back to you.

Unfair Bosses

If you are getting more than your share of after-hours or holiday assignments, instead of accusing the boss of sticking it to you say "Ann, it seems I've been drawing a disproportionate share of holiday assignments. Are you aware that I have been on call on each of the last four holidays?"

If the boss is dumping excessive scutwork on you or delegating too much, ask her to set your work priorities or to provide additional help.

If you think that your boss is discriminating against you, ask him or her point blank something such as "Are you against women in this job?" The answer, of course, will be no. Follow with "If that is true, why do you frequently say that women do not understand mechanical things?" After the boss fumbles with that, say how you feel when he or she makes such remarks. If this gets out of hand, blow the whistle on your boss. Your case must be solid and specific. You must be able to give examples and have corroborative evidence.

The Ones Who Bypass You

These managers frequently give orders to your subordinates without your knowledge, usually when you are not right on the spot.

These skip-level intrusions can be minimized if you sit down and discuss them with your boss. Point out how this undermines your authority and confuses your staff. Give specific examples.

Tell your staff that they are to keep you informed about requests from others and (except in emergency situations) are not to carry these orders out until they have checked with you.

If you feel that your employees can diplomatically tell certain of these order-givers that they must get your approval first, try that approach. You may want to authorize your team members to decide when they should honor extrinsic orders. You can provide a discretionary task list.

Laissez Faire Leaders

These people are not really leaders; they just have the title. They have abdicated their responsibility. They are never around when you need them, and when they are they are no help.

Determine what your authority is, and use it. Revise your position description to include more control over your areas of responsibility. Seek broad approval for your objectives, plans, and schedules, and then go ahead with them.

Pin the boss down when he or she issues vague directives. Gradually assume more responsibility and control.

Bureaucrats

Make sure that you play by the rules. Avoid pushing these bosses into risky things or complaining about lack of action. Know the policies, procedures, and practices thoroughly.

Manipulators Who Fail To Deliver on Their Promises

After receiving verbal approval or promise, send these bosses memos in which you spell out what was approved or promised.

WHEN YOU HAVE SERIOUS LEGITIMATE GRIPES

Recognize that your work environment is not healthy if your boss routinely expects you to do personal favors that have nothing to do with the welfare of the organization. There may be times when you must balk at such assignments (e.g., you are always asked to take notes at meetings or to fetch coffee because you are a woman).

When you register complaints with your boss and do not get satisfaction, keep a detailed record of what transpired.

Avoid end runs, that is, going to the boss's superiors with problems or complaints. This is usually the beginning of the end of a relationship. The most serious variant of the end run is when someone keeps going up the hierarchy until he or she finds someone who gives the answer he or she is seeking.

If you do feel strongly about talking to a higher authority, tell Ann first, or suggest that you both go together.

We will discuss hostile bosses, sexual harassers, and other kinds of unpleasant leaders in subsequent chapters.

NOTE

1. W. Oncken, Jr., *Managing Management Time* (Englewood Cliffs, N.J.: Prentice-Hall, 1984), 238.

Chapter 19

Managing Health Care Specialists and Multicultural Work Forces

- characteristics of health care specialists
- recruitment, selection, and orientation of health care specialists
- appropriate leadership style, recognition, and rewards
- communication
- educational and training opportunities
- coping with the prima donnas and nonconformists
- working with a multicultural work force

CHARACTERISTICS OF HEALTH CARE SPECIALISTS

Their Profession Gets Top Priority

Health care professionals are often loyal to their profession first and to their organization second. It is important for them to be respected by their professional peers.

They are highly focused on their own specialty, and they strive for technical excellence. Most of them are competent and take great pride in their accomplishments.

Health care specialists work for the satisfaction of a job well done rather than for the approval of others. They seek self-direction rather than outside guidance. They often know more than their supervisors about their specific area of expertise.

Their Personalities Do Not Please Everyone

Health care specialists are often impatient and sometimes uncooperative. Because they are impatient with people who seem not as bright or as knowledgeable as they are, they tend not to mix with nontechnical people and are often conspicuous by their absence at staff social affairs.[1] Some of these valuable workers may be ostracized because they do not conform to social standards.

Some health care specialists have big egos, and a few are difficult to control because they develop a prima donna complex[2] (see below).

HOW TO HANDLE HEALTH CARE SPECIALISTS

Recruitment and Selection

Try to detect and exclude those who are most likely to have serious role conflicts. Question them about their goals and aspirations, and match these with those of your organization.

Be frank about the opportunities in your department. Is there a clinical ladder, or are promotions only into administration? Is it publish or perish?[3]

Orientation

During the orientation phase, be explicit as to the responsibilities involved and the degrees of autonomy permitted. If the new hires find that they dislike the restrictions imposed on them or that they yearn for the academic atmosphere that they left behind, it is better for all parties for them to discover this during their probationary period.

Appropriate Leadership Style

Managers who structure professional jobs to ensure maximum challenge and autonomy will probably appeal to most health care specialists.[4] Adopt a delegative or consultative leadership style when dealing with experienced professionals. Minimize supervisory control.

Function mainly as a coordinator and facilitator. Remove obstacles, bend rules, cut red tape, remove distractions, and run interference. Permit flexible schedules when feasible.

Provide them with the freedom to act, challenges, necessary resources, and professional titles that recognize specialized education or responsibilities. Permit as much authority and technical control as each of them merits.

Recognition and Rewards

Support organizational efforts to establish dual career tracks to provide alternative channels for salary increases or promotions without employees having to move into management.

Broadcast congratulatory news such as results of special projects, research developments, and individual achievements.[5]

Communication

Learn the fundamentals and terminology of their specialty. Make important information available to them. Let them pick and choose what they want to digest.

Provide opportunities for them to share their professional knowledge (e.g., to attend professional meetings and to give lectures or workshops).

Educational and Training Opportunities

Encourage their continuing education, but do not force them into supervisory training against their wishes.

These people thrive on attending technical and professional meetings. Approve as many as you can; they deserve higher priority than many health care employers give them.

Provide opportunities for them to use the skills they learn. Make appropriate reference books and periodicals available to them.

If these employees have compatibility problems, encourage them to attend remedial seminars on interpersonal relationships. Be diplomatic but persistent when you suggest these. A good time is at annual performance reviews.

Coping with the Prima Donnas

Confident of their job skills or knowledge, prima donnas feel secure and irreplaceable. They may become abrasive to others, even to customers. These attitudes and behaviors can have a devastating effect on customer service and departmental morale.[6]

Try to identify prima donnas during the selection process by asking applicants to describe their work style and to relate examples of their ability to work as part of a team. Ask their references how they got along with others.

To prevent the development of a prima donna complex, use cross-training so that other employees can substitute for the superstar should that be necessary. A good time to initiate this is before the prima donna takes his or her vacation.

Insist on acceptable performance, and do not reward antiteam behavior. Counsel them on the necessity to pitch in and help when necessary. Use peer pressure to reinforce group norms. Do not bend the rules too far for them.[7]

Coping with the Nonconformist

The nonconformist also requires special handling, and that is not always easy. This is complicated when the nonconformist possesses expertise that is scarce and essential. You know this, and so does the nonconformist.

You can usually spot the nonconformists by how they look. They take great delight in violating dress codes and by becoming very defensive when challenged about their appearance. They are seldom good team players and insist on going about their tasks in their own way. At meetings they stand out as devil's advocates, or they may not show up. On the positive side, many of these individuals are very creative and innovative.

If their idiosyncratic behavior has minimal effect on customers, colleagues, or work results, and their overall contribution more than makes up for their lack of conformity, your best action may be no action.

Let them know that you regard them as valuable members of the work unit. Tolerate their impatience and complaints. Do not accuse them of being stubborn or unreasonable. Bend the rules a bit, but make them accountable for results.

Reinforce any attempt that the employee makes at being more sociable or accommodating.

If their appearance or behavior is not acceptable, hold counseling sessions at which you state exactly what they do or what perceptions they create that are adversely affecting customers or other employees. Warn them that lack of cooperation will not be tolerated. Threats of low performance ratings are usually not effective with these people. They do not pay much attention to or worry about what you or others think about their performance. Firing is often the only effective threat, but you must be certain that you have enough documented proof to justify such drastic action. These individuals also like to file grievances. If you assign them to work that demands rigid conformity, they may leave of their own accord.

WORKING WITH A MULTICULTURAL WORKFORCE

Cultural diversity is the watchword of the 1990s.[8] Increasingly, health care supervisors find themselves directing employees who have language, ethical, and cultural differences. These incongruences can have significant negative operational and interpersonal consequences. Do not assume that minority employees want to "blend in" with the mainstream culture. It is more likely that they will want to maintain a clear cultural identity. We must think in terms of pluralism—a cultural mosaic—not a melting pot.[9]

The following measures will minimize these problems:

- Understand your own cultural biases, and replace outdated stereotypes by learning as much as you can about cultural and language differences, respecting them, and growing more comfortable with them.

- Encourage your employees who have language difficulties to enroll in courses on verbal and written English language.

- Make a sincere effort to learn their languages. For a start, learn greetings and courtesy phrases in key languages. Learn how to articulate positive strokes and to give simple instructions in their tongues.

- Seek out information about cultural variances. For example, eye contact has negative connotations in some cultures. We are amused or annoyed by people who make slurping sounds while eating pasta or soup. In Japanese culture, this is expected. If you give a Chinese person a gift, do not expect it to be opened in front of you; that will be done later to avoid any possibility of embarrassment.[10]

- Do not lump different cultural groups under a generic term such as *Hispanic.* There are wide cultural differences among Hispanics. For example, people from Mexico and the Philippines perceive status symbols as deserved and expected, whereas those from the Argentines criticize or resent such badges of prestige.[11]

- Respect cultural observations (e.g., Black History Month, Asian Pacific Heritage Week, Chinese New Year [in February], and National Hispanic Week).

- Ensure involvement of minority groups in all forms of participative management, team building, and empowerment.

- Encourage these groups to become actively involved in social activities.

NOTES

1. M.M. Broadwell and R.S. House, *Supervising Technical and Professional People* (New York, N.Y.: Wiley, 1986).

2. J.E. Osborne, Supervising superstars: The talent and temperament conflict, *Supervisory Management* 36 (1991): 1–3.

3. J. Raelin, et al., Why professionals turn sour and what to do, *Personnel* 62 (1985): 28–41.

4. Raelin et al., Why professionals turn sour, 32.

5. D. Lea and R. Brostrom, Managing the high-tech professional, *Personnel* 65 (1988): 12–22.

6. Osborne, Supervising superstars, 2.

7. Osborne, Supervising superstars, 3.

8. S.M. Ketchum, Managing the multicultural laboratory, *Clinical Laboratory Management Review* 6 (1992): 287–304, 306.

9. Ketchum, Managing the multicultural laboratory, 291.

10. Ketchum, Managing the mulitcultural laboratory, 293.

11. Ketchum, Managing the multicultural laboratory, 294.

Chapter 20

Conflict and Confrontation

- major sources of conflict
- goals and objectives
- the basic five strategies
- preparations for conflict resolution
- the three keys to assertive confrontations
- the confrontation
- confronting an angry person
- tips for more effective confrontations

Conflict is not all bad. In fact, it is necessary for any progressive organization. It takes place whenever there is change, empowerment, paradigm shifts, team building, or attempts at quality improvement. It forces people to take a second look at situations, and if handled properly it enhances interpersonal relationships.

MAJOR SOURCES OF CONFLICT

- People may not know what is expected of them.
- Policies and rules may be ambiguous, and some may think that they are only for other people.
- Communication is garbled.
- There are hierarchical conflicts. For example, someone with a PhD or MD degree resents taking orders from a young manager with an MBA.
- There are incompatibilities or disagreements based on differences of value systems, goals, temperaments, attitudes, or ethics.
- There are conflicts over funds, space, time, personnel, equipment, or staffing schedules.
- There is competition for power.
- There are operational or staffing changes.

The etiology is not always apparent. Often there is a covert issue hidden by a less important overt factor. Other situations are murky because the etiology is complex.

GOALS AND OBJECTIVES

The proactive goal is to prevent conflicts. When that is not possible, we opt to keep small conflicts from escalating into big ones. Objectives include diffusing anger, venting feelings, and converting conflicts into problem-solving exercises.

THE BASIC FIVE STRATEGIES

Each of the following strategies is appropriate for certain situations. The trick is to pick the right one.

Avoid

This may be to deny that there is a problem, to escape physically, or to pass the buck. This strategy is appropriate when:

- it is not your problem
- there is nothing you can do about it
- it is not important
- additional information is needed
- you or the other individual is emotionally upset
- the situation will probably ameliorate if you can wait it out

Fight

This is risky; you may lose. Even if you win the skirmish, your opponent may wait for another opportunity to retaliate, or he or she may become a saboteur. This strategy is appropriate when:

- quick action is needed (you do not convene a committee meeting when a fire breaks out)
- there must be enforcement of rules, such as safety regulations
- ethical or legal issues are involved

Surrender

This is conceding or accommodating ("O.K., O.K., I'll do it"). This strategy is appropriate when:

- you are wrong
- it does not matter to you but is important to them
- you have little or no chance to win
- harmony and stability are important
- giving in on a minor item means winning a more important one later

Compromise

Compromise permits each party to get part of what it wants, so there is some satisfaction for both. Most union-management disputes are settled in this manner. This strategy is appropriate when:

- opposing goals are incompatible
- a temporary settlement to complex issues is needed
- time constraints call for an expedient solution

Collaborate

Collaboration is working together to find solutions that satisfy both parties. This win-win approach is usually the best alternative, but it often requires a creative solution because the best answer is one that neither side originally considered. This strategy is especially appropriate when:

- the issue is too important to be settled any other way
- commitment is sought via consensus
- different perspectives are to be explored

PREPARATIONS FOR CONFLICT RESOLUTION

What we call conflict resolution others (attorneys, purchasing agents, union officials, and diplomats) call negotiating. Whatever it is called, planning is essential and, in the long run, time saving. The planning process consists of two steps: diagnosis (analysis) and strategy.

Diagnose the situation by asking yourself the following questions:
- What are likely to be the points of agreement and disagreement?
- What do you want to accomplish?

- What are your minimal acceptable resolutions?
- What do you think the other person wants?
- What are the strengths and weaknesses of your stance?
- What false assumptions or incorrect perceptions might the other person have?

First, select a strategy from the previous list of five basic strategies. You may be able to avoid the confrontation, but this is usually a poor choice, and you always have the option of breaking off an encounter at any step of the way.

When you must face an aggressive person or situation, prepare yourself for the encounter, and then make your move. Do not procrastinate.

Prepare the arguments you can make to maximize the value of positive aspects, to minimize the negatives, and to counter the other person's arguments.

THE THREE KEYS TO ASSERTIVE CONFRONTATIONS

1. **Success imagery.** This consists of visualizing a successful confrontation. Picture your body language, hear your words and voice tone, and envision a successful outcome. Athletes and professional speakers have used this technique with great success for years.

2. **Self-talk.** This is simply converting negative thoughts to positive ones when we are talking to ourselves. All of us carry on inner dialogs with ourselves all day long.

   When we are in a passive mode, these internal conversations are negative and pessimistic; our minds conjure up statements such as "I could never say that" or "She'll just blow me away."

   Let your positive affirmations take control. Say to yourself, "I will be in control." Avoid weak statements such as "I'm going to try to stand up to her next time."

3. **Rehearsals.** After you have selected your dialog and appropriate body language, rehearse the anticipated encounter over and over. Do it in front of a mirror. Verbalize out loud. Still better, get a friend or relative to role play with you. Do not be satisfied until your performance is down pat.

THE CONFRONTATION

After outlining the problem, focus on areas of agreement (e.g., "Lynn, I think we agree that we both want what is best for our patients, right?").

Be an attentive listener, keying in on what the other person is saying. Do not be guilty of mindscripting, which is switching your attention from what the other person is saying to what you want to say next. Be empathic. Respect the other person's feelings, but still feel free to respond in a manner of your choosing.

Let the person know that you hear and understand. Validate with something such as "As I understand it, Lynn, you're angry because ———, is that right?" Validating has two benefits: It clarifies the problem, and it lets the person know that what he or she is saying is important.

Seek a solution that satisfies both of you. Often it pays to ask exactly what it is that the person wants. An angry person may have to stop and think when faced with that, or you may find that what he or she wants is less than what you were prepared to offer.

On the other hand, don't neglect to say what it is that you want.

If you feel your heart pounding, face turning red, voice rising, and fists clenching, call a time out. Say "You're making me uncomfortable" or "I need a little time to collect my thoughts, Lynn." The person will usually back off or may even get derailed.

To avoid retaliation, use the strawman technique. This is a way of expressing your opinion indirectly. It is most appropriate when dealing with a strongly opinionated boss or a know-it-all. For example, Instead of saying "Dr. John, I think you are wrong," say "Dr. John, how would you respond to a physician who claims that the therapy you ordered is outdated?"

CONFRONTING AN ANGRY PERSON

People are more likely to express anger toward those who have less power. Sales representatives, service providers, spouses, children, and pets take more than their share of abuse.

Anger is manifested by bitter sarcasm, accusations, crying, sulking, pouting, and walking away (often accompanied by door-slamming and angry words). Yelling, threatening, and physical attacks are, of course, more frightening.

Some people are supersensitive. They may have explosive tempers on short fuses. These individuals take everything personally. Focus on your goal. Do not argue or lose your temper; just press your case. Say "I know you're angry about this, but we must solve this problem."

TIPS FOR MORE EFFECTIVE CONFRONTATION

- Be prepared, just as you would be for a debate.
- Pick the best time and place. Do not meet when your self-esteem is low or when either of you is upset.

- Regard the other person not as an enemy but as a partner in problem solving.
- Clarify the other person's viewpoint and your own. Do not proceed until these viewpoints and the desired outcomes are crystal clear.
- Focus first on a point of agreement, and work from there.
- Be assertive, not aggressive.
- Attack the problem, not the other person.
- Do not cause your opponent to lose face. Don't threaten or issue ultimatums.
- Don't be sarcastic or critical.
- To avoid retaliation, use the strawman technique.
- Watch your body language. Maintain eye contact, sit or stand up straight, and appear relaxed. Do not fidget or squirm. Avoid threatening gestures such as finger-pointing, fist-making, crossed arms, hands on hips, or scowling. Smile when you agree, remain expressionless when you disagree.
- Control your voice. Keep its volume, pitch, and rate under control. Stop if you find it growing louder, faster, or high pitched.
- Be diplomatic and tentative when facing firm resistance. Use words such as *maybe, perhaps,* or *you may be right.*
- When cornered or upset, escape by pleading stress.
- Do not get stuck believing that your solution is the only good one. Focus on the benefits of your argument to the other person.
- Promise rewards ("If you . . . , then I'll . . .").
- End on a positive note.

Chapter 21

Employees with Problems

- the marginal performer
- the older employee
- parents of latchkey children
- the absent employee
- the employee with a personal problem
- company policies
- handling employees with personal problems
- employee assistance programs
- special precautions
- two employees are feuding

Some employees create problems for supervisors because they "can, but don't." Such employees include the marginal performer, the absent employee, and the worker who has an emotional, mental, or drug-related problem.

THE MARGINAL PERFORMER

Among the marginal performers who could do better if they wished are older employees who are just putting in time until their retirement, those who regard their job as interim employment, and those who lack motivation. The first step in dealing with these employees is to get to know them better. Determine their motivational needs:

- Are they bored with their job? Consider job enrichment, cross-training, special projects, committee assignments, teaching responsibilities, job rotation, or participation in research or development.
- Are their social needs being met? Do they prefer solo or group work? How do they get along with their peers? Consider transferring them to a fast-moving team.
- Are their ego needs being met? Do they get the attention and respect that they think they deserve? Are you making a special effort to give it? Maybe they need a status symbol, such as a change in title, a bigger desk, or a name plate.

When necessary, you may have a counseling interview with these employees. **In dealing with marginal employees, it is important to remember the following:**

- Be careful about using marginal employees for orienting and training new employees because a bad attitude may rub off.
- Do not transfer extra work to other employees.
- Avoid awarding satisfactory ratings to marginal employees on performance appraisals because this may create problems later if they are reassigned or discharged.

The Older Employee

Older workers may lack ambition, protect turf, be unwilling to take risks, or have obsolete skills. **In addition to the suggestions that have already been offered, the following may be helpful with older employees:**

- Acknowledge their experience by seeking their advice.
- Get them an understudy, or involve them in orienting new employees or providing on-the-job training (select who and what carefully).
- Explain the need for change, get them involved, and give them training if needed.
- Encourage them to attend professional meetings.
- If they are nearing retirement, approve their requests for time off without pay. Hire part-timers to fill the gaps, if necessary, rather than overload their co-workers while they are away.
- Listen to their plans for retirement. Be sympathetic.

The Excuse Maker

Some employees whose work is not up to par always have a rational excuse, usually one that invites sympathy (e.g., "My wife is sick again," "My son is in trouble with the law," or "My car keeps breaking down.") Do not allow them to trap you into supporting their self-pity or debating the merits of the excuses. Focus on job standards and performance objectives.

Parents of Latchkey Children

Parents of children who go home from school to an empty house are understandably concerned about the welfare of their children. This concern can result in frequent telephone calls and mental distractions that interfere with job performance.

The following may be helpful:

- Talk to the parent about after-school child care. Contact the human resources department to see if assistance is available in the community.
- Explain to the parent that this concern is affecting job performance. Express your desire to help.
- Consider other solutions:
  —Rearrange the parent's work schedule, if possible. For example, coffee breaks may coincide with telephone calls to the child.
  —Assign low-priority tasks at the time of greatest concern.
  —Ask the parent to limit the length of calls and to limit calls to important messages.
  —Be tolerant about permitting the parent to take time off when crises develop, but know where to draw the line.

THE ABSENT EMPLOYEE

It has been estimated that the average American employee takes from 7 to 12 days of unscheduled absences every year, and absenteeism costs American business more than $26 billion annually.[1] Absenteeism may be external (e.g., failure to show up for work, tardiness, or early departures) or internal (e.g., extended coffee or meal breaks, absence from the work area, socializing, and daydreaming).

The absentee rate can be calculated as follows:

$$\text{Total hours absent/total hours paid for} \times 100 = \text{Inactivity rate}$$

A rate of 3 percent is considered a reasonable level by the U.S. Department of Labor. The average absenteeism rate for a group of American hospitals was 2.68 percent in 1982.[2]

The two most common causes of absenteeism are job dissatisfaction and paid sick leave programs. Parkinson's Law of Sick Leave Abuse is that the number of days lost because of sickness increases to equal the number of paid sick days allowed. **Although supervisors have little control over sick leave policy, there are measures at their disposal to prevent sick leave abuse:**

- Stress that sick leave is a benefit, not a right.
- Eliminate causes of job dissatisfaction.
- Set a good example.
- Keep good attendance records. Look for patterns of absenteeism (e.g., Mondays, Fridays, hunting seasons, or paydays).

- When an employee calls in sick, take the call personally. If someone else makes the call and the employee is not very sick, ask to speak to the employee. Ask whether the employee has seen a physician, whether medication is necessary, and when the employee can return. Tell the employee to keep in touch.
- Welcome the employee back. In a friendly way, ask how the employee feels.
- When absence is excessive, follow counseling procedure.

Remember that sick leave cannot be called excessive if it does not exceed that allowed by policy.

THE EMPLOYEE WITH A PERSONAL PROBLEM

A personal problem is any emotional or behavioral condition that limits an employee's ability to perform his or her job. Such problems include family stress, alcohol abuse, misuse of drugs, emotional disorders, and legal or financial difficulties. Supervisors are responsible for detecting and attempting to correct a deteriorating job performance, but they are not expected to diagnose or treat personal problems. A poor job performance is the only reason for which a supervisor should initiate disciplinary procedures.

When normal supervisory efforts do not result in improved job performance and a personal problem appears to be the cause of the difficulty, the employee should be referred to the employee assistance program of the organization. If the organization does not have such a program, the problem should be discussed with the human resources department.

Indications of a Personal Problem

Supervisors should suspect that an employee has a personal problem when they observe the following:

- increased absenteeism
- frequent absence from the work station
- confusion or difficulty in concentrating
- decreased productivity or work quality
- friction with other employees
- unusual behavior (e.g., temper tantrums or emotional outbursts)
- accident proneness
- alcohol on breath

Drug involvement should be suspected when, in addition, an employee:

- is visited by strangers or employees from other areas or meets them in the parking lot
- is suspected of theft
- makes secretive telephone calls
- visits the washroom for long periods
- wears dark glasses indoors
- wears long-sleeved shirts in hot weather
- has blood stains on the shirt sleeves
- perspires excessively

Company Policy on Personal Problems

All organizations should have a well-documented policy and an established procedure (see Figure 21-1) for handling employees with personal problems. Most now have some type of employee assistance program. Employees who utilize the services of the program are guaranteed confidentiality because the information obtained is considered a medical record. Employees are encouraged to seek assistance on their own initiative before problems affect their work. Generally, time off in connection with the counseling services is treated as any other disability absence.

Step-by-Step Procedure

- **Hold a frank and firm performance counseling session:**
  —Make certain the employee knows what is expected, and that documentation is complete (see Chapter 15).
  —Describe the unacceptable behavior or results, not what you think the problem is. Say, "Joe, your daily reports have been 1 to 2 hours late every day for the past week" rather than "Joe, you often have alcohol on your breath. You've got to get off the stuff."
  —Do not accuse the employee of having a personal problem, but encourage an admission with a statement such as "I've noticed that you seem tense recently. Is something bothering you that I can help with?"
- **Here are four appropriate questions to put to the employee:**
  1. Are you aware that your performance has dropped below our standards? (If yes, ask when he or she first observed this.)

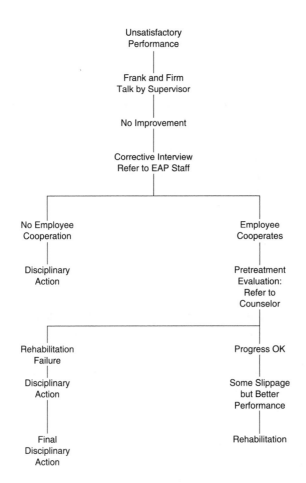

Figure 21–1 Supervisory procedure for employees with personal problems.

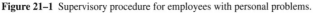

2. Is it possible that a personal problem may be at the root of this? (If yes, ask what he or she has done about it.)

3. Are you aware of our employee assistance program?

4. Is there anything I can do to help?

- **If the employee's performance fails to improve, hold a second counseling session:**

    —If the employee does not volunteer the information that there is a personal problem, say, "If you have a personal problem, I suggest counseling help.

We have an excellent employee assistance program here that is completely confidential and free."

—Emphasize that the employee's job will be in jeopardy, if his or her performance does not improve.

- **If the employee cooperates and progress is satisfactory, continue your support:**
  —As with any medical condition, expect occasional backsliding.

  —Make sure that you acknowledge good work.

  —Resist any temptation to lighten the employee's load. Treat the employee as any other employee, but allow a reasonable transition period after the employee has sought help before expecting job performance to return to an acceptable level.

- **If the employee refuses to seek help or if rehabilitation fails, take disciplinary action.**

In this procedure, you must take certain precautions:

- Use only job performance to initiate disciplinary procedures.
- Do not apologize for bringing up performance deficiencies.
- Do not try to be a diagnostician. You are an expert in the area of performance. Other people can better determine the nature of personal problems.
- In your counseling interview, do not discuss personal problems in depth.
- Do not moralize. There should be no stigma attached to personal problems.
- Be tough, but do not take punitive action until counseling has been suggested.

TWO EMPLOYEES ARE FEUDING

There are many reasons why two people do not get along at work. In addition to differences in race, nationality, religion, age, politics, and gender, there may be competition for attention, promotion, recognition, turf, or resources. Personality differences get blamed most often. Sometimes bystanders are provoking the situation.

Before you attribute the problem to personality clashes, look for external causes. For instance, there may be ambiguous position descriptions that do not indicate who does what or who has what authority.

There are three basic strategies to cope with this situation:

1. **Avoidance.** This is best when it is not your problem or when you lack the authority to act.
2. **Arbitration.** This is analyzing the situation and then taking sides or dictating a solution. This approach often fails, and there can be serious side effects.
3. **Mediation.** You encourage the pair to solve their own problem, keep the pair from exploding, and guide them into mutually agreeable solutions. You must be perceived as neutral by both parties. Never take sides.

Sometimes the problem is solved simply by telling the feuding duo that they do not have to like each other to work together and that you expect them to act as adults and to treat each other civilly on the job.

If that approach does not work, talk to each person individually, looking for an underlying cause of the animosity. A solution may emerge during one of these conversations. Job redesign, clarification of limits of authority, or revising of territorial boundaries may provide the remedy.

If the problem is still not solved, hold a joint meeting. The intent of this meeting is to convert them from adversaries to problem solvers.

Follow this sequence:

1. Warn them that if they don't work out a solution administrative action will be taken, action that will not please either party.
2. Seek some common ground or area of agreement (e.g., "You both agree that our goal is to improve customer service, right?").
3. Listen to both sides impartially. Do not tolerate interruptions, blaming, or name calling. Make each person summarize what the other person said to clarify any miscommunications.
4. Ask each person what he or she wants changed. Review areas of agreement and disagreement.
5. Discuss the pros and cons of each alternative, and get them to agree to one.
6. Clarify future behavior (e.g., "What are we going to do differently?" or "What are we going to do if . . . ?").
7. Congratulate them for reaching an agreement. Say that you have confidence in their ability to resolve their differences.
8. Follow up. Hold additional sessions if necessary.

If they can't solve their differences, you must decide whether you can live with the flawed situation. If not, take whatever administrative action is necessary (e.g., reassign them so that they no longer work together).

NOTES

1. P.I. Morgan and H.K. Baker, Do you need an absenteeism control program? *Supervisory Management* 29 (1984).

2. M.M. Markowich, letter to participants in United Hospitals, Inc., Pennsylvania, October 13, 1987.

Chapter 22
Employees Who Have Bad Attitudes or Habits

- the employee who has a bad attitude
- the colleague with a bad attitude toward you
- the negativists
- the know-it-alls
- the uncooperative silent ones
- the supersensitive ones
- the moody ones
- the jealous ones
- the gossipers
- the incessant talkers and socializers
- the ones whose appearance you dislike

The employees who give supervisors their biggest headaches are not the incompetent ones (those can be trained). They are not the ones who brazenly violate rules (those can be disciplined). They are the subordinates who meet work standards but who drive supervisors up the wall with their idiosyncratic behavior. These harassers are usually described as people who have a bad or negative attitude.

A person with a bad attitude may be a negativist, a goof-off, a hot head, a disciplinary problem, or a disloyal subordinate. The generic term *bad attitude* is used to describe a comprehensive causative factor of any undesired behavior. It is a term that is universally used to excess. When we talk about a person's negative attitude, we are trying to get into that person's head, to see what makes him or her tick.

Negative attitudes may be reflected in low productivity, high error rate, violation of rules and procedures, lack of team spirit, uncooperativeness, public criticism of the organization and its officers, or constant threats to resign—just about any undesired behavior. It's often difficult to draw the line between bad attitude and disloyalty or bad attitude and unethical behavior.

If supervisors had the courage to document what they really thought about their people with bad attitudes, these adjectives would probably appear in their performance reports: *disinterested, inflexible, pessimistic, complaining, indifferent, change resistant, unenthusiastic,* and *nonsupportive.*

199

The quality of supervision has a major impact on employee attitude. Attitude varies directly with morale and motivation. Replacing a weak supervisor with a competent one can lead to dramatic attitudinal improvement.

Before taking any action, determine whether there really is a problem. Previously, we posed the crucial question that comes up whenever we face a difficult person. It is worth repeating: Does the behavior affect to a significant degree the department's work, the employee's teammates, or you? If not, and if you think you can learn to live with it, your best move may be no move.

If coaching alone does not get the desired change, move on to counseling. Discuss the problem with the person candidly. Explain how the behavior affects you, the department, or others. Give specific examples of how you see the person's disenchantment being expressed and how it affects you.[1]

When we tell people that they have a poor attitude, we must be able to provide specific behavioral examples that led to that subjective diagnosis. Failing to do that will elicit defensiveness or anger or will confuse the person. It will not get the desired change.

Detailed record keeping should begin when the results of coaching and counseling are not effective. Cutting these folks loose may be the best solution, but you will need concrete proof of how the bad attitude affected performance or other employees.[2]

EMPLOYEES WHO ARE OVERLY CRITICAL OF THEIR EMPLOYERS

In most instances, this mouthing off by one or two employees is not serious. Often it can be nipped in the bud by a remark such as "For someone with your ability, I can't understand why you would stay with this organization. Don't you find it demeaning?"[3]

There are two instances in which you must take vigorous action before serious harm is done:

- when these people badmouth the organization in front of patients, visitors, clinicians, or other customers
- when they advise other employees to slow down

These two situations justify charges of disloyalty and in most organizations are grounds for dismissal.

THE COLLEAGUE WITH A BAD ATTITUDE TOWARD YOU

There are times when we must work with a colleague who seems to have a bad attitude toward us. This results in little (or not so little) daily skirmishes, which are not conducive to team efforts.

Rapport is the key to getting along better, and it begins with a genuine desire to improve the relationship. Throughout this book we mention the importance of risk taking. Here is a good example of a risk that is well worth taking. Grab the bull by the horns. Ask the other person what it is about you that irritates him or her. You may be in for a surprise. The irritating factor may be as simple as the practice of sending caustic memos or calling him or her by a nickname.

If you get a frank response, thank the person, and promise to modify this behavior. Then ask the person if you can be candid about what change you would like to see on his or her part. Do not unload a gunnysack of complaints.

This tactic may fail or make matters worse, but it is worth the risk.

THE NEGATIVISTS (PESSIMISTS, CYNICS, AND WET BLANKETS)

Negativists may be hard workers who are competent, productive, and even loyal but who have a bleak outlook toward most things and people. They lack excitement in life and happiness at work. If you hang around them long enough, you get infected.

Negativists are convinced that the people in power do not care or are self-serving. In meetings, when any new idea is proposed, Pessimist Polly can always be counted on to come up with "The trouble with that idea is. . . ."

Negativists may be confused with devil's advocates. Both voice concern or ask challenging questions, but the devil's advocate does so with an open mind and is prepared to join a consensus if convinced. The negativist persists in finding reasons for opposing whatever is being proposed no matter what. Even when they lose arguments or are outvoted, they remain unconvinced.

Avoid acceptance of the contrary outlooks expressed by these individuals. Their resistive persuasion not only is depressing and self-defeating but can be infectious. On the other hand, do not dismiss their comments too quickly; this could turn the negativist against you.

When a known pessimist is present at a meeting, do not rush into making suggestions. Pessimists tend to remain silent while a problem is being explored or when alternatives are being asked for. They spring into action only after solutions have been proposed.

Call for solutions from others. Project realistic optimism. Give examples of past successes of the action now being proposed. Concede that every action carries some element of risk.

Using a worst case scenario, show that the possible consequences are not threatening and that the chances for success are great. Explain that current conditions are not like those that were present before when a similar project was not successful. Relate favorable outcomes that other departments or organizations experienced using the same actions.

Avoid arguments by simply stating that the negativist may be right but that you want to go on or that you agree with the others on the best course of action.

If they persist, insist that they come up with alternatives, or assign them information-gathering chores.

Have an open mind. Once in a while they may be right. Use their negativism when you get to discussing pitfalls and contingency planning. They can tell you everything that can go wrong.[4]

If the pessimist is a colleague and the work situation does not demand that you work together, avoid him or her if you value your optimism.

KNOW-IT-ALLS (EXPERTS IN EVERYTHING)

These individuals want you to recognize them as being superior. They try to maintain control by accumulating large bodies of knowledge. They are condescending if they know what they are talking about, pompous if they do not. If you object to what they say, they take it as a personal affront.

Avoid these people as much as possible. Do not pose a threat or argue. Remain respectful, and avoid direct challenges. Resist the temptation to debate with them.

Do your homework. Be certain that you know what you are talking about. Present your ideas tentatively using phrases such as "What would happen if . . ." or "I wonder whether. . . ."

THE UNCOOPERATIVE SILENT ONES (CLAMS)

These people are not those who fail to speak up because they have nothing to say or because they are listening intently. They are not the polite ones who fear that they will say something wrong or will hurt your feelings. *The silent ones discussed here are those who reflect fear or suppressed anger by their silence.*

Their silence may be preceded by a perfectly congenial conversation until you suddenly touch a sensitive area. You are most likely to encounter this glum silence during a counseling or disciplinary session with a subordinate.

If you encounter one of these clams in a counseling session, use Bramson's technique.[5] When it is Irene the Clam's turn to speak but she remains silent, lean forward and counter with your own silence, accompanied by eye contact and raised eyebrows. Maintain this silent expectant stare for at least 10 seconds. If she remains silent, say "You haven't answered my questions, Irene. Is there some reason for that?" If her silence persists, say "Irene, I'm still waiting."

If there is still no response, state the consequences of her remaining silent (e.g., "Irene, you may have a good reason for not talking, but this is not beneficial to our relationship. I'm very concerned about where this is taking us").

If Irene still remains silent, terminate the interview with "I take it that you're not ready to talk to me, Irene. Since we still must resolve this problem, I want to see you here tomorrow at the same time."

THE SUPERSENSITIVES

These individuals take offense at whatever they perceive to be a put-down. They are extremely sensitive to criticism, often bursting into tears, shouting, or dashing off to the restroom. When this behavior is effective for them, these people have a potent tool for manipulating colleagues and superiors.

Handle with care, but do not be manipulated by these reactions. Never withhold negative feedback because of previous overreactions. Do not apologize for what you said or did (e.g., "Gosh, I'm sorry that I hurt your feelings").

For example, if when delivering a reprimand an employee breaks into tears, say "Pat, I find it hard to discuss this when you sob like that. Would you like a few minutes to compose yourself?", or hand Pat a tissue and go on with the discussion.

If Pat jumps up and runs out of your office, do not run after him or demand that he return. Instead, reschedule the meeting, and at that time make no mention of the previous episode. Pat has learned that his inappropriate behavior was not effective.

If Pat loses his temper and starts shouting, wait a minute or so. If he does not calm down, get up and leave your office.

MOODY PEOPLE

Normal people have some mood swings. It is the degree and circumstances that are important. Transient moodiness, such as that during a grieving period, usually does not require any action by supervisors other than a helping hand. *A persistent or markedly depressed state, however, calls for professional help.* Between these two extremes are a variety of moods manifested by sorrow, sullenness, irritability, or other personality changes.

Ignore mild transient moods. If they persist, acknowledge them without agreeing with them. Ask questions, and listen with empathy. Do not flood these folks with sympathy. Sympathy may result in the persistence of the moods, possibly leading to the martyr syndrome. Empathy is more effective. If the situation does not improve, suggest professional counseling.

THE JEALOUS CO-WORKERS

Jealousy is common when employees compete for promotion or recognition. Frustrated people may try to undermine your position by starting ill-founded rumors, publicly berating you, becoming a bottleneck, or turning others against you. When any of these disloyal activities occurs, you must take firm action.

First discuss the problem with your boss and get his or her support, then confront the envious one. Lay it on the line. Say what you have seen or heard and that you want it stopped. Describe your future expectations (e.g., "I don't want arguments in front of staff, patients, or physicians. If you have a gripe, see me in my office").

If the undesired behavior persists, remind the person that it will affect his or her next performance rating and possibly continued employment.

THE GOSSIP

Although a little benign gossip is harmless, when character is attacked or misinformation affects work or morale, something must be done.

Gossips want attention, so supply it in healthy ways. Spike their misinformation by insisting on validation or correcting false comments. Explain how their gossiping is having an adverse effect on the work team and that people are withholding information from them because they fear that what they say will be repeated in distorted forms. Do not encourage gossips by reacting positively to their messages. In some instances it is necessary to shun these people.

THE INCESSANT TALKERS AND SOCIALIZERS

These folks suffer from verbal diarrhea. Monday morning finds them rehashing weekend sports or their recreational activities. They repeat their broadcasts as long as they find listeners. *You must know and act when these time-wasters become bottlenecks.*

Break up the little group discussions in the hallway. Give the verbose ones extra assignments. When they learn that too much talk and too little work result in extra assignments, they will usually modify their abuse of time.

If possible, isolate them from willing ears. Encourage them to do their socializing during breaks (see chapter 33 for advice about how to cut them off at meetings).

THE ONES WHOSE APPEARANCE YOU DISLIKE

Ask yourself these key questions:

- Does the person's appearance offend customers or interfere in the orderly conduct of business (e.g., cause people to stop work and stare)?
- Does it violate any policy or rule?

- Is it a safety hazard (e.g., shoes with high heels that are dangerous on slippery or uneven floors)?

Try not to hire these people in the first place. Applicants who show up for employment interviews looking like something the cat dragged in are exhibiting their best appearance. It will get worse when they report for work.

During orientation of new employees, emphasize the importance of appearance, especially if they have direct contact with customers. Discuss the dress code and what your personal expectations are. Forewarning is proactive, criticizing is reactive.

THE ONES WHOSE WORK AREA IS MESSY

Messiness is in the eyes of the beholder. Before you can get employees to clean up their act, you must convince them that there is a mess (parents know that this is not easy). Some fastidious supervisors make a big fuss over a little disorder. *The key point is whether a disorderly desk or work area has a negative effect on performance,* co-workers, or customers. A receptionist's desk in full view of visitors is not the same as a desk in the corner of the maintenance department.

There may be barriers beyond the employee's control. For example, visiting V.I.P.s may drop their coats on a receptionist's chair, or delivery people may place large cartons in doorways. Help your staff eliminate such barriers.

We will discuss hostile people, sexual harassers, and chronic complainers in subsequent chapters.

NOTES

1. M.M. Danziel and S.C. Schoonover, *Changing Ways* (New York, N.Y.: AMACOM, 1988).
2. Danziel and Schoonover, *Changing Ways,* 229.
3. W.H. Weiss, *The Supervisor's Problem Solver* (New York, N.Y.: AMACOM, 1982).
4. R.M. Bramson, *Coping with Difficult People* (New York, N.Y.: Random House, 1981).
5. Bramson, *Coping,* 73.

Chapter 23

Coping with Hostile People

- the two essentials of successful coping
- the hostile big three
- the Sherman tanks
- the exploders
- the snipers
- the passive-aggressives

THE TWO ESSENTIALS OF SUCCESSFUL COPING

Your unspoken assertive message to hostiles is that you respect their right to have feelings and to speak their minds but that you also have those rights. In addition, regardless of the rank and power of the other person, you do not have to listen to profane, intimidating, or obnoxious language.

To achieve freedom of expression, you need self-esteem and assertiveness. If you lack assertiveness, none of the advice provided here will be of value; your passivity will prevent you from using it. Fortunately, there are numerous and readily available publications, seminars, and audiotapes on this subject.

The hostile big three are called Sherman tanks, exploders, and snipers by Bramson, whose terminology will be used in this chapter.[1] Readers are strongly urged to read Bramson's original work; it is a classic.

SHERMAN TANKS (BULLIES AND DICTATORS)

Of the hostile groups, Sherman tanks are the most difficult to handle because they often have power, usually are professionally or administratively competent, and know exactly what it is that they want. Sherman tanks have had years of successful intimidation; their victims are too numerous to count.

Sherman tanks may be superiors, customers, inspectors, staff coordinators, or even colleagues. Every executive suite and medical staff has at least one.

Sherman tanks have permanently adopted that style because it is so effective. They may be physically intimidating, and they are always psychologically threatening. They are aggressive, abrupt, arrogant, and autocratic. They are contemptuous of their victims. When they attack, they expect their targets either to fight back or to capitulate.

206

The most successful strategy is to stand up to them, but without fighting. In any confrontation you must be assertive enough to get their attention. Then state your own opinions and perceptions while remaining emotionally neutral. When they launch a tirade, do not get defensive or try to counterattack.

Here is a three-step modified Bramson technique for handling Sherman tanks:

1. **Hear them out without interruption.** Hold your ground. Equalize eye level as much as possible by asking them to sit down; you stand up if they refuse. Maintain eye contact, but do not try to stare them down. Hold yourself erect; do not hunch your shoulders or cower. Instead of counterattacking, urge them to continue, or ask them some open-ended questions.

2. **Respond non-defensively.** When they start repeating, break in with a "Doctor, pardon me." Then deliver your reply, turning up your voice volume sufficiently to be heard, but not as loud as theirs. Insist that they listen to your response. Each time they interrupt, say "Doctor, you interrupted me," and go on. Be tentative or noncommittal. Use words such as *it appears, it seems, perhaps,* and *possibly.*

3. **Switch to solving the problems that brought them in.** Remember that their behavior is designed not only to humble you but also to get something done. Now that you have taken the fun out of the former, they are ready to discuss what they brought with them. *When their complaints are legitimate, apologize briefly,* and move to solutions as quickly as possible. *Do not put up with offensive language or profanity.* Walk away from it. If the person has much power, tell your boss what you did and why.

EXPLODERS (VOLCANOS, GRENADES, AND TIME BOMBS)

Like Sherman tanks, exploders manifest anger, but there are significant differences. Sherman tanks always exhibit the same overbearing attitude, whereas exploders are gentle between attacks. The anger of Sherman tanks is contrived and under their complete control; the anger of exploders is real. They are partially to completely out of control. They sometimes push or strike.

The exploder suffers from childlike temper tantrums. Exploders discovered that people often did not take them seriously unless they got mad.

These people have a tremendous need for respect. They explode when their self-esteem is threatened, for example when they are the target of a joke, are kept waiting, or are ignored or when their competency is questioned.

Coping is a matter of helping them regain their self-control. Exploders are like wind-up toys: They wind down if you can wait them out. After their explosions, they may become pussycats. They often become apologetic and may break down and weep.

If they appear to be out of control, respond as you would to a hysterical person. In a loud voice call out "Stop! Stop!" or "O.K.! O.K.!" or keep repeating their name; even wave your arms to get their attention.

A clever tactic is to say that you need a note pad to write down what they are saying because it is important. This buys still more time for them to wind down, and it also boosts their self-esteem.

If they continue to rant and rave, their voices will be loud and fast. Say that you cannot write fast enough when they speak so fast and that they must slow down. As soon as they slow down, the pitch and volume of their voice also plummet. Anger drains away. Often they will now sit down for the first time.

Listen carefully for two essentials: what is setting them off (their "hot button"), **and what it is that they want.** You may hear a word clue that is repeated over and over, such as *policy, schedules, recognition,* or *consideration.*

Do not get involved in a verbal boxing match in which accusations or threats swing wildly back and forth without any attempt at compromise. Do not try to explain things while they are still upset; their listening mechanism is out of order. After they have calmed down and become rational, find out exactly what they want. Use their name frequently.

If an apology is in order, make it, but add that you get upset when people act as they did. Show that you are intent upon helping by stating what you intend to do to correct the situation.

If they remain irrational, say loudly that you want to help, but not when they are in such a state. Call a break ("Julie, let's take a 15-minute break. I'll come back after we've both calmed down"), or leave immediately if they become verbally or physically abusive. Over your shoulder call back that you will talk to them later.

Do not forgive them for their behavior, even when they return all apologetic. Forgiveness reinforces the explosive behavior. Do repeat "I'm always willing to listen to you, but not like that."

If you discover what their trigger mechanism is, try to avoid it in the future.

Some employees have an explosive temper on a short fuse, and they become angry at the slightest provocation. These individuals often are job hoppers. They stay on a job only until they blow up, tell the boss off, and quit or get fired.

Emotional immaturity, low self-esteem, and marginal competence are characteristic of these firecrackers. They have intense feelings of frustration, fear, prejudice, or guilt.

Thorough employment screening usually weeds out these people. If you are stuck with one, keep him or her away from customers. They can do a lot of damage.

Do not take personally what they say in fits of temper. Reply with "I'm sorry you said that. I'd think that over if I were you. You've nothing to gain by offending me."

If the session continues to degenerate, end it. Do not judge, criticize, or moralize; just end it. Simply say that the interview is no longer productive and that you will meet again later. Get up and move toward your door.

Professional counseling in my experience is not often helpful in chronic cases, but it is worth recommending. More often these employees are terminated via the disciplinary route. If they resign during one of their rages, do not let them change their minds.

SNIPERS (FOXES, SABOTEURS, AND NEEDLERS)

Snipers would like to be in control, like Sherman tanks, but they lack the courage. The sniper's weapons are sarcasm, snide remarks, and sick humor. "They throw snowballs with rocks in them."[2(p.26)] Snipers have discovered that using sharp, stinging remarks lets them get away with attacking you without assuming any responsibility. They do most of their dirty work in front of other people, who provide their cover.

Snipers utilize innuendoes, sotto voce remarks, not-too-subtle digs, and nonplayful kidding. Their remarks usually drip with sarcasm. Their assaults are not always carried out in your presence. They often talk behind your back, knowing that what they say will reach you. When you respond angrily, they retort, "Can't you take a joke?"

Sniper's victims tend not to fight back because they do not want to make a scene. They smile weakly, wonder what's going on, and later find out that they have taken some hits. They lie awake nights thinking of what they should have said or done.

Your goal is to flush them out and blow them away.[3] Recognize the zingers when you hear them. Say to yourself, "Well, here comes one of Larry's little zingers." Do not laugh, even if it is a little funny or if all the other people giggle or snicker. Don't ignore it either.

Bypass your sense of politeness. Immediately stop what you are doing or saying, turn toward the sniper, and repeat exactly what you heard; these jokes lose their punch when repeated.[4] Then say, "Larry, that seemed to be a barb aimed at me. Is that what it was?" or "Are you making fun of what I just said?"

As soon as you have called snipers on this, you have blown their cover. Now they must either confirm what they said or try to weasel out of it with something such as "I was only kidding" or "Where's your sense of humor?" Respond with a sour smile and something such as "Well, it didn't sound funny to me."

If they back up what they said, you may learn something important. Critical feedback can be worthwhile. If they back down, you have turned the tables on them.

Alternatively, ask the sniper what his or her remark has to do with the subject under discussion (the relevance question) or what the purpose of the remark was (the intent question); for example, "What are you really trying to say?"

Ask for help from your associates. When you overhear the sniper say "What a stupid idea, she's in a dream world," say to the group, "Anyone else see it that way?"

If the sniper's criticism gets support, you can search for more information about it. If the others do not agree, follow with "I guess there is a difference of opinion" (not "See, you're wrong").[5]

After a snowball-throwing meeting, get the sniper aside and make a direct accusation. Snipers do not function well in one-on-one situations; their camouflage is missing. Do not buy their "Oh, you're just too sensitive." Reply that you enjoy a good joke like everyone else but that what you are hearing are not good jokes.

PASSIVE-AGGRESSIVES

Passive-aggressives represent a subset of snipers. Like snipers, they conceal their antagonism. Passive-aggression does not mean fluctuations between passivity and aggressiveness. The behavior is constant. Wetzler aptly calls this behavior sugar-coated hostility.[6] *Passive-aggressives are manipulators who pretend to be helpless while they infuriate their superiors and associates.*

Passive-aggressives believe that they are getting a raw deal by their bosses, whom they perceive as dictators; this causes them to feel angry and resentful.

They lack the confidence to challenge authority directly, so that their resistance surfaces indirectly and covertly. They play many psychological games. Typical things they do to try your patience are showing up late for meetings, submitting late reports, getting angry with you but refusing to tell you why, or fouling up a procedure. They apologize superficially, give you endless excuses, or just clam up. Inwardly they enjoy your anger or discomfort.

You are not likely to change their personality; it is even resistant to psychological help. Your goal is to insist on behavior that meets your expectations and not to let them get you upset when they play their mean psychological games. Do not accept their excuses, and never give them the satisfaction of witnessing the anger or frustration you feel when they upset you.

NOTES

1. R.M. Bramson, *Coping with Difficult People* (New York, N.Y.: Random House, 1981).
2. Bramson, *Coping,* 26.
3. R. Brinkman and R. Kirschner, *How To Deal with Difficult People* (Boulder, Colo.: CareerTrack, 1988). Video program.
4. Brinkman and Kirschner, *How to Deal.*
5. Bramson, *Coping,* 30.
6. S. Wetzler, Sugarcoated hostility, *Newsweek* (October 12, 1992): 14.

Chapter 24

Personnel Retention

- the importance of personnel turnover
- why do they leave?
- proactive remedial measures
- the four major objectives for coping with employee exits
- treat resignations as minicrises
- answer their questions
- how to maintain quality and efficiency during the transition
- exit interviews

"The deadly enemy of great performance on the front line is high turnover."[1(p.121)]

The dollar cost of replacing an employee is high, often more than the annual salary of the position being filled. Angry former employees can wreak havoc. For example, one departing employee from an oil company erased a computer database worth millions of dollars.[2] It is more difficult to estimate the cost of loss of morale, quality, and service continuity.

WHY DO THEY LEAVE?

Personnel retention depends on a number of external and internal factors. Job turnover is higher when jobs are plentiful, when specific skills are in great demand, and when organizations are handicapped by low compensation, poor working conditions, or inept leadership. A typical turnover rate for hospital nurses is 30 percent. This is much higher in some health care institutions and in some hospital units, especially those with high employee burnout rates.

Turnover is a push-pull situation. Attractive outside offers pull people elsewhere, while discontent pushes employees out. The push may be stronger than the pull. For a number of reasons, employees are reluctant to blame their immediate supervisors for their resignations. Yet, in one study 24 percent of employees quit because they did not like their supervisors; this was double the number leaving for better jobs.[3]

Many professionals leave because there is no dual career ladder; only promotions to administrative positions are available. Other employees become frustrated when they see the higher-salaried posts all going to outsiders.

211

Organizations with high turnover often have inadequate employee recruitment and selection systems, weak orientation and training programs, and a hierarchy riddled with incompetent managers.

Other reasons for leaving include lack of recognition, regressive or outdated benefits packages, salary freezes, reductions-in-force, underqualification, overqualification, transportation or parking problems, unsafe work environment, job stress, spousal transfers, and vocational changes.

PROACTIVE REMEDIAL MEASURES

Supervisors have little impact on measures that only top management controls. Even so, they can minimize the turnover due to leadership failures by practicing the principles discussed in this book. Often a department with revolving-door turnover is transformed into a stable unit when a new supervisor takes over.

THE FOUR MAJOR OBJECTIVES FOR COPING WITH EMPLOYEE EXITS

1. To avert the loss of a valued employee, or at least to keep the door open for a return.
2. To maintain good public relations. This includes ensuring that the departing employees are aware of their rights and benefits and know what kind of references they will receive.
3. To determine the real reason for resignations, and to institute changes that can eliminate the negative aspects of the job.
4. To minimize the effects of the loss on the work team, and to achieve smooth transitions.

TREAT RESIGNATIONS AS MINICRISES

Regard any resignation of a valued employee as an emergency. Remember that your employees are your clients. When one of them resigns, you have just been fired!

Follow these three steps as soon as you learn about resignations:

1. Immediately meet with your boss to formulate a plan for reversing the resignation. Your goal is to come up with a persuasive argument for convincing the resignees that it is in their best interest to remain on board.

2. Meet with the employees as soon as possible. Tell them how much you value their services and how much you want to retain those services. Probe at length into the reasons for the resignations. Find out how their family members feel about the move and what apprehensions they have; there are always some.

3. Make your pitch. State what changes can be made in their work or work environment. If salary is a factor, inform them of any upcoming raises, but usually it is unwise to negotiate salaries; there are too many pitfalls or complications to such action. Focus and build on their apprehensions about the change. Compare what they now have with what they may be getting into, if that is to your benefit. Invite their spouses to additional discussions if you sense resistance on the part of the spouses.

ANSWER THEIR QUESTIONS

Departing employees have many questions about their rights and benefits. Answer all that you can. If there are some that you cannot answer, refer them to the appropriate sources.

Express your appreciation for what they have accomplished. If you really would like them back, tell them so, even when they do not ask. Being needed and feeling wanted are always a tonic for one's self-esteem.

HOW TO MAINTAIN QUALITY AND EFFICIENCY

Managers are always concerned when there is a long time lag between employee departures and when their replacements are in place and able to perform adequately. Here are some measures that can help you achieve a smooth transition.

Learn about the Resignations As Early As Possible

To achieve efficient employee replacement, encourage employees to announce their plans as soon as possible. One survey reported that more than 40 percent of respondents knew they were leaving up to 4 months before they informed anyone in the company.[4]

Employees often withhold this information for a variety of reasons. They may dislike their bosses or fear that they will be mistreated during the interval between their revelation and the day of their departure. Some resignees have seen how previous individuals were mishandled. Others may want to take advantage of that interval to attend subsidized meetings, to take educational courses, or to use other benefits such as sick leave.

Although supervisors usually like to keep people as long as possible, there are exceptions. Low performers often become nonperformers or bottlenecks in their last days on the job. In these situations, the sooner the person leaves, the better.

Compromise on the departure date may be necessary. The optimal date for one party may disadvantage the other.

Do Not Sever Relations

Employers may opt to work out an arrangement for the employees to serve as consultants, to work part time, or to make periodic visits to train a replacement, help with inventory, prepare for an inspection, or assist on weekends. Resignees may be flattered by such offers.

React to the Effects of Departures on Work and Work Groups

Once an employee's decision to leave becomes general knowledge, team relationships change. Supervisors must anticipate and monitor these changes. There may be alterations in cohesiveness, group roles and norms, and communication patterns.

Subordinates and others who rely on the resignees are likely to experience stress and a decline in performance if personnel changes occur without their knowledge.[5] Keep your staff informed, and help them adjust to the changes.

Some co-workers will draw away from the resignee, whereas others will perceive the person as a hero to be envied and will become friendlier toward that individual.

Resignations affect people in other departments, especially when the employee has been a member of interdepartmental committees, focus groups, or task forces. Make certain that these people are informed of the change.

If resignees have community contacts that should be maintained by your organization, you or the resignees should contact these organizations or individuals to inform them of the change and whom they should contact in the future.

Make Maximum Use of the Resignee's Remaining Time

Usually it is best to treat short-timers just as you did before their resignation. Excluding them from meetings or no longer asking for their input is counterproductive. Assure resignees that their contributions are still expected and valued.

Review work projects, current and planned, that involve the departing ones. Decide which of these should be continued and how that will best be achieved. Failure to plan ahead may result in setbacks or tasks suddenly being dumped onto unprepared persons (maybe you, the supervisor).

Ask Resignees To Update Their Position Descriptions

Ask them who they think could take over each of their major responsibilities right now or how long it would take them to train someone.

Ask Resignees To Prepare Lists of Their Activities Not Listed in Their Position Descriptions

These include the following:

- new tasks that the employee was getting ready to assume
- assigned role in upcoming projects or new services
- special duties the person can take care of before leaving (e.g., orienting and training replacements, organizing records, or revising procedures; supervisors are often surprised at the number of discretionary activities their employees were involved in)
- computer accounts and any other accounts for which the person was responsible

Assist Recruiters in Locating and Screening Candidates

A major and recurring frustration voiced by managers is the time it takes to recruit, hire, and train new employees. Yet most managers think that their responsibility ends when they fill out a request for a replacement employee and send it to the human resources department (how long would Notre Dame have had winning football teams if Lou Holtz used that procedure for getting players?).

Supervisors can improve this process by providing the human resources department with a concise abstract of the position description together with a list of the attractive features of the job and a list of recommended publications for announcing the opening. They can also help by ensuring that the qualifications for the candidates are not too high and offering to help with the screening process by answering telephone inquiries about the job.

EXIT INTERVIEWS

Objectives of the Exit Interview

- to make a final attempt to reverse the resignation
- to provide information about severance and earned vacation pay, vested pension rights, insurance, and other entitlements
- to discuss references, job leads, and outplacement counseling
- to provide the employee with the opportunity to vent his or her feelings
- to clarify charges or complaints against employees who are being separated involuntarily
- to discover the real reasons why the employee is leaving
- to maintain good relations
- to ensure completion of housekeeping details (e.g., documents that must be signed, such as permission to release information for references, and notification of various departments of changes in address and phone numbers)
- to acquire information that will identify problem areas, including the job and its rewards, the supervision, and the work environment (see Exhibit 24–1 for a list of appropriate questions)

Exhibit 24–1 Questions for Exit Interviews

- Does your job description accurately define your responsibilities?
- How well did we train you for the job?
- How adequate was your authority to get the work done?
- What opportunities did you have to develop your special abilities?
- How would you describe your supervisor?
- What did you think of your last performance review?
- Was your good work recognized? How?
- How would you rate our teamwork (customer service, managerial support, compliance with safety rules)?
- Was your unit adequately staffed?
- How did you feel about your work (vacation, holiday) schedules?
- Are our salaries and benefits competitive?
- Do you have any comments about our policies, rules, or procedures?
- What are the best (worst) features of this job?
- How could the job or working conditions be improved?
- How can this position be made more attractive?
- What was the main factor in your decision to leave?

The Exit Interviewer

Exit interviews should not be conducted by the immediate supervisor because that person may be one of the reasons for the departure. Interviewers should be experienced in personnel counseling and are usually personnel specialists who are familiar with personnel policies, benefits, and procedures.

Interviewers first collect information concerning the position description, performance appraisals, current salary, and other pertinent information. Ideally, the employee's supervisor and some co-workers are contacted to learn more about why the employee is leaving.

Conducting Exit Interviews with Resignees

The best strategy is to divide the interview into two phases. The first is the administrative phase and is for the benefit of the departing employee. The employee learns what he or she wants to or should know. This phase is not threatening, avoids sensitive areas, gets employees to relax, and enhances the shift into the second and more sensitive phase.

The dialog in the first segment is handled in a highly directive fashion using a question-and-answer format. **The second phase is the fact-finding segment, designed to reveal the real reasons for the departure.**[6]

This segment is conducted in a nondirective fashion, providing employees with the maximum opportunity to express themselves (e.g., "Before you go, I'd like your help in making the job more attractive for the next person").

Close the interview by summarizing what was discussed. End on a positive note.

Because resignees often withhold true information to avoid saying anything that might jeopardize their return or getting favorable references, some organizations contact resignees again 6 months or a year after they have departed.

The Involuntary Separation

The primary objective when an employee must be involuntarily separated is to minimize ill will. Such separations traumatize self-esteem and create hostility that may lead to grievances, adverse publicity, lawsuits, and even sabotage. Furthermore, the employee often maintains relationships with remaining members of the staff and can poison the attitude of these people.

At the meeting, one must be prepared, compassionate, and concerned. Do not stall or feel guilty or intimidated. Never react defensively or emotionally. Do not apologize for the action.

You should:

- let them vent their anger or frustration without comment or interruption. Empathize by saying something such as "I can understand how you feel," but do not review the chain of events that led to the decision to let the person go.
- ask them if their rights and benefits have been explained to their satisfaction. If not, get them the information they seek.
- tell them how their separation will be announced (e.g., "Louise has departed as of [date], and her replacement will be named as soon as the choice has been made" or "The position has been eliminated").
- state how reference inquiries will be handled. Often only dates of employment will be released. If more information is given to prospective employers, invite the employees to include pertinent information about their responsibilities and accomplishments. Make certain that you have their signed permission to release such information. Ideally, they are given copies of the exact statements that will be released.
- if appropriate, provide advice on obtaining employment or improving work skills.

NOTES

1. W.H. Davidow and B.K. Uttal, *Total Customer Service: The Ultimate Weapon* (New York, N.Y.: Harper & Row, 1989), 121.
2. A. Farnham, The trust gap, *Fortune* (December 1989): 66.
3. J.L. Zaradona and M.A. Camuso, A study of exit interviews: Does the last word count? *Personnel* 62 (1985): 47–48.
4. C.L. DeVater and A.G. Bateson, Employee job change: Effectively managing the transition, *Society for Advancement of Management Advanced Management Journal* 57 (1992): 30–35.
5. DeVater and Bateson, Employee job change, 33.
6. J.P. Zima, *Interviewing: Key to Effective Management* (Chicago, Ill.: Science Research Associates, 1983).

Chapter 25

Cost Control and Budgets

- the functions of budgets
- budgets and supervisors' competency ratings
- principles and rules of budgeting
- revenue budgets
- preparing forecast budgets
- capital expenses
- wages, benefits, and overhead
- variances and control

The cost-containment measures that have been imposed on health care providers have intensified the importance of cost control. Supervisors are key people in the control and reduction of expenses. They usually participate in the preparation of departmental budgets, suggest cost-cutting measures, and direct the implementation of control measures.[1]

FUNCTIONS OF BUDGETS

The Planning Function

The preparation of a budget is part of the planning function. A budget provides a financial map of future activities. It also contains data vital to the determination of new charges.

Budget planning normally starts at executive levels and trickles down to first-line managers. It should coincide with the review of major policies and the reassessment of plans and goals.[2]

The Controlling Function

The actual administration of a budget is part of the control function. The most powerful tool for controlling costs, a budget creates a greater awareness of costs on the part of employees and helps them achieve goals within stated cost expenditures.[3] As Townsend writes[4(p.173)]

A tight budget brings out the best creative instincts. . . . Put him under some financial pressure. He will scream in anguish. Then he'll come up with a plan which, to his own amazement, is not only less expensive, but is also faster and better than his original proposal.

The accounting department usually provides supervisors with weekly or monthly cost reports. These reports highlight variances that serve as red flags for remedial actions.

The Evaluating Function

The performance ratings of supervisors include determinations of how accurately they forecast their expenses and how well their expenditures match the monies allocated. Variances reflect poorly on financial skills, unless the deviations result from factors that are not under the supervisors' control. Staying under budget is not always a cause for celebration because having funds left over often indicates poor budgeting practice rather than good management.[5]

PRINCIPLES AND RULES OF BUDGETING

When planning a budget, supervisors should always remember the following principles:

- Expenses are charged to the department or cost center that incurs the expenditures.
- Every item of expense must be under the control of someone in the organization.
- Managers responsible for complying with expense budgets should participate in their preparation.
- Supervisors are not responsible for expenditures over which they have no control.
- Ordinarily, unused funds may not be carried over from one annual budget to the next.[6]
- Unused funds for capital expenditures may not be transferred to operating expenses or visa versa.[7]
- Requisitions for individual expenditures may have to be approved by some authority.[8]
- Slush funds are disallowed, or at least looked on with disfavor, but supervisors should try to allocate some monies for unexpected needs.

Revenue

Revenue figures may come from accounting or from data-processing departments. Patient billing is usually computerized, which makes it possible to calculate the revenue figures for each section.[9]

Supervisors are usually not directly accountable for revenues but can be helpful in computing charges for the services that their departments render. Without the supervisors' cost data, finance departments have no legitimate basis for determining charges or for forecasting profit or loss. In predicting revenue and costs, supervisors should consider not only historical growth trends but also changes in workload anticipated as a result of the introduction of new services, procedures, or equipment.[10]

Preparation of Budgets

A breakdown of expenses charged to a department by categories, such as salaries, benefits, and supplies, is essential (Table 25–1) and expenses must be recorded on an ongoing basis. A budget cannot be adequately prepared the week before it is due.[11] To prepare an itemization of expenses, it is necessary to collect expense figures for several months and to annualize the figures by dividing the year-to-date expenses by the number of months recorded and multiplying by 12.[12]

Thoughts, suggestions, or ideas conceived during the fiscal year that involve additional expense or provide opportunities to cut costs should be recorded.[13] Furthermore, increases in supply expenses, service contracts, and continuing education or training expenses must be taken into account when a forecast budget is planned.

Table 25–1 Example of a Forecast Budget: Chemistry Section

Item	Annual Expense ($)
Medical/surgical supplies	300
Employee welfare	20,640
Pension	2,112
Postage, freight, express	408
Salaries and wages	281,572
Departmental supplies	367,800
Quality control	28,667
Travel	672
Publications	100
Education	336
Repairs and maintenance	12,000
Total Direct Expense	714,607

Capital Equipment

There is usually a separate budget, or part of a budget, for capital equipment. Most capital equipment budgets are now projected for a 5-year span. Supervisors who must determine the rate of obsolescence of major pieces of equipment often seek this information from manufacturers or suppliers. Replacement items or new equipment are among the most expensive budgetary items for some cost centers (e.g., laboratory or radiology services), and the capital equipment budget should reflect the costs of these items.

Wages, Benefits, and Overhead

The figures for salaries, benefits, and overhead are added to the budget by the finance department, not by the operating section. This is appropriate because supervisors have no control over these items and cannot be held responsible for them.

Salaries represent more than 60 percent of operating expenses for most cost centers. Therefore, when administrators want to cut costs, the first area to be scrutinized is usually the salary expense. It is essential to keep detailed records to justify work hours and overtime.

Furthermore, management is loath to approve requests for additional staff, even when there is a projected increase in workload, unless records substantiate the need. Reports of crises that have occurred because of personnel shortages can help in the justification process. This also holds true for equipment problems and requests for new apparatus.

THE CONTROLLING PROCESS

Supervisors must always be prepared to defend the figures that they have submitted. With or without modifications by higher authorities, the budget will revisit supervisors at least monthly in the form of a responsibility summary (Table 25-2). This report shows the budget estimates by month and year to date, pairs them with the actual expenses for the month and the year to date, and indicates variances for each item. When variances exceed a certain amount, supervisors generally must submit a written or verbal explanation.

Supervisors must study these reports as soon as they are received. If an item is not clear or seems to be in error, the supervisor should seek clarification from the accounting or data-processing department. In addition, the supervisor should be prepared to discuss the variances with his or her immediate superior.

Table 25-2 Responsibility Summary

	Current Month Actual	Current Month Budget	Current Month Variance	YTD Actual	YTD Budget	YTD Variance	Total Budget	Budget Balance
Inpatient revenue	160,414	167,081	6,667*	349,943	348,725	1,218	2,186,346	1,837,621
Outpatient revenue	106,591	78,129	28,462	233,294	169,937	63,357	1,021,120	851,183
Total patient revenue	267,005	245,210	21,795	583,237	518,662	64,575	3,207,466	2,688,804
Medical/surgical supplies	207	25	182*	289	50	239*	300	250
Employee welfare	2,299	1,663	636*	3,875	3,319	556*	20,640	17,321
Pension	1,059	1,059	0	2,112	2,112	0	2,112	
Postage, freight, express	31	34	3	55	68	13	408	340
Salaries and wages	25,166	23,263	1,903*	50,084	46,423	3,661*	281,572	235,149
Departmental supplies	43,788	30,650	13,138*	69,925	61,300	8,625*	367,800	306,500
Quality control	211		211*	211		211	28,667	28,667
Travel		118	118		318	318	672	354
Publications					50	50	100	50
Education		59	59		159	159	336	177
Repairs and maintenance	49	1,000	951	3,115–	2,000	5,115	12,000	10,000
Total direct expense	72,810	57,871	14,939*	123,435	115,799	7,636*	714,607	598,808
Total patient revenue	267,005	245,210	21,795	583,237	518,662	64,575	3,207,466	2,688,804
Direct expense	72,810	57,871	14,939*	123,435	115,799	7,636*	714,607	598,808
Operating gain or loss	194,195	187,339	6,857	459,802	402,863	56,939	2,492,859	2,089,996

*Unfavorable variances (i.e., low revenue or high expenditures).

NOTES

1. L.W. Rue and L.L. Byars, *Supervision: Key Link to Productivity* (Homewood, Ill.: Irwin, 1982).

2. J.E. Newell, *Laboratory Management* (Boston, Mass.: Little, Brown, 1972).

3. K. Karni, et al., *Clinical Laboratory Management* (Boston, Mass.: Little, Brown, 1982).

4. R. Townsend, *Up the Organization* (New York, N.Y.: Fawcett, 1971), 173.

5. Newell, *Laboratory Management,* 134.

6. Newell, *Laboratory Management,* 134.

7. Newell, *Laboratory Management,* 134.

8. Newell, *Laboratory Management,* 145.

9. J. Sattler, *Financial Management of the Clinical Laboratory* (Oradell, N.J.: Medical Economics, 1980).

10. Sattler, *Financial Management,* 24.

11. Sattler, *Financial Management,* 123.

12. Sattler, *Financial Management,* 124.

13. Newell, *Laboratory Management,* 134.

Part V
Developing Employees

Chapter 26

Job Redesign: A Paradigm Shift

- the paradigm shift
- job satisfaction and enrichment
- meeting motivational needs
- job fit
- quality of work life
- job redesign

Health care is undergoing a paradigm shift from a technical model to a sociotechnical model. Advances in instrumentation and automation are not enough. To satisfy our major external customers—patients—we need more high-touch. To satisfy our major internal customers—employees—we need job enrichment.

Job enrichment is not a project. It is a continuous process of encouraging employee participation in multiple activities. It capitalizes on, and makes full use of, professional abilities and individual skills.

Job satisfaction and enrichment involve taking a second look at how we assign people and how we design jobs. Job satisfaction and enrichment are perceived differently by different employees. One person's meat is another person's poison. We must know the motivational needs of individual team members (see Chapter 14). For employees who want more control, we provide delegation and empowerment (see Chapter 11). For those who want more task achievement, we provide training, challenge, and job enhancement. Those who have a strong affiliation need we involve in group efforts (see Chapter 10).

JOB FIT

Before we embark on cross-training and other job enrichment measures, we must place the right people in the right jobs. We start with accurate position descriptions (see Chapter 4) and comprehensive recruiting and selection of new hires (see Chapter 8). We assign people to tasks that take advantage of their strengths and make their weaknesses irrelevant (see Chapter 7). We ensure that employees are not handicapped by oppressive or restrictive policies and rules (see Chapter 6).

227

QUALITY OF WORK LIFE

The physical work environment, social relationships, kind of supervision, and other morale factors determine the quality of work life. Employees now take these for granted. They and their unions fight to maintain them. These generic factors must be favorable before significant sociotechnical breakthroughs can be achieved.

Quality of work life programs and Japanese-style management represent macro models of organizational design. We turn to job redesign for micro models.[1]

JOB REDESIGN

> *"An effective job design meets both the requirements of the tasks and the social and psychological needs of the workers."*[2(p.56)]

Job Redesign Measures

- cross-training
- rotation of work stations, departments, or shifts
- job transfer
- changed work hours (flex time)
- switches from full time to part time, or vice versa
- deletion or addition of specific duties
- new locations of work stations
- improved instrumentation, flow patterns, communication, and methodology
- changed team membership or roles
- support of creativity and entrepreneurship
- delegation or more challenging assignments
- appointments to committees, quality circles, or other work groups
- involvement in research or development
- assignments to teaching or training roles

When Should Changes Be Considered?

Anytime! The considerations may be formal or informal, planned well in advance or on the spur of the moment. There are some more opportune times. These include the latter phases of probationary employment, at the time of performance reviews, when salary discussions are initiated by employees, when new services are contemplated, when employee cut-backs are necessary, and when organizational expansions, mergers, acquisitions, or other restructurings take place.

Key Questions To Be Answered

- Does this employee want more authority or autonomy?
- Does this employee prefer to work alone or on a team?
- Will both the organization and the employee benefit?
- What can be achieved without an immediate change in the job classification?
- Will the budget and current staffing permit changes?
- How will the changes affect work flow and other people?
- Will the results improve customer service, costs or charges, or employee morale?
- Will the changes enhance total quality management (continuous quality improvement) measures?

Guidelines or Cautions

- Do not attempt to use job redesign or enrichment as a cure-all.
- Ask whether the answers to the above questions are favorable.
- Tailor the changes to the needs and wants of the employees and the organization.
- Know the motivational drives of each person.
- Consider the effect of the change on others.
- Ensure that the employee endorses the measures.
- Be certain that the employee has a good chance to succeed.
- Make the goals and plans flexible and reversible.
- Update the position descriptions as appropriate.
- Provide feedback and support.
- Do not promise what you cannot deliver.

NOTES

1. J.B. Cunningham and T. Eberle, A guide to job enrichment and redesign, *Personnel* 67 (1990): 56–61.
2. Cunningham and Eberle, A guide, 56.

Chapter 27

Complaints, Grievances, and the Chronic Complainers

- common causes of employee complaints
- the supervisor's role
- the seven essential steps
- complaints about salary
- when complainers gang up on you
- when an employee goes over your head
- chronic complainers
- grievances
- sexual harassment

Complaints represent a major source of customer feedback, and employees are among our most important internal customers. Legitimate or not, complaints are signs that somewhere something is wrong and demands attention.

COMMON CAUSES OF EMPLOYEE COMPLAINTS

- policies and rules
- working conditions
- compensation and benefits
- leadership
- relationships with other employees

THE SUPERVISOR'S ROLE

The supervisor's role is to respond effectively and promptly to both legitimate and imagined complaints. This avoids formal, and often costly, grievances. Increasing numbers of lawsuits are being registered by disgruntled employees, often after disciplinary action has been taken against them.

Gripes may be articulated during staff meetings, performance reviews, exit interviews, and daily contacts. Observant supervisors suspect problems when they note that an employee is unusually silent, irritable, or depressed.

Caring managers engage in naive listening when they realize that they have been tuning out long-term patients, loquacious colleagues, or boring bosses. Naive listening is nothing more than listening as though one is meeting these people for the first time, without preconceived notions.

THE SEVEN ESSENTIAL STEPS

1. Listen carefully. The initial complaint is often only a trial balloon to see how you will react. You may have to dig deep to find what is under the surface.
2. Investigate. Is the complaint legitimate? Are there less obvious but more serious ones trailing behind? Are other people affected? Is the situation getting better or worse?
3. Decide on what, if any, action is needed. Get help if you need it. Ask the complainer what he or she would like done. Make certain that your solution will not make matters worse.
4. Inform the complaining employee about your findings and what you propose to do. Do this without undue delay. If your remedy is not satisfactory to the employee, seek alternatives.
5. Implement your decision.
6. Check the effectiveness of your action.
7. Record what has transpired.

COMPLAINTS ABOUT SALARY

Every supervisor has been faced with these. They are heard most often when salary changes are announced or when competitors give larger raises. The greater the difference between expected and real salary increases, the more strident are the voices. If favoritism is thought to be at play, tempers flare.

Pay-for-performance strategies may exacerbate salary dissatisfaction. Employees who do not receive the maximum merit increase are often dissatisfied with their performance ratings. Even more unhappy are those who were told that their work had been outstanding and then found a minuscule increase in their paycheck.

The following are some suggestions for avoiding or handling salary controversies:

- Do not overrate employees or make unrealistic promises.
- Know what competitors are paying.
- Try to get more pay for your outstanding performers by other means, such as promotions, title changes, or revision of position descriptions.
- Let employees blow off steam. Be empathic.
- Refuse to discuss salaries of other employees.
- Do not be guilty of favoritism.
- Know exactly how salary increases are determined in your organization.

Here is an example: "Dolores, although salary increases are based largely on performance, there are other factors that must be considered. These include the availability of certain specialists, budgetary restrictions, and the relative numbers of employees in each performance level."

If the raise is not deserved, state the reason very clearly. The person should know exactly why he or she was passed over and how the deficiency can be overcome.

WHEN COMPLAINERS GANG UP ON YOU

When confronted with a group of complainers, Bernstein and Rozen practice what they call creative ignoring. The supervisor just sits still and looks thoughtful. This response gets the group to quiet down and become more manageable. If it is a group of customers or colleagues, the supervisor asks for each person's individual input before responding, calling on the least hostile person first. If it is a bevy of angry subordinates, ask them to pick one spokesperson because you insist on a one-to-one confrontation. Request that the rest leave your office.[1]

WHEN EMPLOYEES GO OVER YOUR HEAD

Ideally, your boss will send these complainers right back to you as soon as he or she realizes that the employee has not given you an opportunity to respond. Unfortunately, some managers are all too willing to lend an ear to employees who bypass their supervisors, especially when the manager and the supervisor do not get along.

As soon as you become aware of this situation, confront your boss. Present your side of the situation. Urge him or her to send for you on these occasions so that you can respond in front of the person.

Let the employee know that you know what is going on and how you feel about it. Illustrate how such activities are counterproductive and ultimately backfire.

CHRONIC COMPLAINERS

The characteristics of true chronic complainers are that most of their complaints lack validity, and that they are more interested in registering feelings than in getting problems resolved. They rarely participate in finding solutions, and their daily conversation consists predominantly of negative comments. Chronic complainers constantly use words such as *never* and *always*. Their favorite starts with "Why doesn't someone. . . ."

The occasional griper can often be stopped with a "Well, what are *you* going to do about that," but this does not stop certified chronic complainers. They bounce right back by telling you that they have no influence in the organization or that their suggestions are never taken seriously.

The typical chronic complainer is a conscientious and competent worker. His or her work is usually acceptable unless flexibility and risk taking are required. This also makes it difficult to get rid of these annoying people.

The Best You Can Hope To Accomplish

Although you rarely cure bona fide chronic complainers, you can often achieve the following:

- Their complaining decreases to a tolerable level.
- They limit the complaints that they to bring to you to those that you can do something about.
- They bring solutions with the problems.
- They spend more time performing and less time griping.
- They develop a bit more confidence in their own ability.
- They refrain from complaining in front of customers or your boss.

Practical Suggestions

Use the seven step approach outlined above. **Active listening is essential, and that is not easy.** If you ignore their complaints, however, not only will you aggravate the situation but you may divert the complaining to customers or competitors. If their complaining bypasses you and goes to your superiors, your reputation as a leader will suffer.

Listen to their main points. Write the complaints down in their presence. It is good for their self-esteem. Sometimes simply listening can silence the complainer. Do not agree or disagree with them. Avoid approval nods or sympathetic grimaces. Maintain a noncommittal facial expression.

Direct your attention more at their feelings than at the object of their complaints. They are reassured when their feelings are validated (e.g., "I can understand why you are upset about that)". Validating feelings is not the same as agreeing with them. It is only acknowledging their right to have those feelings.

Stop them when they start repeating or if they try to move to another topic. Rein in rambling discussion by asking, "What's your point?" Acknowledge that you understood what they said by paraphrasing and summarizing their main points.

Trying to argue them out of their negative stance, or trying to placate them, or explaining everything seldom works.

Force them to help solve the problem. After acknowledging that a problem exists, move quickly into problem solving. Ask specific, open-ended questions. These are the who, when, where, and how questions. Avoid the whys because they get you into deep water. True chronic complainers are not comfortable with problem-solving questions; they just want you to agree with their complaints.

Encourage them to research the problem. If they say that they do not have the time, respond by saying "Well, if you change your mind let me know."

Be honest when you say what you can and will do or what you cannot do. Ask them what it is they want you to do. When they say that what you propose will not succeed, ask them what is the worst that can happen, and then indicate that you are not worried about that state of affairs. Another ploy is to narrow the options to two and to ask which they think is the lesser of the two evils.

When solutions are beyond your control, say so. At times you must make statements such as "We've simply got to make the best of it."

GRIEVANCES

A grievance is a formal complaint by an employee for which redress or relief from management is sought. Grievance procedures are needed to ensure fair treatment of employees, to maintain good morale, and to avoid costly court litigation.

Employers must abide by the limitations placed by collective bargaining agreements, antidiscrimination legislation, civil service regulations, and employment contracts. Grievance procedures are spelled out in every union contract. Most nonunion organizations have a formal grievance protocol, and supervisors must be familiar with it.

Supervisors who are vigilant for conditions that induce employee dissatisfaction, who handle gripes expeditiously and fairly, and who rarely have to take disciplinary action against their subordinates seldom have grievances filed against them. When they do, they are able to defend their actions because they have documented all discourses with the aggrieved employee and have followed mandated procedures.

When employees are not satisfied with a supervisor's response to a complaint, it is the supervisor's duty to make them aware of the appeal process. Most employees who file charges will have investigated their rights and studied the organization's policy manual.

Employers frequently lose litigation cases because supervisors have been guilty of inconsistent rule enforcement, unreasonable application of rules, or excessive penalties in terms of policies. Poor documentation is the most common cause, however.

SEXUAL HARASSMENT

There are two forms of sexual harassment.[2]

1. *Quid pro quo* occurs when an employee is expected to grant unwanted sexual demands or suffer the loss of job or some tangible job benefit.
2. *Hostile work environment* occurs when an employee is exposed to a work environment that is hostile or abusive because of sexually oriented verbal, visual, or tactile activities.

Verbal abuse includes sexual language, innuendoes, epithets, or jokes. Phone calls are frequently mentioned. Visual offenses consist of provocative gestures and sexually oriented posters, letters, notes, or graffiti. Tactile harassment can be sexually oriented touching, patting, pinching, rubbing, or pressing.

The procedure for receiving and investigating complaints of sexual harrassment must be prompt, fair, and confidential. Every supervisor must be aware of the policies and procedures relating to this form of discrimination and must enforce them vigorously and with sensitivity while not forgetting the rights of the alleged harasser.

Sanctions may include verbal warnings, letters placed in personnel files, demotions, suspensions, or dismissals.[3]

Here is a step by step procedure:

1. Listen carefully to the complaint. Ask the accuser to put it in writing and to include dates, places, names of witnesses, and the exact statements or behavior of the alleged harasser. Note: If the complainant later decides to withdraw the charge, get that decision in writing.
2. Investigate as soon as possible. Interview witnesses and other alleged victims.
3. Confront the harasser, and inform him or her of the complaint. Listen carefully to the rebuttal. If appropriate, tell the alleged harasser that this must stop immediately. Often you find that they simply were not aware that what they were doing constitutes sexual harassment.

4. Document what transpired at the meeting, including the exact words the person used in his or her defense.
5. Get back to the complainant, and relate what happened. If no supporting evidence is found, explain this. Reaffirm the commitment on your part and that of the organization to the preventing of sexual harassment. Tell the complainant to report any further incidents.
6. Report the affair to your superior and to the human resources department.

Here is what to do when you must cope with a potential sexual harasser:

- Do not encourage the person or remain silent.
- Clarify your position and what you want out of the relationship. (e.g., "I prefer to keep our relationship on a strictly professional basis").
- If the solicitations continue, review your personnel policy and follow the recommended procedure, or ask the advice of a senior member of the human resources department.
- Warn the person that if he or she persists you will regard the activities as sexual harassment and will report it.
- Document each episode. Get witnesses if possible. Remember that a single incident rarely suffices to make a case.
- If you filed a complaint and you feel that it was not handled to your satisfaction, notify the human resources department that you intend to take the complaint to the local Equal Employment Opportunity Commission representative or to contact a legal service agency, a state discrimination agency, or a lawyer. If you have a union, complain to your union representative. As soon as legal action is threatened, things usually start happening.
- If you are still dissatisfied, do what you threatened to do!

NOTES

1. A.J. Bernstein and S.C. Rozen, *Dinosaur Brains* (New York, N.Y.: Wiley, 1989).

2. *"Discrimination because of sex under Title VII of the Civil Rights Act of 1964* as amended: Adoption of final interpretive guidelines," U.S. Equal Employment Opportunity Commission Part 1604, *Federal Register,* November 10, 1980.

3. K.E. Lewis and P.R. Johnson, Preventing sexual harassment complaints based on hostile work environments, *Society for Advancement of Management Advanced Management Journal* 56 (1991): 21–26.

Chapter 28

Introduction of Change

- the good and bad effects of change
- the need for change specialists
- how not to direct change
- what change requires
- goals and objectives of change
- the planning process
- stages of employee responses
- steps in enlisting help from your team
- resistance to change

*"Directing and controlling change in an organization
has been likened to managing in white water."*[1(p.24)]

Health professionals and managers are continually faced with change: new governmental regulations, standards promulgated by accrediting and licensing agencies, technological advances, new reimbursing systems, managed medical care, "point of care," and burgeoning new services.

The tides of change are augmented by waves of new management approaches, such as quality management, team building, empowerment, customer satisfaction, awareness of cultural diversity, and paradigm shifts. The sales representatives hurrying down hospital corridors are now joined by consultants hired to help the executives carry out their new grand plans.

Threats of new and old competitors challenge hospitals like never before. Acquisitions, mergers, reorganizations, and staff reductions cause tremors throughout health care institutions.

In all too many institutions, new administrators are hired while nursing and housekeeping staffs are reduced. Public relations staffs and budgets are increased at the expense of educational programs. These changes pose a still greater challenge for the health care supervisor.

To have a flexible, responsible, and adaptive team, changes must be quick, effective, and pervasive.

THE GOOD AND BAD EFFECTS OF CHANGE

Change can improve productivity, quality, morale, motivation, and teamwork. On the other hand, not only can it fail to improve the bottom line, it can result in perceptions of loss of control by managers and supervisors. A pervasive sense of helplessness, pain, and anxiety may arise. Such negative results are more likely to occur when changes are sudden and information is lacking[2]

THE NEED FOR CHANGE SPECIALISTS

New areas of specialization spring up, and older ones phase out. When hospitals offer new and complex services such as advanced trauma care or open heart surgery that require more interdepartmental and interservice cooperation, employees who previously had only been vaguely aware of each other now find themselves on special work teams or task forces together. *Cross-functional* has become a buzzword.

Adaptability and flexibility are required at all hierarchical levels. Relearning and retraining are the orders of the day. Some employees must be completely recycled. Thus today's health care managers must be change specialists.

Motivating people to change is a major challenge of leadership. Managers must understand why people resist change. They must persuade employees to view change as normal, and they must be prepared and know how to introduce innovations.[3]

Actually, supervisors are more involved in changes than top managers. Major changes are promulgated from the executive suites, but it is up to department heads, supervisors, or self-directed teams to implement these initiatives. Also, for every company wide innovation, there are hundreds of changes that originate within departments or small units.

Change masters are individuals who succeed because of their ability to adjust to change.[4] They are good planners and delegators who readily accept the risks needed to produce change. Their subordinates are willing followers who do not need to be coerced or threatened.

HOW NOT TO DIRECT CHANGE

Management should not introduce change by tell-only directives or sell-only attempts that rely on persuasion or coercion. Nor should management deny employees an opportunity to participate in decisions about the nature of the change and when and how it will take place.

Dalziel and Schoonover list the following typical oversights[5]:

- failure to consider the people who must implement the change

- failure to consider all the people or activities affected by the change
- failure to delegate or empower
- failure to plan or to document plans
- failure to get support for plans
- failure to consider constraints, opposition, and setbacks
- consideration of only short-term effects
- failure to address complaints or suggestions

WHAT CHANGE REQUIRES

Change requires that new agreements be negotiated and that tools for action be found beyond what it takes to do the routine job of maintaining already established strategies and processes.[6]

Change efforts have to mobilize people and add to what is not yet known. Be wary of excessively logical how-to approaches. Intuition, brainstorming, and creative thinking are often needed.

Ownership is essential. The employees must buy in. As employee input into change increases, the employees acquire more ownership of, and commitment to, decisions about change. They want to see their ideas flourish. Before employees buy in, they must trust their leaders and have faith in their integrity.

Security is so important. When it is absent, all kinds of negative feelings may be experienced. When job security is provided, there is more employee flexibility, lower resistance to change, and greater willingness to risk it.[7]

Major changes take time, patience, and persistence, and even lesser changes often take longer than expected. Many people learn slowly and forget easily. There is almost always some dragging of feet or outright resistance.

A culture of pride encourages the willingness to risk change. Such a culture is nurtured when organizations are successful, when people are made to feel important, when there are many promotions from within, and when managers seek ideas first from inside.

Change requires a system that rewards the change makers. See Chapter 14 for more on reward systems.

GOALS AND OBJECTIVES OF CHANGE

A well-defined goal is a prerequisite for productive action and arches over four critical objectives:

- *selecting the right people*
- *preparing and motivating people to change*

- *obtaining the necessary resources*
- *implementing the change.*[8]

THE PLANNING PROCESS

Gather information from past experiences. Focus on activities that were instrumental in success and those that were barriers. Assess the compatibility of your proposed change with the current organizational culture and goals. Change should not violate cultural norms.

Strategies have limited impact unless they are rooted in specific activities that individuals perform. Detail the training that is needed to help prepare employees for the change. Consider contingencies for displaced people. Design incentive and reward systems into the plan.

Successful changes start with answering the following "W" questions[9]:

- What will it cost? What do we hope to achieve? What are the risks, constraints, and barriers? What additional data are needed? What resources are essential? What did we do wrong last time? What additional training will be necessary?
- Who wants the change? Why? Who will benefit? Who will be affected adversely? Who will resist? Who will support the change?
- When should planning start? Will we have enough time? By what date must official approval be obtained? When should the implementation start, and when should it be completed?
- Where will we find the space, funds and people?
- Will the change provide an opportunity to utilize available skills better? Will people have more autonomy over how they do their work? Will the changes make employees' jobs (and yours) easier or more difficult? Will the change increase or decrease profit, motivation, morale, quality, and productivity?

Test your plan by asking these questions:

- Is it concise and clearly written? Does it include action steps?
- Was it distributed to the right people?
- Has there been sufficient input from others?
- Is there both a formal and an informal network to lend credence and support?
- Does it include training specifics, such as applications of planning tools (flow charts, histograms, and cause and effect diagrams)?

STAGES OF EMPLOYEE RESPONSES

Harper and Harper[10] describe the following four stages in the development of change:

Stage 1. *contentment:* liking things as they are
Stage 2. *denial:* resisting new ways
Stage 3. *experimentation:* trying new behaviors
Stage 4. *integration:* feeling comfortable with change

STEPS IN ENLISTING HELP FROM YOUR TEAM

1. Discuss the need for change with a few close associates, including people who would be involved in or affected by the change.
2. If you are the originator of the change, prepare a mission statement or goal(s). If successful, how would the change improve the situation as it currently exists?
3. Prepare a list of alternative strategies for accomplishing the goal. Document possible benefits and disadvantages of each alternative.
4. Discuss it with your entire team. Establish the urgency to change, but do not overdo it. Encourage complete discussion, including criticism. Invite additional alternatives or modifications of those already offered. Select an alternative, by consensus if possible, and try to get everyone's pledge of support.
5. Formulate and document a plan, and get its approval from your team and your superiors.
6. Provide reassurance to those who may be concerned about the change. Listen carefully, and encourage full expression of their apprehensions.
7. Assign responsibilities. As much as possible, get people to volunteer. Modify position descriptions where appropriate.
8. Prepare and publicize the agenda and time table.
9. Implement and follow up. Recognize individual and group contributions as your plan is carried out. Do not wait for the change to be completed before giving praise and recognition.

RESISTANCE TO CHANGE

"It is not change that people resist so much as they resist being changed."[11(p.237)]

Why Do They Resist Change?

At the very least, change is uncomfortable for everyone. Although some people thrive on change, the majority of employees do not. There is always some pushing and shoving. Employees are not obstinate or uncooperative; rather, they fear the unknown and how it may affect them and their work group. Change shakes up their comfortable and predictable daily routines. The more a change affects established habits and relationships, the more the complaining. Resistance is highest in organizations ensconced in bureaucratic tradition.

People often balk because they receive too little information or are omitted from the planning process. Employees with a strong need for affiliation fear the break-up of their comfortable and supportive work group.[12]

Previous negative experiences may have taught employees that change is hazardous or harmful. Some individuals merely fail to see the rationale for change or any payoff. They are perfectly content with the status quo.

Even changes that individuals have been asking for can be psychologically upsetting. A new instrument does not live up to your expectations or the promises of the vendor. A promotion elicits mixed feelings. The pride and paycheck are nice, but the altered relationships with former co-workers may be upsetting.

How Might They React?

Some employees will show a degree of support, others will take a wait-and-see attitude, while still others will actively reject the process. When change is first mentioned, many staff ignore it, hoping that it will go away or that they will not be affected. When the typewriters start disappearing and the computer keyboards move in, these people feel annoyed, depressed, or even angry. We hear statements such as "I'll be damned if I'm going to learn to operate that monster."

There may be increased absenteeism, turnover, and grievance filing. Hostility, moodiness, and slowed output may result. Subtle sabotage is expressed in a myriad of ways: forgetting to do things, inciting resistance, doing exactly what is ordered while knowing that such action is wrong, and setting up roadblocks.[13]

If the change is a major one, such as a reorganization that involves relocations and disrupted work groups, you hear people talk about early retirement or job change.

Reactions are more negative and intense when changes reduce employee control. Employees may applaud the installation of a new air conditioner, but that applause changes to loud protestations when they find that they cannot change the control settings.

As people find that they can cope with the situation, their attitude becomes more positive. They begin to see why the change was needed and how it may actually improve their jobs. Later, they fight to prevent return to the old system. A computer breakdown that requires a temporary return to the old manual backup causes consternation in the ranks.

How To Overcome Resistance

If rational and emotional concerns are ignored, those concerns will magnify and make the change more difficult. Concerns are minimal when employees have been involved in the planning right from the beginning. They are alleviated when supervisors listen patiently and empathically. Employees breathe a sigh of relief when they are told that their concerns are normal and will pass.[14]

Encourage participation and involvement. Participation should occur when alternative solutions to a problem are being developed. Solicit insightful and creative suggestions.[15]

Communication is essential. Sending and receiving are equally important. Explain the need for change in pragmatic terms. Discuss issues that led to the decision.

When you hear grumbling in the background, investigate the problem, and address it without delay. Tap into your grapevine, and tune into your network.

Sometimes highly vocal critics or negativists can be ignored. The team's initial enthusiasm may overcome these nay-sayers. It helps to have some team members discuss their initial successes during the early phases of the change. Sometimes the critics can be converted by giving them more of the action. Success is also an excellent antidote to procrastination.[16]

Provide sufficient opportunities for employees to learn how to use new facilities or to become familiar with new routines. It is important to let people become familiar with new equipment and processes in the early phases. Do not let the information filter down through third parties.

Explain the functioning of new equipment to each person who is going to use it. Give your optimistic informal leaders the hands-on experience first. Make training manuals and other instructional materials available, and give people the time to get acquainted with them.

Provide support. Begin with assurances and progress reports. Enlist the group in helping to make the change.[17] Reduce stress resulting from changes by expecting it and treating it as a natural sequence of events. Listen to employees blow off steam without reacting adversely. Be honest and humane. Instead of taking credit for the implementation of the change, lionize others.

When diversity of opinion is the principal resistance, it may be time to negotiate. Discuss all aspects of the change, and try to understand other points of view.

Sometimes an authoritarian approach is necessary even though you know that resistance will be generated. When the Office of Safety and Health Administration comes up with inconvenient new safety measures that your employees feel are unnecessary and inconvenient, you have no choice but to enforce the regulations. Coercion is usually the strategy of last resort, however. Coupling coercion with education and communication may mitigate some of the threatening aspects of the change. Coercion applied independent of other implementation strategies produces resentment.[18]

When you must champion a change that you feel is inappropriate, avoid making remarks about "the jerks upstairs" who issued the orders. This only increases resentment, lowers morale, and delays implementation. Your prestige is not enhanced by such exhibitions of disloyalty. Do your best to explain the purpose or need. Maybe you should get more information about the reason for the change or what is involved.

Use Your Reward System Effectively

Focus attention on vision-supporting behaviors. Be a credible role model. Expect, measure, and reward those who use the vision. Measure only what you really want. Keep it simple.

Autonomy is a powerful reward. Delegate authority to those who demonstrate use of the vision. For real achievers who relish challenges, the strongest reward may be to get them involved in another change, and a bigger or more difficult one. Watch pinball machine addicts, however. Their only reward is winning the opportunity to play another game.

Preferred work assignments, expanded turf, one's own desk or office, opportunities to meet the upper brass, a new title, opportunities to get away from the immediate work site, simply spending more time with you or with others, or being given more responsibility and authority can all be strong rewards (different strokes for different folks). At the same time, remove the rewards for clinging to the old behaviors.[19]

NOTES

1. G.P. Boe and C.G. Hudson, Managing change in troublous times, *Medical Laboratory Observer* 23 (1991): 24.

2. R.M. Kanter, *Change Masters* (New York, N.Y.: Simon & Schuster, 1983).

3. W. Umiker, *The Customer Oriented Laboratory* (Chicago, Ill.: American Society of Clinical Pathologists Press, 1991).

4. Kanter, *Change Masters,* 183.

5. M.M. Dalziel and S.C Schoonover, *Changing Ways: A Practical Tool for Implementing Change within Organizations* (New York, N.Y.: AMACOM, 1988).

6. Kanter, *Change Masters,* 192.

7. Kanter, *Change Masters,* 203.

8. Umiker, *Customer Oriented Laboratory,* 108.

9. Umiker, *Customer Oriented Laboratory,* 109.

10. A. Harper and B. Harper, *Skill-building for Self-Directed Team Members* (New York, N.Y.: MW Corp., 1992).

11. C.R. McConnell, *The Effective Health Care Supervisor,* 2d ed. (Gaithersburg, Md.: Aspen, 1988), 237.

12. Dalziel and Schoonover, *Changing Ways,* 119.

13. Boe and Hudson, *Managing Change.*

14. Kirby, 71.

15. Boe and Hudson, *Managing Change.*

16. J. Belasco, *Teaching the Elephant To Dance* (New York, N.Y.: Crown Publishing, 1990), 46.

17. Boe and Hudson, *Managing Change.*

18. Boe and Hudson, *Managing Change.*

19. Belasco, *Teaching the Elephant,* 166.

Chapter 29
Encouraging Creativity

- the creative process and intuition
- characteristics of creative people
- the effective innovative supervisor
- principles of managing creative people
- communication precautions
- how to reward creative people
- barriers to creativity

"Imagination is more important than knowledge."[1]

The person doing the job has the best opportunity to see what can be improved about that job and the step that precedes it. Only employers with tunnel vision think that all worthwhile ideas are generated in executive suites or in research departments. Effective cost control, quality improvement, increased productivity, and better customer service can be achieved only when employees have input.

Although all workers at all levels have ideas about how things can be improved, some are blessed with a high charge of innovativeness, intuition, or entrepreneurship. These creative employees can be among the most valuable members of an organization if they are treated intelligently.

Organizational infrastructures are shifting to make room for people who are innovative. Innovative potential now outranks graduate degrees in some progressive institutions.

Your goal as manager is to keep these people flooding you with great ideas without letting them get out of control.

THE CREATIVE PROCESS

Just as a kaleidoscope forms new patterns from many disconnected pieces, the creative person forms new patterns from many seemingly unrelated ideas. The process usually starts with a problem (problems are opportunities in disguise). Edwin Land invented the Polaroid camera because his young daughter asked why she could not see pictures as soon as they were taken.

Creativity adds vision to planning, uniqueness to the organization, and daring to decision making. It is most dynamic when it is associated with an individual's need for achievement, satisfies self-esteem, and earns recognition.

When employees are challenged to think creatively about their work, they seek to learn more about their jobs and, in the process, become more competent and efficient. It is creativity that leads to new services and products.

When creativity is suppressed in favor of conformity, it resurfaces outside the workplace in hobbies, recreational activities, and artistic endeavors. Back on the job, stifled operational creativity may be expressed in unique ways to annoy bosses or to circumvent policies and rules.

INTUITION

Intuition has been regarded as a mystical, magic power that originates below the conscious level. It is euphemistically referred to as flashes of insight, hunches, and gut reactions. Intuition is not judgment but knowledge gained without rational thought or logic. It may be thought of as experience stored in the unconscious mind. Intuition + logic = common sense.[2] See Chapter 34 on problem solving for more about intuition.

CHARACTERISTICS OF CREATIVE PEOPLE

People who are creative have a sort of restlessness. Confident that there is always a better way of doing things, they challenge systems, processes, procedures, tradition, practices, policies, and rules.

Most share the following characteristics:

- They have innumerable bits of information (the pieces in the kaleidoscope) that relate to the focal point of their interest.
- They blot out what to them seems irrelevant or unimportant, sometimes to the annoyance of their supervisors.
- They are curious, open, and sensitive to problems. They may bombard their supervisors and others with questions, many starting with "why," "why not," or "what if. . . ."
- They are optimistic risk takers who like challenges and rarely talk about failure.
- They often appear preoccupied, and at other times they work furiously. Their ideas usually come in spurts.
- They dislike rigid routines, monotonous tasks, restrictive policies, and bureaucratic interference.

- They tolerate isolation and ambiguity. Independence and autonomy are important to them.
- They often enjoy the innovative process more than the results of the innovation.
- They are sensitive to intuitive nudges. They sense when things are right and when they are not.
- They bounce ideas off others and build on the suggestions of their associates.
- They are voracious readers.
- They are often nonconformists, regarded by their peers as different. At meetings they are likely to play the role of devil's advocate.

THE EFFECTIVE INNOVATIVE SUPERVISOR

Effective supervisors strive to increase their own creativity and that of the people who report to them. To avoid job blindness, they occasionally step back and take a new look at processes, systems, and people. They seek fresh insights into nagging problems.

Supervisors can increase their own creativity by enhancing the creative characteristics previously listed. In addition, they:

- believe that there is always a better way and are always on the lookout for new ideas
- overcome ideonarcissism, which is the egotism of thinking that your idea is unique and that, because of your increased experience, it must be the right one
- view problems as challenges rather than annoyances, and chalk up failures as learning experiences
- utilize brainstorming techniques for making decisions and solving problems
- are tolerant of ambiguity and the idiosyncrasies of teammates
- challenge rules, including their own, and cut red tape
- are skilled at negotiating and persuading people, especially those who control the purse strings
- set aside some time each day for reflective thinking
- talk to customers daily (i.e., they practice management by wandering around)
- inject humor into situations (some of the best ideas start off as jokes)
- are willing to take risks

PRINCIPLES OF MANAGING CREATIVE PEOPLE

Creativity flourishes only when employees feel secure and free of the fear of failure. Ideally, this is accomplished by establishing a corporate culture that supports new ideas. To switch from a culture that endorses conformity and compliance to one that fosters innovation is not easy.

Identify your innovative people, and strive to know them better. Focus on each person's unique expertise.

Emphasize creativity during the orientation and training of new employees (Chapter 9). Encourage all your staff to become change specialists. Present problems as challenging opportunities. Be alert for, and encourage, employee statements that begin with "Maybe we could . . ." or "What if . . .?" These indicate that a creative idea is about to be born.

Give them a loose rein to pursue and develop new ideas. Tolerate some daydreaming. They need this to fire up their creativity or to retrieve information stuck in the catacombs of their unconscious minds.

Do not nit pick or demand perfection. When they neglect routine duties in favor of a pet project, you may have to tighten the rein. But do not say "You can't do that." Instead, say "You can get back to your project when you have completed ___."

Let them take risks and make mistakes without risking their jobs. Tolerate failure and mistakes as the costs of innovation and progress. Use idea traps, such as quality circles, brainstorming sessions, incentive awards, and suggestion boxes.

Provide necessary resources and psychological boosts. Give them some discretionary time for nondirected research. The ones who are already spending weekends so engaged are the most deserving.

Expose them to in-house and outside learning; including:

- seminars and professional meetings
- consultants and guest speakers
- publications
- audiotapes and videotapes
- customer input
- vendors and sales representatives

Protect them. Employees and managers may harass people who are different. Expect some creative ideas from everyone, and tell them that. For those supervisors who complain that their people never come up with creative ideas, let me pose this question: If you walked around your department with a roll of $100 bills and offered one for each idea they came up with that day, would you get any suggestions? You bet!

COMMUNICATION PRECAUTIONS

Do not say yes or no too quickly. A quick no leaves the employee feeling that you have not given his or her idea serious consideration. When you quickly say yes too often, you may find yourself in hot water or forced to renege on your promises.

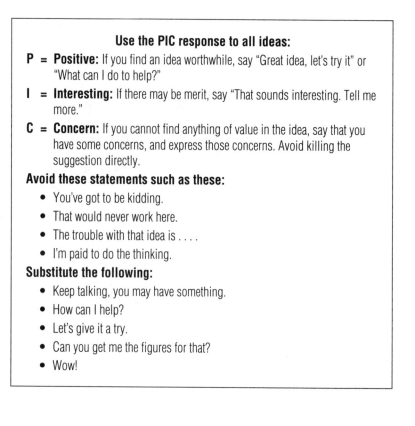

Use the PIC response to all ideas:

P = Positive: If you find an idea worthwhile, say "Great idea, let's try it" or "What can I do to help?"

I = Interesting: If there may be merit, say "That sounds interesting. Tell me more."

C = Concern: If you cannot find anything of value in the idea, say that you have some concerns, and express those concerns. Avoid killing the suggestion directly.

Avoid these statements such as these:

- You've got to be kidding.
- That would never work here.
- The trouble with that idea is . . . .
- I'm paid to do the thinking.

Substitute the following:

- Keep talking, you may have something.
- How can I help?
- Let's give it a try.
- Can you get me the figures for that?
- Wow!

HOW TO REWARD CREATIVE PEOPLE

Give prizes not only for suggestions but for criticisms that lead to improvements. Creative people are likely to have reward values that differ from those of their colleagues. For example, they usually value financial support of their projects more than salary increases.

Shower them with recognition. Encourage them to publish. Permit them to attend meetings where they can associate with other creative people.

Other appropriate rewards are increased work space, equipment, availability of resources, personal library, appointments to teaching staffs of academic institutions, and relief from tedious tasks, boring committee assignments, and other bureaucratic time-wasters.

Because creativity is usually expressed in bursts, rewards of all kinds are best delivered in bursts. Recognition should not be delayed until the next performance review, and bonuses that follow specific accomplishments are better than annual merit raises.

BARRIERS TO INNOVATIVE THINKING

- Prejudging ideas (we tend to accept ideas from authority figures or people we respect and to reject those from marginal performers or individuals below us in the organization)
- Fear of failure (this is one of the greatest inhibitors of creativity. An oft-quoted statement of Tom Watson, Sr., the founder of IBM, was "The way to accelerate your success is to double your failure rate.")
- Restrictive policies, rules, rituals, and procedures
- Strict controls and limited budgets
- Approval procedure for suggestions and projects
- Demands for consensus
- Understaffing and excessive work group assignments
- Long chain of command
- Group norms
- Disparaging remarks

NOTES

1. B. Eigen, *How To Think Like a Boss: And Get Ahead at Work* (New York, N.Y.: Carol, 1990).
2. W. Umiker, *Applied creativity, Society for Advancement of Management Advanced Management Journal* 53 (1988): 9–12.

Chapter 30

Career Development of Staff

- the benefits of career development programs
- the planning process
- who is accountable?
- needs assessment
- useful tools
- mentoring
- practical tips for supervisors
- stress reduction

"It is only as we develop others that we permanently succeed."

Harvey S. Firestone

Career development is a combination of planned and implemented education and experience. The short-term consideration of an education completed at the end of college has evolved into a philosophy of lifelong education and training.[1]

THE BENEFITS OF CAREER DEVELOPMENT PROGRAMS

Career development programs for employees benefit the employees by making them more eligible for promotion, increasing their self-esteem, and injecting more interest into their jobs.

Employers benefit by having a more talented and flexible roster. Some executives express concern over the loss of talented employees whom they trained only to see leave for better jobs. This disadvantage, however, is more than balanced by the increased personnel retention that results from better morale, the enhanced expertise of those who do not leave, the goodwill of the resignees, and the beneficial effect on recruitment when candidates learn about the educational advantages available at the institution.

As employees become more highly qualified, supervisors can delegate more and therefore have more time to spend on other high priority responsibilities. They also have the pride and satisfaction that all coaches and teachers derive from watching their charges mature.

Some form of career development is needed to enhance morale and motivation and to increase personnel retention, productivity, and service quality.

THE PLANNING PROCESS

Some health care workers desire promotion to managerial positions; others eschew supervisory responsibilities. They prefer steps up the clinical ladder if these are available. All employees want some growth within their current positions to make more important contributions to patient care and to other customers. The point being made is that career development should be tailored to individual needs.

Supervisors who are busy reviewing position descriptions to comply with guidelines under the recent Americans with Disability Act may find this an ideal time also to consider revisions in the titles and responsibilities that will establish the criteria necessary for employee career advancement.

Discussions of career development should first be broached when new employees are being interviewed for employment. Candidates' career goals, as perceived by the candidates at that time, are best discussed when candidates ask about opportunities for promotion. By the end of the probationary period, these goals should be clearer.

Goal changes or modifications should also be discussed at annual performance reviews. Action plans for helping the employees work toward those goals represent one of the most important outcomes of these meetings (see Chapter 16).

Plans are essential for successful promotions. Employees are motivated more strongly when their desire to move up in the organization is accompanied by an expectation of success. Failed promotions are as much the fault of the managers who awarded the promotions as of the promoted persons.

WHO IS ACCOUNTABLE FOR THE PROGRAM?

Upper management is accountable for providing the facilities, staff, and resources for formal programs. Supervisors share the responsibility for developing and implementing the program for their units with the educational or personnel department of their institution.

Career development is primarily self-development, however. The true test of professionals is not what they know how to do but how they behave when they do not know what to do.[2] I have little sympathy for health care workers who wail about not being trained for supervisory jobs when they knew that they would be offered such positions eventually and had years to seek the necessary training.

NEEDS ASSESSMENT

Any training program worthy of the name should be preceded by a needs assessment. *This assessment should consider the following:*

- the expertise needed by the unit, now and in the future. This involves obtaining product or service forecasting information from top management. Skills inventory charts are highly recommended. They list the employees who are qualified to perform each major responsibility. These charts are invaluable for planning skills enhancement, cross-training, and work station rotation.
- what is needed by individual employees to meet or exceed the requirements of their jobs or to be ready to assume greater responsibilities
- what is needed to bring oldtimers up to date. Job obsolescence occurs at an ever increasing rate; and because women play a major role in health care institutions, many positions are filled by employees who have interrupted their careers to start or raise families.
- what is needed to energize plateaued or marginal workers whose work interest needs rekindling
- what is needed to make you dispensable! The highest-order career development program is succession planning. Supervisors who make themselves dispensable by training successors are more eligible for, and worthy of, promotion.

To help determine how well your current training program meets basic needs, answer the questions in Exhibit 30–1.

USEFUL TOOLS IN THE CAREER DEVELOPMENT PROCESS

- orientation and on-the-job training of new employees
- in-service education, including the use of guest speakers and consultants
- workshops and seminars
- formal programs at educational institutions
- job rotation and cross-training
- self-education
  - books, journals, computers, audiotapes, and videotapes
  - participation in any educational endeavor
- special assignments
  - committees and other special work groups
  - assignments as trainers, instructors, or lecturers
  - duties as coordinators or facilitators (e.g., quality assurance, safety, or data processing)
  - temporary assignments at satellite facilities or elsewhere
  - temporary loans to other managers
  - substituting for absent employees

Exhibit 30–1 Questions Related to Skills Enhancement of Your Staff

1. Do you have an in-house educational program for each staff member? Does it include a minimum number of hours of participation or some results evaluation method? Are records kept? Are you satisfied with the results?
2. Are training materials (books, journals, tapes, and other teaching tools) easily available? Do you know how frequently these are used? Are they frequently updated?
3. Is there an on-going professional and/or management training program readily available?
4. Do your employees have the time to make use of the training materials? to attend lectures, demonstrations, and other educational sessions?
5. Is there financial support for continuing education? Are schedules flexible enough to permit employees to attend programs of educational institutions?
6. Do your employees get intellectual stimulation through problem-solving sessions?
7. Do your employees have the opportunity to cross-train? to rotate work stations? to assume greater responsibilities? to serve on committees, quality circles, task forces, and other work groups?
8. Do you delegate tasks that provide valued educational experiences for your employees? Do they assume greater responsibilities? Do you empower them sufficiently to carry out these responsibilities?
9. Are educational subjects presented at routine staff meetings?
10. Are there real opportunities for promotion? Do you have dual career tracks? Can your employees be promoted within their current grades?
11. Does each employee have an individualized career growth plan that is jointly formulated?
12. When employees plan to attend outside seminars or workshops, do you jointly establish practical goals for that experience? Are these discussed when the employee returns? Do you provide opportunities to put those new skills to work?

MENTORING

Mentoring is a powerful instrument for fostering careers. Most successful people readily admit that they owe some of their success to help they received from one or more mentors. A mentor can be any experienced person, not necessarily someone directly associated with the organization and not necessarily a person of power.

The mentor must be willing to share time and expertise with a protegee. Many active and retired executives and professionals are more than willing to do that.

The value of mentorship increases when supervisors lack the time, willingness, or ability to provide the advice needed by employees. The current trend toward enlarging managerial span of control has resulted in less supervisory time being available for individual employees. Thus the need for mentors has increased.

During orientation programs, encourage your new employees to be on the lookout for people whom they would like to have as mentors.

Mentors wear several hats. As teachers and guides, they share knowledge, especially the kind of information that takes years to acquire. On a local level, this includes unwritten practices, rituals, managerial idiosyncrasies, policies that can be ignored, and rules that must be obeyed to the letter.[3]

As sponsors, mentors provide introductions to the right people, invite their protégées to serve on cross-functional committees or projects, and invite them to make presentations where they can display their talents.

As counselors and advisors, mentors not only give advice on career building but can also serve as sounding boards, provide empathic support, and encourage protegees to develop problem-solving skills. They also comment on innovative ideas that protégées are reluctant to propose through official channels.[4]

When mentors work in the same area as their mentees, they can observe skills. This provides opportunities for constructive criticism.

Five factors perceived as barriers to mentoring are lack of access to mentors, fear of initiating a relationship, unwillingness to mentor, need for approval of others, and misinterpretation of approaches.[5]

PRACTICAL CAREER-BUILDING TIPS

- Work on easier skills first to ensure early success.
- Ask others to help.
- Maintain a high ratio of praise to criticism.
- Correct errors before they become habits.
- Be patient. Expect plateaus in progress.
- Serve as coach, facilitator, advisor, and cheerleader, not as task master.
- Use adult training methods. Employees are not school children.
- Consider using the educational tools listed above.
- Encourage mentorships.

STRESS REDUCTION

A major and common barrier to career development in health care institutions is stress and burnout. Supervisors can do much to alleviate job stress, especially the stress that they themselves cause.

Here are twelve important ways to prevent or reduce employee stress in the workplace:

1. Eliminate or modify the stress factors presented in Exhibit 30–2.
2. Encourage humor and laughter.
3. Reinforce good performance with praise.

Exhibit 30–2 Stress Factors That Supervisors Can Affect

- Too little or too much communication
- Too little or too much responsibility
- Lack of leadership, resources, job security, time, respect, recognition, praise, training, performance feedback, authority, psychological support or credit for accomplishments, opportunity for input into decision making
- Excessive demands for conformity or perfection (nit picking)
- Failure of leaders to keep promises
- Unethical practices
- Unclear or excessive performance expectations, including short deadlines and turnaround time and excessive paperwork
- Territorial disputes
- Unsafe working environment or practices
- Favoritism, discrimination, or harassment
- Rapid technical, procedural, cultural, or organizational changes without sufficient preparation
- Bad or unfairly enforced rules, policies, and practices
- Stiffled creativity, job enrichment, or career enhancement
- Working with difficult people
- Lack of protection from outside forces (physicians, patients and other customers, senior officials)

4. Be careful how you react to their mistakes.

5. Give them more leeway in how they get the job done.

6. Empower them.

7. Reduce the workload of the overachievers.

8. Protect them from abusers.

9. Be certain that they know how to do their work.

10. Prepare them for change.

11. Do not assign stressful tasks to people with low stress thresholds.

12. Be alert for signs of stress or burnout. Take quick action when you spot them. Get burned-out employees professional help.

NOTES

1. J. Naisbitt, *Megatrends* (New York, N.Y: Warner, 1982).

2. W. Oncken, Jr., *Managing Management Time* (Englewood Cliffs, N.J.: Prentice-Hall, 1984).

3. W. Umiker, Mentoring: A tool for career development. *Medical Laboratory Observer* 18 (1986): 71–72

4. Umiker, Mentoring, 71.

5. B. Ragins and J. Cotton, "Easier said than done: Gender differences in perceived barriers to gaining a mentor, *Academy of Management Journal* 34 (1991) 939–951

Part VI
Special Supervisory Skills

Chapter 31

Verbal Communication

- on-the-job information
- formal and informal communication systems
- characteristics of good verbal communicators
- how to energize your verbal power pack
- barriers to verbal communication
- listening skills
- use of telephone and voice mail

Communication is, by far, the most important managerial skill. Without it, all other skills are inoperative. Supervisors spend most of their day communicating.

ON-THE-JOB INFORMATION

Communication is the cornerstone of cultural shaping and participative management. To seek improved quality, better customer service, increased productivity, more teamwork, and acceptance of change, we must take a second look at our communication systems and how we utilize them.

Most employees feel that bosses hold back things that they, the employees, should know about. Subordinates may withhold important information from their superiors if they dislike or mistrust them or if they fear that the information will adversely affect their relationship.

Effective information sharing must be[1]:

- multidirectional (up, down, lateral, and diagonal)
- objective, factual, and true
- comprehensive, but not excessive
- credible
- timely

FORMAL AND INFORMAL COMMUNICATION SYSTEMS

There are serious limitations to formal communication systems. These depend largely on written messages and formal meetings. Supervisors who depend entirely on this source are soon out of touch with what is going on in their organization. Generically written, watered-down newsletters or notices on bulletin boards are not enough. Information from electronic bulletin boards, voice mail, and one-on-one "grapevine" modalities is more effective.[2]

A common managerial problem is placing too much reliance on the computer. Unfortunately, a lot of significant information never gets into the computer.

The Grapevine

Although the grapevine transmits rumors and gossip and is subject to distortions and omissions, it is rapid and up to date and enjoys pervasive circulation. It is a valuable channel to disseminate information quickly and is invaluable as a source of current information

Supervisors must know who the grapevine's principal receivers are and keep tuned into them. Secretaries of V.I.P.s, for example, are excellent sources of fairly reliable information.

When you hear distorted or false news, put out corrections promptly via both formal and informal channels. This aborts false rumors and discredits the rumor mongers. Label a portion of each staff meeting as the gossip mill, and verify, discredit, or clarify rumors.

Use the grapevine not only to counter misinformation but also to disseminate good news, to make pronouncements that are not appropriate for newsletters or memos, and to test the waters. For example, if you have reservations about an action you are considering and are hesitant to go directly to others, have an aide pass on that information and tell you what the reactions are.

The Open-Door Policy

Implement your open-door policy in locations other than your office. Be available in the lounge during breaks or in the cafeteria. Some people are more comfortable talking to you there. Best of all, be available to your people at their work stations.

CHARACTERISTICS OF GOOD VERBAL COMMUNICATORS

Effective verbal communicators are enthusiastic and have good voice quality and expressive facial expressions, gestures, and other manifestations of body language. **Best of all, they are great listeners.**

They convey directions that are precise and clear as to what must be done and who is to do it. They seldom hear "Oh, I'm sorry, I thought you meant . . . ."

They often ask for help. Their colleagues may occasionally say "I told you so," but they rarely say "I *could* have told you so." Their delivery connotes genuine respect and concern for others, regardless of rank or power.

Communicators who have high self-esteem are not afraid to say "I don't know," "I made a mistake," or "I'm sorry."

HOW TO ENERGIZE YOUR VERBAL POWER PACK

Get people's attention:

- Establish and maintain eye contact.
- Praise them for something they did, are doing, or will do.
- Promise them something.

Exhibit confidence by word and body language:

- Use the person's name often.
- Speak firmly and clearly, not too fast or too slow.
- Avoid "weakeners" such as "I wonder if I could . . . ."
- Offer alternatives other than yes or no (e.g., "Would it be O.K. if I take off Friday" is not as effective for you as "Should I take off Monday or Friday?")

Show that what you want will help them (e.g., "If I attend that seminar, I can bring back some diagrams that you can use in your presentation").

BARRIERS TO VERBAL COMMUNICATION

There are three major categories of communication barriers: *physical, semantic, and psychological.*

Physical Barriers

Physical barriers include background noise, visual distractions, poor lighting, and environmental discomforts such as excessive heat or cold.

Semantic barriers

The most obvious semantic barrier is a foreign language. The percentage of workers who do not speak English is increasing at a rapid rate. This is compounded by the reluctance of recent immigrants to learn English and by the cultural variances that accompany language differences. These workers are often intimidated by the difficulty of making themselves understood. Supervisors must use simple vocabulary and sentence structure, use the active rather than the passive voice, and articulate slowly. They must be patient and prepared to repeat messages. Feedback from the employees is necessary to ensure their understanding. Workers should be encouraged to learn to speak English, and ideally supervisors will master at least a few important phrases in the foreign tongue.

Although foreign languages are the most obvious barriers, other semantic barriers include jargon, computerese, acronyms, and professional terminology. Some of us even have difficulty understanding our professional colleagues in other departments.

Psychological Barriers

Physical and semantic barriers are often easier to overcome than psychological barriers. *Potential psychological barriers include perceptions and assumptions.*

Perceptions are based largely on our personal and ethical values and our past experience. Two people witnessing the same scene may perceive entirely different messages depending on their values and experience.

Values are what we were taught to believe is right or wrong. Cultural, racial, and gender differences affect value systems. To learn more about the value systems of others (and our own), listen for the shoulds and should nots in conversations (e.g., "Length of service should count more around here").

Assumptions are things taken for granted, or how people interpret things. Frequently assumptions are false or distorted. When we say "Do you understand?" or "Do you have any questions?" we assume that a yes to the first question and a no to the second question indicate that our message was understood. Experienced teachers know that other modalities must be used to get that information, such as asking specific questions, giving examinations, or watching performance.

Other psychological barriers include mixed messages (inconsistencies between words and facial expressions, voice tone, or body language), kidding and sarcasm, put-downs ("Don't be ridiculous"), judgmental responses ("The trouble with you is . . ."), stereotyping ("Women just don't understand instruments"), and inflammatory utterances ("I demand that you . . .").

LISTENING SKILLS

Most of us are terrible listeners. We talk when we should be paying attention. Even when we are not talking, we often are merely waiting to speak rather than listening. We are often guilty of mentally writing a script, that is, formulating a response while the other person is still verbalizing.

Listening is visual as well as auditory. In fact, when what we see is different from what we hear, the visual messages are usually the genuine ones. Here are some commonly observed visual messages:

- clearing the throat and blinking the eyes ("I'm nervous")
- tugging on the ear ("I'm not listening")
- rubbing the nose ("I don't believe that")
- clasping the hands behind the head ("I'm in charge here")
- rubbing the palms ("Let's go" or "I'm winning")
- arms folded across the chest ("The answer is no")
- rubbing the back of the neck ("I'm frustrated")
- moving the foot in a circle ("I'm getting impatient")
- raising one eyebrow ("I can't believe this")
- raising both eyebrows ("That surprises me")

A caveat: *Do not rely on a single visual message.*

The same gesture can have different interpretations. Always look for confirming groups of visual observations before drawing conclusions. For example, a head tilt accompanied by pursed lips and ear tugging usually indicates suspicion. On the other hand, when a head tilt is combined with a shifting gaze, it usually means boredom or annoyance.

Touching

Touching is powerful, but it must be done in a way that is not interpreted as having sexual or aggressive overtones. Important factors in the appropriate use of touching are the anatomical location, the kind, and the context. Safest touch zones are the forearm, elbow, upper arm, and shoulder. Use light, transient touches. Do not hold, pat, or massage. Handshakes are almost always appreciated, except when they produce pain (arthritics dread them) or are prolonged.

The context of the conversation is important. The touch should reinforce the verbal response. Touch is especially appropriate when one is expressing appreciation or support.

The Value of Silence

How often have we wished that we had remained silent? But let us not get into that. Instead, we want to focus on the importance of the silent pause. Psychiatrists know the value of silent pauses to get patients to reveal what is on their minds. In an earlier chapter, we mentioned the value of silent pauses during interviews or counseling sessions.

Phonetics

*How one says something is just as important as **what** one says.* Voice tone, volume, and rate vary with one's emotional state. For example, a subordinate may say "I'm O.K.," but the phonetics say "I feel miserable."

Try to mirror the other person's volume and rate of speech.

Here are some verbal patterns that reduce power:

- posing questions to make requests or demands: "Would you like to get me a cup of coffee?"
- using disclaimers: "I know this sounds silly, but . . . ."
- using weak qualifiers: "sort of," "maybe"
- tolerating interruptions

The Three Strategies for Effective Listening

1. *Attentive Appearance*

Face the person. Stand or sit upright, lean toward the person, and maintain eye contact. Good eye contact is not staring down the other person. It is shifting the gaze from the eyes to other parts of the person's face or occasionally glancing away from the face entirely.

Avoid a poker face. Let your facial expressions show your feelings. Your body language must be congruent with your verbal messages.

2. *Attentive Words*

Use responders such as "Uh-huh," "Yes, go on," and "I see" or phrases such as "Tell me more."

3. *Feedback*

This is the most effective of the three. Only when feedback is provided does the speaker know that the right message has been received.

Use echoing (repeating exactly what was said), paraphrasing (repeating what was said, but in your own words), interpreting, and summarizing.

Kinds of Responses

- defensive: "That's a damn lie!"
- judgmental: "You are too sensitive."
- advisory: "I'll tell you what I would do."
- questioning: "Be more specific."
- empathic: "You seem upset. I can understand that."

Skilled listeners make frequent use of empathic (supportive) responses and minimize defensive, judgmental, and advisory ones. Questioning is appropriate unless it sounds like cross-examining. They also listen carefully for underlying feelings.
Avoid the following:

- criticizing
- diagnosing
- falsely praising
- ordering
- name calling
- advising
- moralizing
- threatening
- cross-examining
- diverting
- insincerely reassuring
- feigned listening

THE TELEPHONE

The importance of the telephone and telephone courtesy cannot be overemphasized. I strongly recommend that every supervisor either attend a seminar on phone etiquette or read a book on the subject, such as the one listed at the end of this chapter.

Tips on Telephone Efficiency and Courtesy

When you are the receiver:

- have paper and pencil next to the phone to take notes

- answer within three rings; apologize if you do not
- identify yourself and your department or your title as appropriate
- sit up straight and smile; the caller "sees" it
- sound enthusiastic (pleased to receive the call)
- use all the listening skills described above
- when you transfer a call, do not hang up until the connection has been made
- if the person being asked for is not available, offer to help or to find someone else
- never cut people off with statements such as "You'll have to call back," "I don't know," "You have the wrong department," or "There's nothing I can do about that"
- before you put callers on hold, give them the choice of being put on hold, calling back, leaving a message, or being called back
- take notes

When you are the caller:

- stand up during the call, you will sound more businesslike
- state your business first, saving social talk for later; by that time you will have sensed how busy the person is
- use the person's name frequently
- be concise; do not waste the person's time
- let the other person hang up first

Avoid phone tag by:

- using an answering machine or voice mail
- picking the best time to call; most people are in their office just before lunch and late in the afternoon
- asking the person's secretary for the best time to call
- leaving a note
- telling the person who answers the phone the exact time you will call again or stating the best time to be called
- asking that the person be paged

Voice Mail

Many callers are irritated by voice mail. Some refuse to leave messages. When used well, however, voice mail can eliminate frustrations for both caller and call recipient.

Use voice mail effectively by[3]:

• changing your greeting regularly to let callers know your situation (e.g., "I'm on another call right now," "I'll be back in my office at noon," or "I'll be out of my office until Monday, February 12")
• stating—in addition to your name, organization, and phone number—the time and date, the nature of your call, when it is convenient for you to be called, or when you will call back
• substituting a message for a request to be called back
• suggesting a fax response if a response is needed; give your fax number
• letting your callers know when you make call-backs (if you screen calls as a time management technique)

NOTES

1. F. Sonnenberg, The essentials of on-the-job information, *Supervisory Management* 37 (1992): 8–9.
2. Sonnenberg, The essentials, 8.
3. D. Deeprose, Making voice mail customer friendly, *Supervisory Management* 37 (1992): 7–8.

SUGGESTED READING

Payne, E., et al. 1987. *Body language: "The Silent Communicator."* Fort Collins, Colo: TransVision.
Scott, D. 1988. *The telephone and time management.* Los Altos, Calif: Crips.
Walther, G.R. 1986. *Phone power: How to make the telephone your most profitable business tool.* New York, N.Y.: Putnam's.

Chapter 32
Written Communication

- selection of communication channels
- letter versus memo
- the standard format for memos
- the ABC rule for getting action
- the four key steps in writing
- editing a staff member's report
- when to follow conversation with memo or letter
- bulletin boards and bar coding
- computer applications

SELECTION OF COMMUNICATION CHANNELS

On a daily basis, managers must choose among various channels of communication. Efficiency, effectiveness, speed, and cost are affected by this selection process. *Here are some of the selections managers face:*

- verbal, written, or both?
- if verbal, one-on-one? group meeting? intercom? word-of-mouth? teleconference?
- if written, memo? letter? fax? computer? bulletin board?

VERBAL VERSUS WRITTEN COMMUNICATION

Verbal communication is usually faster, permits complex dialogs, and transmits feelings better. Booher recommends verbal communications when you want immediate feedback, when you want to persuade or question, and when you do not want your words to come back to haunt you.[1]

Written messages can mute hostility or emotion, are permanent, and usually are less susceptible to misinterpretation. They do not interrupt the work of recipients as verbal messages frequently do. Busy people are annoyed by telephone interruptions or summons to unscheduled meetings.

Note: Do not use memos to deliver bad news, such as a firing, reprimand, or unpleasant assignment. Deliver these in person.

LETTER VERSUS MEMO

Letters are for external, private, or formal purposes. A useful rule is that anything that requires a stamp should be a letter. Memos—"messages in shirt-sleeves"—are preferred for in-house or nonprivate messages. See Exhibit 32–1 for a format for memos.

THE ABC RULE FOR GETTING ACTION

A = **Attention:** You must get it.
B = **Behavior:** What do you want from the reader, or what are you going to do?
C = **Convince:** Provide facts, logic, statistics, or references.

THE FOUR KEY STEPS IN WRITING LETTERS, MEMOS, OR REPORTS

1. Freewrite a Rough Draft

The first paragraph gets the most attention, so frontload it by including the purpose of the report and a summary sentence.

Early on, use the reader's name or "you." Try to deliver some good news, a compliment, or an expression of appreciation for something the person said or did. Write in a conversational mode. Imagine the reader sitting across from you. Prepare a strong closing statement.

Exhibit 32–1 A Standard Format for Memos

To:	Night supervisor
From:	Lab manager
Date:	August 1, 1993
Subject:	New procedure for . . .
Message:	The new procedure will be demonstrated on 8/15/90 in the chemistry lab.
Action:	Please review the attached . . . , and please attend the demonstration.
Attachments:	Procedure sheet for . . .
Signature:	Sue Smith, Lab Manager
Copies to:	Medical director/Chemistry supervisor

Do not waste time correcting grammatical or spelling errors in the first draft. Concern yourself only with content and clarity at this point.

2. Rewrite with Emphasis on Content

Check the rough draft for brevity, clarity, and personal touch. Is it complete? Does it answer what, who, when, where, why, and how?
Improve the readability by:

* using stroking words, such as the reader's name, "you," and "we"; compliments, and expressions of appreciation
* converting negative or impolite statements into positive, tactful, and courteous ones
* strengthening vague or abstract wording
* using gender-neutral language

3. Edit for Structure

* Check the paragraphs. Keep them short with one major thought for each.
* Check the sentences. Vary their lengths to avoid telegraphic sound. Break up the long ones.
* Convert passive to active voice.
* Convert *-ion* nouns into verbs (e.g., change "It is my intention." to "I intend").
* Eliminate:
    —archaic, pompous, or overused phrases ("bizlish" and "legalese")
    —unnecessary words (e.g., "The consensus *of opinion*")
    —redundant phrases or modifiers (e.g., "*There are* too many people arriving late")
    —weak words (e.g., "We provide *good* service")
    —slang, jargon, and acronyms
    —buzzwords or hackneyed phrases (e.g., "down the tube," "out of this world," and "belly-up")
* Use contractions (e.g., "you're").
* Emphasize by underlining, highlighting, and using bold or italic print.

4. Edit for Grammar, Spelling, and Punctuation

Use computer software to check spelling and grammar.

Note: See the Suggested Reading at the end of this chapter for excellent explanations of proper punctuation.

HOW TO EDIT A STAFF MEMBER'S REPORT INOFFENSIVELY

Refrain from sending it back marked up like a school paper. Go over it in person. Have the writer sit next to you while he or she holds the paper.

Focus on major defects. Is it organized logically, supported by data, and clear as to its purpose?

Avoid finding too many flaws. The writer will think you are nitpicking. End with an encouraging comment about how the person's reports have improved in content, readability, or promptness.

WHEN TO FOLLOW CONVERSATIONS WITH MEMOS OR LETTERS

- When a permanent record is needed.
- When the receiver is a poor listener or is forgetful.
- When the oral communication may have been flawed.
- When more details are needed.
- When no action followed a verbal request.
- When you want to make certain that you get credit for an idea.
- When the message is one that involves risk or might be denied by the recipient.

BULLETIN BOARDS

Bulletin boards, which once were largely ignored, are making a comeback. Total quality management (continuous quality improvement) programs often make use of charts and graphs to illustrate progress or accomplishments. Bulletin boards are ideal to display these.

To increase interest in the displays, place these charts and other important information next to work or vacation schedules, which must be viewed frequently. Add news items such as commendations or thank-you notes from patients, letters from former employees, newspaper clippings of interest, and personnel changes. People always are interested to hear more about their friends and colleagues.

BAR CODING

Managers in laboratories, blood banks, supply departments, and elsewhere are finding that bar coding can reduce costs and increase efficiency.

COMPUTER APPLICATIONS IN HEALTH CARE

Most health care professionals have personal computers. Anyone who cannot speak computerese or perform basic computer functions is severely handicapped (but not protected by the Americans with Disabilities Act). Here are some of the major uses of computers at work.

Word Processing

This is the principal use for most people. In addition to typing of routine letters and reports there are special applications such as the following:

- lists (e.g., "to do" lists, rosters, schedules, and inventories)
- newsletters, charts, certificates, special forms, and other graphics
- policy manuals and directories
- medical and blood donor records
- position descriptions
- schedules that can be in calendar format or listed under tasks (a project can be defined in PERT or Gantt charts)[2]
- transfer of printed data and drawings into computer-readable messages using optical character recognition programs (this is achieved through the use of flatbed or hand-held scanners, which are essentially photoduplicators for computers)

Spreadsheet Programs

Spreadsheet programs are useful for the following:

- budget control and forecasting
- staffing needs
- productivity measurements

Database Management

Database management allows users to define records to be retained and to store, recall, and change the information with just a few strokes. It also enables users to define fields of data that can be sorted and later manipulated independently or in concert with other pieces of information.[3] *Databases are useful for the following applications:*

- management information systems
- project tracking
- facilities management
- quality management
- financial management

Communication

- electronic mail (the electronic bulletin board permits one to tap into information banks, such as poison control centers, and to receive other diagnostic or therapeutic information)[4]
- telecommunications (local area networks and wide area networks)

Training

Computers are being used increasingly to supplement orientation programs on either a generic or a specific departmental basis. This ensures uniformity and quality of instruction and saves much instructor time.

Problem Solving

In addition to database management, so-called expert intelligence programs are being developed that permit users to use the same sequence of problem-solving steps as that applied by experts in the field.

Special Departmental Uses

Each hospital department has some specific uses for computers. For example, the pharmacy may have a program that keeps track of pharmaceuticals that have been issued to floors and another that credits patient accounts for medications that have been returned. Blood banks maintain donor inventories. Human resources departments may have programs to screen job applicants or to record exit interviews.

Problems with Computer Systems

In addition to hardware breakdowns, incompatible interfacing systems, limited memory, power failures, inadvertent erasure of stored data, and lack of back-up systems, there are problems of time sharing, security, and training new people to use computer systems.

NOTES

1. D. Booher, *Send Me a Memo: A Handbook of Model Memos* (New York, N.Y.: Facts on File, 1984).
2. W.W. Christensen and E.I. Stearns, Microcomputers in Health Care Management (Gaithersburg, Md.: Aspen, 1984).
3. Christensen and Stearns, *Microcomputers.*
4. Christensen and Stearns, *Microcomputers.*

SUGGESTED READING

Iles, R.L. 1988. *Techniques to improve your writing skills.* Shawnee Mission, Kan: National Press Publications.
Strunk, W. Jr., and E.B. White. 1979. *The elements of style.* New York, N.Y.: Macmillan.

Chapter 33

How To Be More Effective at Meetings

- use and misuse of meetings
- the four components of a meeting
- purposes of meetings
- meeting preparations
- the agenda
- getting started
- encouraging participation
- maintaining control
- use of visuals
- important do nots for chairpersons
- ending the meeting
- postmeeting activities
- problem members
- you as a member
- power in meetings
- committees and committee meetings

Most managers think they spend too much time in meetings and that most meetings are a waste of time, and they are right! Nevertheless, the higher one rises in an organization, the more time he or she spends in conferences.

Insecure managers call meetings for the sole purpose of getting moral support or sharing responsibility. Perhaps the biggest time-waster is the regularly scheduled meeting held when there is nothing important to discuss.

If a meeting is to discuss viewpoints, it is probably necessary. If it is strictly to distribute information, it is probably not necessary. Meetings are generally not an efficient way to dispense information; information can be disseminated more effectively by other channels.[1]

Many decisions can be made and problems solved without group dialogues. When fast action is needed, meetings can impede progress. Nor do they often produce great ideas or resolve crises. On the other hand, meetings can be valuable for decision making and problem solving. This is explored in the next chapter.

THE FOUR COMPONENTS OF A MEETING

1. **Purpose:** the reason for the meeting (if you cannot state it, you do not need the meeting)
2. **Process:** how the meeting is conducted
3. **Content:** what is discussed.
4. **Product:** the outcome (if it does not involve some kind of action, the meeting has been a failure)

PURPOSES OF MEETINGS

* to disseminate information; to explain new policies, laws, services, protocols, and the like; to introduce new personnel; and to report on inspections, restructuring, or construction progress
* to accept reports or recommendations
* to get help to make decisions, solve problems, allocate resources, prepare plans, establish priorities, generate ideas, or assign tasks
* to persuade, gain acceptability, or obtain commitment for an idea, program, or proposal
* to teach, train, demonstrate, or explain

MEETING PREPARATIONS

In addition to preparing an agenda and ensuring that meeting space and facilities are available, participants can improve their effectiveness in meetings by getting input from others before the session and by campaigning for their proposals.

Reviewing your proposal with members who are already in agreement locks them into the position and makes it harder for them to change their minds. Getting support from leaders of the opposition is even more important.

Sometimes getting input from members or enlightening these participants before the meeting eliminates the need for the meeting.

The selection of members is important. Significant cost can be decreased and displeasure avoided if attendance is limited to people who are needed and willing. The group should collectively have the needed knowledge and experience, and members should be people who can be depended on to show up and participate.

Avoid power disparity; it inhibits free wheeling discussions. Avoid negativists, but welcome devil's advocates who are not obstructionists and who can spot problems and raise important issues.

If terminating sessions has been a problem, schedule meetings just before lunch or quitting time. If the agenda is brief, hold a stand-up meeting.

THE AGENDA

Think of the agenda as a device to steer your meeting, as the rudder of your discussion boat. The agenda is to a chairperson what a recipe is to a cook. Encapsulate the topics in action or goal-oriented statements. Try using a one-sentence purpose statement (e.g., "to prepare the final draft of our mission statement"). Avoid the word *discuss* when the purpose of the meeting is to propose some action.

After each item on the agenda, indicate the expected results (e.g., decision needed, action, or information only). Distribute the agenda several days before the meeting.

At the meeting, use the agenda sheets for making margin notes during the meeting.

GETTING STARTED

Arrive early to ensure that everything is in readiness. If there has been a change in the meeting room, make certain that members are guided to the right place. Stand at the door to meet arrivals. Introduce new members and guests.

Have your opening statement memorized. It should include the purpose statement and a comment about how important the meeting is. Sound and look enthusiastic.

Review the highlights of the previous meeting, and ask for any comments or corrections. Note any progress that has been made since that meeting.

ENCOURAGING PARTICIPATION

Some great ways to get members to speak up include the following:

- Go around the table, calling on each member by name.
- Respond enthusiastically to all suggestions.
- Split into breakaway groups.
- Let others lead some of the questioning or chair the session.

- Reinforce input from reserved members, (e.g., "Thanks, Erica, for speaking so candidly. That took courage").
- Use nonthreatening, open-ended questions (e.g., "How do you think someone who was opposed to that idea would respond?").
- Withhold your opinion until everyone else has spoken.
- If a person's suggestion cannot be accepted, try using part of it.
- Encourage members to build on the ideas of others.
- Preserve the ego of all members.

MAINTAINING CONTROL

Keep people from going off on a tangent. When they stray, say something such as "Jessica, that's interesting. We ought to look into that further. Now about . . . ."

Summarize progress periodically by using a flip chart or blackboard. Call for a break when things stall.

Ask whether anyone needs more data before making a decision. Invite each person by name to state his or her position. Try to reach a consensus. Consensus is not always good, however. The urge to reach consensus may be so strong that insufficient attention is paid to eliciting individual opinions and encouraging dissenting viewpoints. We will discuss consensus more in Chapter 34.

If you are in a meeting for an hour and no one has made a recommendation, you are not in a productive session.

An effective leader says, "I take it you're recommending . . . ." Ensure that recommendations are phrased in specific terminology. This is especially important when you are dealing with customer service. For example, "to improve emergency department service" is too general; "to decrease waiting time in the pediatric clinic to an average of 15 minutes" is much more specific.

USE OF VISUALS

A good visual should assist, not replace, the presenter. Visuals are like the headlines of a newspaper story.

Use visuals to open presentations, channel thinking, emphasize key points, present financial or statistical data, make comparisons, simplify complex processes, and explain new concepts.[2]

Good design criteria include the following[3]:

- letters large enough to be seen by everyone (at least 1/4-inch letters on a transparency to be readable at 20 feet)

'

- one idea per visual
- maximum of seven words per line
- maximum of seven lines per visual
- short words

SOME IMPORTANT DO NOTS FOR CHAIRPERSONS

- Do not try to dominate the meeting.
- Do not state your opinion before others have given theirs.
- Do not tell a participant that he or she is wrong.
- Do not instruct or lecture unless that is the purpose of the meeting.
- Do not argue (disagreeing is acceptable).
- Do not ridicule, kid, or be sarcastic.
- Do not take sides early in the discussion.
- Do not fail to control problem members.
- Do not allow the meeting to run overtime.

ENDING THE MEETING

Summarize the discussion to avoid confusion, and state the decisions. If no decisions were made, give the reason. Indicate the areas still requiring consideration. Review assignments, and select the date for the next meeting.

POSTMEETING ACTIVITIES

Send thank-you notes to individuals who made excellent presentations, clarifying remarks, or an outstanding effort or who supported you.

Prepare the minutes without delay. Copies should be available within 24 to 48 hours. State important facts briefly but thoroughly. Include the following:

- the names of attendees and members who were absent
- a statement that the previous minutes were read and approved
- a discussion or presentation of each item on the agenda
- a record of agreement or disagreement
- a record of vote or decisions made
- the date, place, and time of the next meeting
- the time of start and adjournment

PROBLEM MEMBERS

There are all kinds of participants: incisive thinkers, impatient doers, chronic objectors, speech-makers, shoot-from-the-hip decision makers, and ultraconservatives; you can probably name others. Let us take a closer look at the ones who give chairpersons the most difficulty.

Latecomers

It is sometimes better to declare an intermission and brief the latecomer than to halt progress.

Members Who Offend Others

No member has the right to mock or insult others. The leader should immediately interrupt the errant behavior and apologize to the person who has been ridiculed (e.g., "Jack, that is uncalled for. I don't appreciate that remark, and I'm sure the rest here agree. Let's keep this on a professional level").

Members with Secret Agendas

As soon as a secret agenda becomes apparent, the moderator must bring the announced agenda back into focus.

Intimidators

Intimidation is one of the most common methods of trying to force an opinion. The three tactics are to appear to be angry, to assume a superior attitude, and to ridicule. The chair must stop this quickly.

Hostile or Angry Members

If you know who these people are, plan ahead what you are going to say. Practice by saying it out loud several times before the meeting. Visualize a successful confrontation.

At the meeting, encourage venting. The more anger that pours out, the less there is left. Do not interrupt the person, and insist that he or she not interrupt you.

Nonparticipants

Their thoughts are elsewhere. Some of these people should not have been invited. Bring their minds back on track by posing questions or asking for their opinions.

Side Conversationalists

Some private conversation is natural. Timid members may be afraid to speak up, so they whisper to each other. They may be bored or just discourteous. If you stop in the middle of a sentence and glare at them, this may work. If not, ask them to share their conversation with the group.

Comics

We all enjoy a little humor, but individuals who overdo this can be disruptive. They can be stopped in their tracks if you fail to laugh, give a wry smile as you shake your head, or state that you want to get on with the business.

Motor Mouths

These people are enthralled by their own voice and never seem to run out of gas. Their comments are endless, and their questions are really just more comments.

Jump in when they pause for breath. Say "Just a minute, Rita, let's hear what others have to say," "We're getting bogged down, Rita, please make your point," or "Please put that in the form of a motion."

Destroyers

Some participants become emotionally rather than rationally involved. They play psychological war games and demand attention by criticizing, interrupting, or taking offense at innocent remarks. One of them may say "I resent that" or "If you people approve that, I'm walking out." Ignore their outbursts. Do not argue or get excited. Let them say their piece, and then go on.

YOU AS A MEMBER

All managers, including the chief executive officer, serve on committees and other groups as members. Members have almost as many responsibilities as the moderators. Effective participation begins when you receive an agenda.

Think about what you can contribute. Collect data or references. Be prepared to ask pertinent questions, and answer queries in your area of expertise. If you cannot attend, notify the chair as soon as possible. *Good members:*

- question the need for their attendance
- do their homework
- arrive on time
- listen thoughtfully to others and try to understand their points of view
- ask for clarifications
- are tolerant of opinions with which they disagree
- offer honest opinions, even when these are unpopular
- try to separate facts from perceptions, assumptions, or opinions
- have the courage to disagree without being disagreeable
- remain rational and assertive, even when harassed
- seek win-win solutions but are willing to compromise
- accept special assignments such as searching literature or serving as recorder
- never, never become one of the problem members described above

POWER IN MEETINGS

Be a participant, not a spectator. If you observe the members who wield the most power at meetings, you will note that while others veer off to other issues they are not dissuaded from their goals.

Take up space. Do not go into a shell. Spread your materials on the table.

Sit next to, not across from, an opponent. When addressing that person turn your body, not just your head, 30 degrees toward him or her.

In large groups, stand up when you talk; eye level is important.

Make eye contact first with the group leader, then move to others, return, move away again, and return. A smile helps put your eyes in the right mode of friendliness and adds to eye contact.

If you are usually passive and rarely participate, get going by asking questions. That makes it easier to comment later.

Be positive in what you say and how you say it. Know when to come on strong and when to be tentative.

Use effective hand movements, but do not wave your arms.

Avoid disclaimers (e.g., "I know this sounds silly, but . . ."), weak words (e.g., "sort of" or "pretty sure"), and inflammatory phrases (e.g., "You have to" or "I demand").

When negotiating:

* state your case
* listen while others state their cases
* list similarities between positions
* define points of disagreement
* attack ideas, not people
* be willing to concede on some points (those that concern you least); if what you offer is not met by like concessions or is met by enhanced demands, resist
* if you cannot get a win-win solution, seek at least a compromise; that is better than a loss
* if you must resist, use the broken record technique of repeating your response (e.g., "No, I can't agree") after each argument from your opponent; do not hesitate or waver (these are signs of weakness)

Discussions become arguments when objectivity is lost in favor of inflexibility and repetition. End arguments by accepting responsibility for them (e.g., "Sally, I'm afraid we're arguing, not discussing. I'm sorry. I wasn't even hearing you. Let's start again").

COMMITTEES AND COMMITTEE MEETINGS

Committee meetings are subject to the same rules and conduct as other meetings. Standing committees are relatively permanent and meet on a regular basis. Many are required by the Joint Commission on Accreditation of Healthcare Organizations. They deal with matters such as quality, safety, infections, ethics, and credentials. Ad hoc committees are temporary, created to deal with a single issue such as a threat of unionization. Task forces represent a special kind of ad hoc committee.

It is unfortunate that so many health care workers dislike committee assignments because committees are constantly growing in number and importance as departments and services become more complex, accrediting agencies make more demands, and the increased need for interdepartmental cooperation demands more cross-functional committee input.

The functions and responsibilities of standing committees are usually spelled out in bylaws, union contracts, and operational procedures or protocols. Ad hoc committees are usually appointed by managers at any level.

The person who appoints a committee should be specific about what he or she expects. The following questions should be answered:

- Who is chairperson, and does that person have the power to appoint members, schedule meetings, and prepare agendas? If you are appointing the committee, select the chairperson carefully.
- Is membership voluntary?
- What is the goal or mission of the committee?
- When is a report due? Are there to be interim reports? If so, at what intervals?
- If it is only a decision-making committee, what are the alternatives to be considered?
- If it is a problem-solving committee, does the convening authority want only what is deemed to be the best solution or a list of all the alternatives that are considered?
- Will the findings be implemented or used by the convening authority only as he or she sees fit?
- What facilities and fiscal support are available?
- If the committee is to serve permanently, have terms of tenure and plans for rotation of membership been provided?

NOTES

1. C.W. Burleson, *Effective Meetings: The Complete Guide* (New York, N.Y.: Wiley, 1990).
2. 3M Meeting Management Team, *How To Run Better Business Meetings* (New York, N.Y.: McGraw-Hill, 1987).
3. 3M Meeting Management Team, *How To Run,* 136.

Chapter 34

Decision Making and Problem Solving

- why decision making is more important now
- decision making and leadership
- the two big myths
- when to avoid decisions
- the essential trinity for effective decisions
- what is judgment?
- logical versus intuitive problem solving
- coping with daily problems
- steps of rational problem solving
- the computer and other problem-solving tools
- using your intuitive process
- group problem solving

Problems are inevitable when people work together. The hallmark of a well-managed team is not the absence of problems but whether the problems are resolved effectively.

WHY DECISION MAKING IS MORE IMPORTANT NOW

- The rate of organizational, technical, legal, and operational change constantly increases.
- It is more difficult to reverse some decisions (e.g., hiring employees).
- Our society grows ever more litigious.
- Critical shortages of certain specialists demand quick hiring decisions or competitors snatch them.
- Financial pressures, especially those relating to capital expenditures or cost containment, have increased.
- Factors of employee and patient safety, satisfaction, and ethics have been increasing in number and complexity.

People decisions are by far the most important. The success of organizations is dependent on people decisions. Hiring, training, disciplining, promoting, and discharging of employees all demand careful consideration by managers at all levels.

DECISION MAKING AND LEADERSHIP

Autocratic leaders make decisions without soliciting help from others. Consultative leaders get input before deciding. Democratic leaders participate with their staffs in making decisions. Delegative leaders turn the process over to others.

Upper management deals chiefly with decisions that relate to end results or long-range strategies: the what. Supervisors deal principally with operational processes: the how.

THE TWO BIG MYTHS

Managers claim that most of their problems would be solved by larger staffs, space, or budgets. Any observer of governmental agencies knows that this is not true.

Employees are blamed for most problems, but the real villains are faulty processes, which are the responsibility of leaders.

WHEN TO AVOID MAKING DECISIONS

Avoid making decisions when:

- the problem will probably correct itself, or interference is likely to make matters worse (if it ain't broke, don't fix it)
- it is not your problem
- you or the others are emotionally upset, or there are serious communication distractions
- more information or advice is needed
- the problem should be delegated (most decisions should be made at the lowest organizational level—as close to the scene of action as possible—provided that the delegates are capable and willing)

THE ESSENTIAL TRINITY FOR EFFECTIVE DECISIONS

An effective decision must be:

1. a quality decision (the sine qua non)
2. timely as to when it is made and when it is implemented (professionals often procrastinate because they are looking for all the data available; they often fall prey to paralysis from analysis because of this endless pursuit)

3. acceptable to the people affected (many managers are adept at making decisions but fail to persuade people to carry them out)

JUDGMENT

Sound judgment requires a combination of knowledge, experience, and intuition. Practical knowledge is gained through experience, and intuition is experience buried in the unconscious mind. For that reason, seasoned veterans usually find it easier to make the daily decisions than do neophytes.

THE DUAL COGNITIVE FUNCTIONS

There are two cognitive approaches to decision making and problem solving: analytical and intuitive. Analytical or left-brain function provides rational, logical, scientific thinking; intuitive cognition or right-brain function provides creativity and inspiration.

Left-brain thinking is a flowchart process. Analytical people rely on algorithmic processes, plans, reports, computer printouts, and step-by-step procedures. Judgment is exercised at each step, and anything that is irrelevant is excluded. Managers and investigators who treat problem solving as a science often fail to come up with creative ideas because they depend entirely on this rational approach.

Intuitive thinking depends on data buried in our unconscious minds, which are like computers with almost unlimited memory storage capability. Unfortunately, what is filed in these cerebral banks cannot be readily recalled by us, like a computer program for which we lost the password. Unlike computer-stored data, brain information is constantly and unconsciously analyzed, synthesized, and reformatted.

Innovative people have deeper insight or stronger gut reactions. They visualize more than their rational counterparts. They prefer diagrams to printouts. They often throw logic out the window. An intuitive thought process can seldom be flowcharted; rather, it is hop, skip, and jump.

Common sense is a combination of logic and intuition, the left and right brains working in tandem.

COPING WITH THE NUMEROUS DAILY PROBLEMS

Any supervisor worth his or her salt is faced with innumerable little problems and decisions every day. Solving problems is the supervisor's most important responsibility. Their subordinates bring them into their office by the carload. Better training, planning, coaching, delegating, and policy making can do wonders in cutting down on the number of these daily interruptions.

Use the stop-look-listen approach that used to be posted at all railroad crossings. Stop what you are doing, look interested, and then listen carefully. If the problem is still unclear, ask pertinent questions.

Then ask what they think should be done. Most of the time they will have thought through the problem and may have a better solution than you can offer on the spur of the moment. Approve their suggestion and congratulate them if you agree. If it is something that only you can solve, give them your answer on the spot, or get back to them without undue delay. Follow up when appropriate.

THE LOGICAL PROCESS: KEY STEPS IN SOLVING LARGE PROBLEMS

Step 1. Prepare a problem statement. Diagnosis is the most important part of problem solving, and it is often the most neglected part. Novice problem solvers jump to solutions before they have identified and delineated the problem. Poor problem statements can lead people astray. For example, the problem statement "Lack of clear policy relating to sick leave" is not likely to lead to solving a problem of excessive absenteeism due to poor leadership.

Step 2. Obtain and interpret the facts or data by asking the following questions:

- When was problem first noted?
- How serious is it?
- Is it getting better or worse?
- Is it more complicated than first appeared? In what way?
- What is the cause? (This is the most important question.)
- How was this handled in the past ? What were the results?

Step 3. Generate alternatives (as many as possible).
Step 4. Formulate criteria to evaluate the alternatives.

- absolute criteria: criteria that must be met by an acceptable solution (e.g., "No increase in costs or personnel")
- differential criteria: criteria used to compare and contrast the various alternatives (e.g., turnaround time, schedule convenience, availability of supplies, and degree of expertise required)

Step 5. Evaluate the alternatives, and select the best.
Step 6. Look for flaws in the choice. Ask a lot of "what ifs." Avoid the jigsaw puzzle fallacy. The latter is based on the false assumption that there is only one good

solution, i.e., a jigsaw puzzle must have four straight edges. Often there are several equally satisfactory solutions: The edges of life's puzzles are seldom straight.

Step 7. Develop an action plan.

Step 8. Implement the plan. If there is hesitation about implementing the plan, ask what would be the worst possible thing that could happen if the plan is implemented and the worst possible thing that could happen if the risk is not taken.

Step 9. Follow up. If what you are doing is not working well, make the needed changes.

USEFUL TOOLS FOR PROBLEM SOLVING

Bar Graphs

Bar graphs (Figure 34–1a) display the values of a number of related items, such as the number of patient visits on each day of the month. When a bar graph shows the distribution of a variance, it is called a histogram (Figure 34–1b).

Pareto Diagrams

Pareto charts (Figure 34–1c) display the frequency of occurrences listed in order of importance or frequency.

Scattergrams

A scattergram (Figure 34–1d) shows the correlation between two variables.

Run Charts

Run charts (Figure 34–1e) plot data over periods of time. They exhibit trends, cycles, or other patterns in a process (e.g., attendance records, turnover, or customer complaints).

Control Charts

Control charts (Figure 34–1f) illustrate values that are either in control or out of control. In Figure 34–1f, the solid horizontal line represents an average or normal value. The spaces between the solid line and the dotted lines are acceptable values,

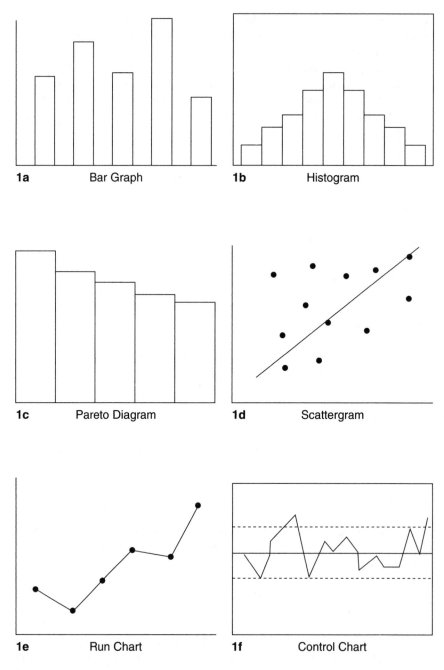

Figure 34–1 Useful tools for problem solving

usually plus or minus two or three standard deviations. Any value outside the dotted lines is an out of control value.

Flowcharts

A flowchart (Figure 34–2a) represents a series of steps or events arranged chronologically.

Cause and Effect Diagrams

Also known as fishbone charts, these devices are useful in an early stage of problem solving or when one is considering potential problems (Figure 34–2b). A cause and effect diagram forces a focus on potential causes. On each leg (fishbone), possible factors are recorded and grouped according to different categories (e.g., process, human, equipment, or policies).

Pie Charts

Pie charts (Figure 34–2c) illustrate relative numbers or percentages.

Gaussian Curve Charts

The bell-shaped curves show frequency distributions. These are among the most common quality control charts (Figure 34–2d).

Force Field Charts

When one is considering the advantages and disadvantages of a new service, process, procedure, or piece of equipment, the opposing considerations can be illustrated and quantified by a force field chart[1] (Figure 34–2e).

Checklists

Checklists (Figure 34–2f) are used as reminders or for documentation of activities. Shopping lists, daily "to do" schedules, and validation of records are just a few uses for this ubiquitous tool. Figure 34–2f is a partial list of tests that a new laboratory technician must be qualified to perform.

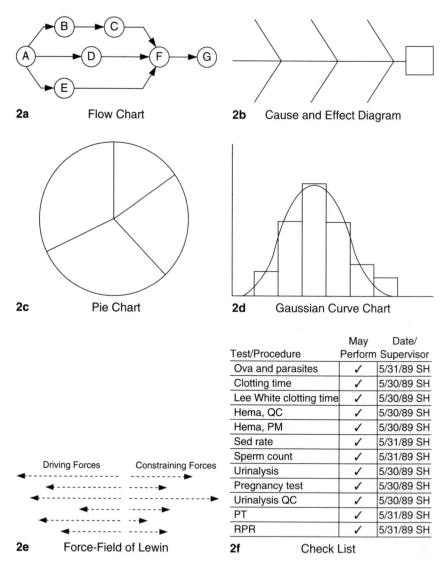

Test/Procedure	May Perform	Date/ Supervisor
Ova and parasites	✓	5/31/89 SH
Clotting time	✓	5/30/89 SH
Lee White clotting time	✓	5/30/89 SH
Hema, QC	✓	5/30/89 SH
Hema, PM	✓	5/30/89 SH
Sed rate	✓	5/31/89 SH
Sperm count	✓	5/31/89 SH
Urinalysis	✓	5/30/89 SH
Pregnancy test	✓	5/30/89 SH
Urinalysis QC	✓	5/30/89 SH
PT	✓	5/31/89 SH
RPR	✓	5/31/89 SH

2a Flow Chart

2b Cause and Effect Diagram

2c Pie Chart

2d Gaussian Curve Chart

2e Force-Field of Lewin

2f Check List

Driving Forces   Constraining Forces

Figure 34–2 Useful tools for problem solving

Gantt Charts

The Gantt chart[2] (Figure 34–3) is a graph with activities listed on the vertical axis and time units on the horizontal axis. It is used to determine the shortest total time required to reach a goal by showing how much time each activity requires and which activities can and cannot be performed simultaneously. In Figure 34–3, note the overlapping of several of the activities.

PERT Charts

PERT (program evaluation and review technique) charts (Figure 34–4) were developed to minimize and control the time required for large projects. The PERT chart is composed of activities and events. Events are represented by circles. Arrows show the time necessary to complete events. When there are steps that are carried out simultaneously, different times are needed for each of these parallel steps. In Figure 34–4, the lines could represent the following steps:

A–B = time for a request to reach a work station
B–C = time for blood collection and delivery to laboratory
C–D = time for serological testing
C–E = time for immunohematological testing
E–F = time for delivery of blood product to patient

The critical path represents the sum of the times for individual steps in the path that require the most time. In Figure 34–4, the critical path is A–B–C–D–F because it takes longer to perform the serological tests than to do the routine compatibility tests.

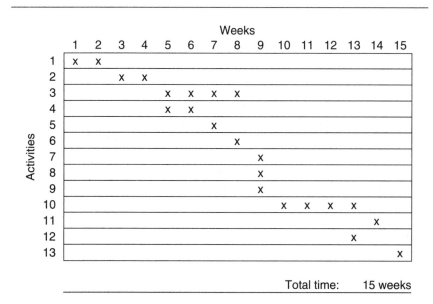

Figure 34–3 Gantt chart

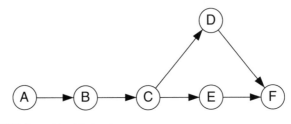

Figure 34–4 PERT chart with critical path

Breakeven Charts

This chart is a scattergram in which the revenue and the expenses—variable and fixed—are plotted against a line drawn at a 45 degree angle (Figure 34–5). The point at which the total expense line crosses this ascending line represents the financial breakeven point.

Likert Charts

Likert charts[3] (Figure 34–6) are useful when one is comparing and contrasting multiple factors of performance at two different times (e.g., before and after a change).

Computer Applications

Computers have been used for a long time to file data, to reassemble information into new formats, and to perform logical operations and calculations. An exciting trend for the use of computers in problem solving is in the area of expert systems. These rely on stored facts and rules of thumb to mimic the decision making of human experts. This has been successful when applied to narrowly defined tasks, but we still lack a system that possesses common sense.

YOUR INTUITIVE PROCESS: KEY TO CREATIVE PROBLEM SOLVING

Pay attention to the nagging doubts you get when you are trying to make a decision. They may represent experience stored in your unconscious mind.

Give your intuitive process time to act. Set aside some think time each day.

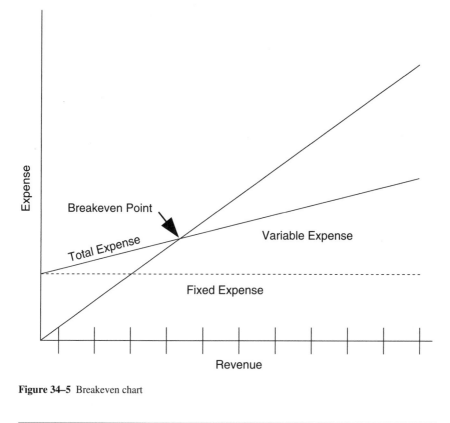

Figure 34–5 Breakeven chart

Capture thoughts as they occur, like the ringing of a muted telephone. These are most likely to pop up when your logical thought process is on hold. Turn off conscious cerebration to let your cerebral energy flow into your unconscious mind. Daydreaming, relaxation, and meditation help. Walking, jogging, and other exercise increase cerebral blood flow.

Solitude can be effective, particularly when it is enhanced by listening to ocean sounds (real or recorded) or background music.

A strategy espoused by Dr. Joyce Brothers, the well-known T.V. psychologist, is to think about a problem just before dropping off to sleep.[4]

Document your problem at the top of a sheet of paper. Under the problem, number the lines 1 through 20. Now force yourself to write down 20 solutions. The first few will come easily (these are usually the ones that you have already discarded). Subsequent alternatives surface with increasing difficulty and are more likely to have originated in your unconscious mind and to be more inspirational.[5]

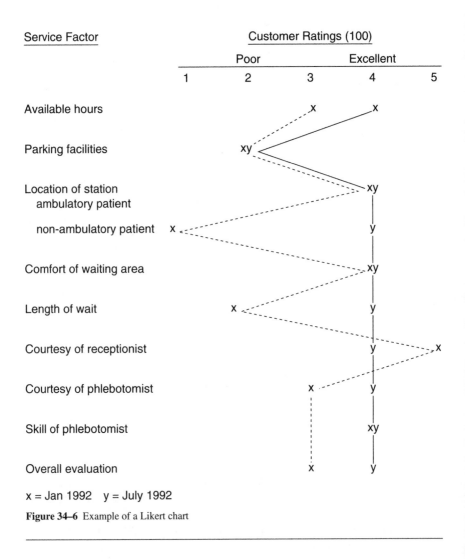

Figure 34–6 Example of a Likert chart

GROUP PROBLEM SOLVING

A problem is like a world globe. From any one spot, you cannot see all the globe. No one person has an all-encompassing view. In groups, more ideas are generated, and the group is more likely to support the choice that is made.

Group meetings increase the likelihood of serendipity, which is the fortunate situation when two events accidentally come together to create an opportunity. This is also a matter of synergy (1 + 1 = 3). When people put their heads together, they come up with more solutions than when they work individually.

The Importance of Seeking Consensus

A group often makes decisions before all the opinions of the members have been explored. Participants who are not heard from may leave the meeting angry, may balk at the decision, may fail to support it, or may even sabotage its implementation. A consensus prevents this.

A consensus is a genuine meeting of the minds. It is not reached by voting. Even a unanimous vote does not represent a consensus if some members are denied an opportunity to speak up. With a consensus, a member may prefer an alternative solution, but after full and fair discussion the member agrees that he or she can live with what the group has decided.

Here are the basics of consensus decision making:

- Ensure that each person expresses his or her viewpoint fully.
- Avoid hasty conclusions or agreements.
- Explore the positive features of each alternative.
- Expose and analyze each alternative's negative features.
- Resolve disagreements.
- Avoid techniques of voting, averaging, or bargaining.
- Insist that each member agree that he or she can live with the solution that is selected. If any member balks, you do not have a consensus.

Be Wary of the Abilene Paradox

The Abilene paradox occurs when members of a group decide on an action that is contrary to what they really want because each individual assumes that the others want that action but for some reason does not speak up during the meeting. A domineering chairperson is a frequent cause.

CREATIVE PROBLEM-SOLVING GROUPS

Unstructured Brainstorming Groups

This is nothing more than a beer-and-pretzel discussion group: lots of talk, lots of wandering off the topic, and not much action. All too many committee meetings degenerate into these. There are exceptions, especially when a group of entrepreneurs or creative people gets together.

Structured Brainstorming Groups

These groups generate ideas guided by certain rules. Here is one technique[6]:

1. A problem is presented to the group.
2. Each member thinks about the problem and records his or her ideas on a sheet of paper. No comment or discussion is permitted at this time.
3. Each member reads one item from his or her list. Each of these is recorded on a flip chart. No comment or discussion is permitted at this time, but members may piggyback on the ideas of others.
4. This sequence is repeated until all the ideas are displayed on the chart.
5. Each item is discussed, amplified, or modified. The originator of each item may be asked to leave the room when his or her idea is discussed. Criticism is now permitted and encouraged.
6. Each member ranks the items that are regarded as feasible.
7. The votes are recorded on the chart.

Note that there are two phases: the generation phase (steps 1 through 4) and the evaluation phase (steps 5 through 7).

To get the maximum benefit, alert participants before the meeting, and set a good example by bringing a large packet of your own ideas, including some really wild ones. Lead off with your wildest one.

NOTES

1. K. Lewin, *Field Theory in Social Science* (New York, N.Y.: Harper & Row, 1951).
2. H. Gantt, *Industrial Leadership* (Easton, Pa.: Hive, 1973).
3. R. Likert, *New Patterns of Management* (New York, N.Y.: McGraw-Hill, 1961).
4. D. Sullivan, *Work Smart, Not Hard* (New York, N.Y.: Facts on File, 1987).
5. E. DeBono, *Lateral Thinking: Creativity Step by Step* (New York, N.Y.: Harper & Row, 1970).
6. A.L. Delbecq, et al., *Group Techniques for Program Planning* (Glenview, Ill.: Scott, Foresman, 1975).

Chapter 35
Time Management

- importance of time management
- limitations of time management programs
- the two aspects of time management
- chronologically handicapped supervisors
- your office or work station
- planning and scheduling
- delegating
- be prepared to say no
- procrastination
- time-wasters
- visitors and other interruptions
- meetings
- fine tune your communication skills
- twenty-two tips for saving your time
- time abuses by others

IMPORTANCE OF TIME MANAGEMENT

Supervisors are well aware of the importance of time. Their days are filled with deadlines, turnaround times, emergencies, and interruptions. There never seem to be enough hours to complete tasks. Most managers put in more than 50 hours a week on the job and still take home unfinished work. We are not including the many hours that supervisors spend at home worrying about problems back at work.

LIMITATIONS OF TIME MANAGEMENT PROGRAMS

Time management programs, like weight reduction programs, succeed only if one commits to reaching a goal. Time management is not managing time, it is managing oneself. Gurus can provide instructions, but the supervisors must supply the discipline. To lose weight, people are required to sacrifice things they like to eat. To gain time, they must give up things they like to do or are comfortable with.

Many time managment programs fail because they require endless lists and logs of activities. Others attempt to impose rigidity on one's life when it is flexibility that is needed.

THE TWO ASPECTS OF TIME MANAGEMENT

There are two aspects of time management: managing your time, and minimizing the waste of your time by people who report to you.

CHRONOLOGICALLY HANDICAPPED SUPERVISORS

Unfortunately these people are not protected by Americans with Disability Act regulations, but they do need help. Managers who practice management by crisis are one subset. Because of poor planning and failure to anticipate problems, these firefighters spend most of their time running around trying to solve crises (putting out fires) instead of preventing them.

Then there are the perfectionists, who are not satisfied with excellence, and who seek perfection: an impossible and time-consuming effort.

Members of the largest group are supervisors who fail to delegate or who try to do not only their own work but that of others. This category includes supervisors who find it impossible to give up their technical or professional tasks after they have been promoted into management. Nonassertive individuals who cannot say no to requests for their time also belong in this class.

YOUR OFFICE OR WORK STATION

The best place to start a time management program is in your office, where results can be observed quickly.

To avoid distractions, move your desk so that it does not face the door, or keep your door closed. Arrange filing cabinets and other furnishings to provide ready access to them.

Organized clutter is O.K. A messy desk does not necessarily mean a messy mind. If you can quickly find what you are looking for and you have enough surface space, let the mess stay and ignore the jibes from your associates.

AN ACTION-ORIENTED FILING SYSTEM

The average supervisor spends an inordinate amount of time looking for things in his or her office.

Instruct your secretary and others on how you want papers, manuals, office supplies, and other items stored. Revise your filing system so that you can find things quickly. Use a desk drawer file for papers you refer to often. Other papers go to file cabinets. Set aside a drawer as a slush file for documents that may or may not be used. Clean out that drawer each month. Sort and batch using folders that are labeled appropriately.

PAPER FLOW

Filing begins when you sort your incoming mail. Do not let disorderly piles of papers accumulate. Try to handle each item only once. Practice the 3D concept: do, delegate, or discard. When you hesitate to discard, ask yourself "What's the worst thing that could happen if I don't have this?"

Do not let your hold basket or folder get out of control. Review the items there daily, and act on as many as you can. Place a throw-out date on major filed items. Clean off your desk every night to avoid chaos when you arrive on the next day.

PLANNING AND SCHEDULING

When you fail to plan, you are planning to fail. Establish goals, priorities, schedules, and deadlines for all major undertakings. More time spent preparing for meetings, interviews, and instructional sessions equates to less wasted time at those meetings.

Experienced supervisors make good use of slack time (e.g., Friday afternoons) to catch up on correspondence, inventory, files, and low-priority items (busywork). They get their administrative tasks out of the way early or late in the day.

We each have daily hours when our productivity and ability to concentrate are greater than during the rest of the work day. Use those hours to work on major problems, research, presenting ideas to the boss, creative thinking, high-priority discussions, and important correspondence. During periods of low productivity, work on handling mail, making routine telephone calls, filing, and other routine chores.

Schedule blocks of daily time for paperwork, private think time, and taking care of unpleasant tasks.

Differentiate between real deadlines, such as payroll data, and less stringent ones, such as the minutes of a meeting. Avoid too much planning. Leave time for unexpected things.

Use "To Do" Lists

Group similar things together on a to do list. Set priorities by number, or at least be labeling each item as must, should, or maybe. Do not expect to accomplish everything on your list every day. Remake or update the list daily.

DELEGATING

The greatest time-saver of all is delegation. Every hour that someone else does something that you previously did is an hour saved. See Chapter 11 for a discussion of delegating.

BE WILLING AND ABLE TO SAY NO

To avoid overcommitment of your time and other resources, you must be able to say no diplomatically and emphatically, especially to superiors. In the case of subordinates, this often means not permitting them to delegate upward. That is not easy if you are easily flattered or manipulated.

Offer alternatives to colleagues. When a superior makes a request that creates a problem, nail down priorities (e.g., "Should I stop working on the. . . ?").

PROCRASTINATION

At the very least, procrastination results in spending your time doing tasks that have a lower priority than the one you should be working on. This is compounded when you are immobilized because you have placed the topic on hold.

Here are some practical suggestions for avoiding or minimizing procrastination:

- Use daily prioritized task lists.
- Start the day with the high-priority or unpleasant tasks.
- Avoid the temptation to stall.
- Do not get involved with trivia.
- Block out enough time to complete time-consuming tasks.
- Slice a big task into thin slices that are more easily completed.
- Convince yourself that the task needs doing.
- Challenge your excuses
- Do not reward procrastination. Do not permit yourself to engage in pleasant activities while you delay action. Sit in a straight chair without coffee or conversation.
- Set a timer for 5 minutes, and force yourself to start when it goes off.

TIME-WASTERS

Use a time log to determine how you spend your time. This enables you to ferret out your wasted time and to alter your time schedules.

It takes 21 days to establish a habit. Select your top five time-wasters, and work on them for 3 weeks. Here are the principal offenders:

- doing things you do not need to do:
  —things that could be delegated
  —trivial things that could be eliminated
  —things you should say no to
  —excessive socializing
- inefficient planning, organizing, and scheduling
- unnecessary or poorly run meetings
- interruptions
  —visitors
  —unexpected problems
  —the telephone (see Chapter 31)

VISITORS

Do not call all visitors annoyances or time-wasters. Most visitors are external or internal customers and should be treated as such. Some of the most effective managers save time elsewhere so that they can devote more time to visitors.

Here are some techniques for controlling visitors who do abuse your time:

- Decrease the need of your staff to get your help by delegating, empowering, and training.
- Meet people in their offices.
- Shut your door when you really need privacy.
- Intercept visitors outside your office. If you have kept them waiting, apologize. Once people get in your office, the transaction time increases. Remain standing. Once visitors sit down, the visit time increases still more.
- Train your secretary and others to help visitors when you are not available immediately. You may not even be needed.
- Use verbal and nonverbal language to signal that you wish to end the meeting.
  —Reduce eye contact.
  —Glance at the clock or your watch.

—Start shuffling papers, tapping a pencil, or drumming your fingers.

—Put your hand on the telephone.

—Say "Could we continue this later when I'm not swamped?" or "I won't take any more of your time."

—Stand up and extend your hand.

—Come out from behind your desk and walk toward the door.

MEETINGS

Limit group meetings to 45 minutes. People get restless after that. If you must go on, call a break.

If you are not the chair and the meetings always start late, either come late yourself or bring busy work with you.

Send members of your staff to represent you. For more on meetings, see Chapter 33.

FINE TUNE YOUR COMMUNICATION SKILLS

Good communications prevent misunderstandings, mistakes, and the need for repeats, all of which are big time-wasters.

If you tend to be verbose on the telephone, put an egg timer next to the phone. When you are trapped in a corridor by windy talkers, summarize what they said and start moving away. If that does not work, ask to be excused. Say that you have an appointment (maybe with yourself?).

TIPS FOR SAVING YOUR TIME

- Avoid procrastination or perfectionism.
- Delegate what others can do or can be trained to do.
- Plan, schedule, and prioritize more.
- Express as much appreciation to people for saving your time as you do to people who help you save money.
- Minimize interruptions by coming to work early or staying late, by finding a good hiding place, or by using a "thank you for not disturbing" sign.
- Learn to say no.
- Monitor your time usage. Keep a log.
- Reduce wasted time at meetings.
- Use waiting times to read or do short tasks.

- Make phone calls in bunches.
- Use margin replies for informal written correspondence.
- Keep your desk ready for action.
- Refer calls and visitors to others.
- Do not regard visitors as interruptions unless they are serious time-wasters.
- Decrease your socializing time.
- Select the most appropriate channel for communication.
- Study and streamline your work flow patterns.
- Improve your general communication skills.
- Use videotapes for repetitive teaching (e.g., orientation and training of new hires).
- Use dictation instead of doing the typing yourself.
- Use the telephone for conference calls.
- Ask for help when you need it. Some supervisors are stubborn about this and make every effort to avoid asking others to help. Be equally willing to help others.

TIME ABUSES BY OTHERS

Time theft may be America's biggest crime. Half writes, "The average worker in the U.S.A. has an average of 7–12 unscheduled absences each year. He wastes 18 percent of the time he is supposed to be working. That equals nine 35-hour weeks . . . a 'vacation' of more than two months per year **at work.**"[1(p.7)]
Major time thefts include the following:

- unjustified sick days
- tardiness or leaving early
- long breaks or meals
- leaving one's post for personal trips (e.g., shopping)
- doing personal tasks on the job
- excessive socialization and idle conversation
- interrupting others
- wandering around the building
- excessive personal phone calls
- personal or family visitors
- daydreaming

Bad habits should be nipped in the bud by better coaching and counseling. Remember, however, that your subordinates are your customers and should be treated with kindness and consideration. A little compassion must be shown when dealing with employees who have latchkey children or other special situations.

The first step in eliminating or decreasing this time waste is to be aware of it. Our old strategy of managing by wandering around pays off handsomely. Merely appearing on the scene will squelch idle conversations and let people know that you are aware of their absences from the work area.

Changes in work stations can often help. People accomplish more alone than in groups when the work is boring. That is not the case when the work is interesting or urgent.

Study your work flow patterns and other systems to determine whether greater efficiency can be achieved.

NOTE

1. R. Half, Management roundup, *Management Review* 73 (1984): 7.

SUGGESTED READINGS

Bittel, R. 1991. *Right on time: The complete guide for time-pressured managers.* New York, N.Y.: McGraw-Hill.

Onchen, W., Jr. 1984. *Managing management time.* Englewood Cliffs, N.J.: Prentice-Hall.

Scott, D. 1988. *The telephone and time management.* Los Altos, Calif.: Crisp.

Part VII

Self-Enhancement

Chapter 36

Assertiveness, Stress, and Burnout

- definitions of nonassertiveness, aggressiveness, and assertiveness
- suggestions for enhancing assertiveness
- handling criticism
- how to say no and mean it
- an Assertive Bill of Rights
- susceptibility to stress
- the four stages of coping
- the importance of frustration and negative emotions
- stress resistance
- burnout

THE NONASSERTIVE PERSON

Nonassertiveness, or passivity, is permitting others to violate one's rights. The nonassertive person expresses thoughts and feelings in such an apologetic manner that others can easily disregard them. The life script for these individuals is "You're O.K., I'm not O.K."

Nonassertive people avoid conflict and focus conversation on noncontroversial topics. Their characteristics include evasive eye contact; hunched shoulders; backing off; rigid posture; low, tremulous voice; and much sighing or throat clearing. They interpret their nonassertiveness as courtesy or cooperation.

Nonassertive managers are not highly respected by associates, subordinates, or superiors. They often lose power to informal leaders. They are afraid to delegate responsibility or authority, to impose discipline, or to make unpopular decisions. They accumulate real and imagined hurts, and then explode in unpredictable ways.

THE AGGRESSIVE PERSON

The person who violates the rights of others is exhibiting aggressiveness. The usual goal of aggression is domination and winning. This is achieved by belittling or overpowering people. The life script for this group is "I'm O.K., you're not O.K."

311

Aggressive people confront others physically, move forward, interrupt, stare down, point their finger, clench their fist, and fold their arms across their chest. They talk in a loud voice, often with a sarcastic or condescending tone. Their expletives are "Listen here" and "Let me tell you."

Aggressive managers practice autocratic management. They surround themselves with weak, highly dependent people. They are constantly at war with other strong-willed persons. They may enjoy short-term success (e.g., as a trouble-shooter), but they often fail in the long haul because morale falls and employees leave. Eventually, productivity declines.

THE ASSERTIVE PERSON

Assertiveness is standing up for one's personal rights and expressing one's feelings and beliefs in direct, honest ways that do not violate the rights of others. The predominant life script is "You're O.K., I'm O.K."

Assertive people are not only better leaders but also more helpful followers. If you feel that the lack of assertiveness is hampering your career, enroll in an assertiveness training program. These programs are offered in almost all communities, often at little or no cost. Most medical centers have annual sessions for their personnel.

SUGGESTIONS FOR ENHANCING ASSERTIVENESS

If you want simply to fine tune your assertiveness skills, the following suggestions should be helpful:

- Adopt an Assertive Bill of Rights (Exhibit 36–1).
- Do not downgrade yourself. When you make a mistake, simply say, "Nobody is right every time." Avoid disqualifying prefaces, such as "I'm not an expert, but . . . ," say, "I suggest that we . . ." Do not issue orders as requests. Instead of "Do you mind finishing up for me?" say, "Please complete this for me."
- Do not let others downgrade you. When someone says, "That's a dumb question," reply, "That may be so, but I want an answer."
- Use basic assertive statements. Simply state what you want: "Pardon me, but I would like to finish what I started to say." Repeat, if necessary.
- Use empathic assertive statements. While acknowledging the other person's opinion or feeling, state what you want: "I know you don't like weekend work, but I have to include you in the rotation."

Exhibit 36–1 An Assertive Bill of Rights

I have the right to say what I think and feel.

I have the right to be treated with respect.

I have the right to say no without feeling guilty.

I have the right to ask for what I want.

I have the right to get what I pay for.

I have the right to disagree with others.

I have the right to be listened to and taken seriously.

- Use dual-message assertive statements. State both what you want and how you feel about it: "When you grumble out loud about your assignments, I get upset. Please stop it."
- Use assertive body language. Stand or sit erect with shoulders back and muscles relaxed. Maintain eye-to-face contact. Use gestures that are meaningful, but nonthreatening. Keep your voice at a moderate pitch, with rate and volume variations. Do not mumble, squirm, or fidget.
- Use strong expletives occasionally.
- Practice assertion in social settings:
  —Speak up when ignored by clerks or attendants.
  —Ask a server to take back lukewarm soup.
  —Remonstrate when someone pushes ahead of you in a line.
  —Return a purchased item.
- Get involved in activities that can develop leadership:
  —education or training courses
  —community service
  —committees and task forces

SPECIAL SITUATIONS

Handling Criticism

When you have been criticized, separate yourself from the criticism. If you must be upset, be upset with your mistakes, not with yourself. If the criticism is vague or general, insist that the critic be more specific. Ask questions such as "How many times?" or "Can you give me an example?" "Do not be afraid to disagree or to say how you feel. Say, "I just can't buy that" or "I'm not comfortable with [or willing to listen to] your evasiveness."

Saying No

Do you find it difficult to say no when:

- your boss asks you to do something, and you are already overwhelmed with work?
- a friend wants your help, but your work will suffer if you give it?
- someone asks for information that you should not release?
- an employee tries to manipulate you by sulking, crying, or getting angry?

If you have trouble handling such situations, you can choose one of these solutions:

- Be tentative: "Let me think about it and get back to you."
- Say no firmly and calmly, without apologizing. Saying "I'm sorry" weakens your stance. Use phrases such as "I'm not comfortable with that," "I don't have the time," or "I don't care to do it." Do not hesitate to repeat the same phrase if necessary.
- Offer an alternative: "Not now," "Perhaps another time," "Ask Sue," or "Yes, I'll help, but I won't be available until. . . ."

SUPERVISORS' STRESS AND BURNOUT

We all have different thresholds of stress resistance, and certain categories of people are more susceptible to stress than others. These sensitive groups include perfectionists, workaholics, martyrs, overachievers, and anyone with low self-esteem. Low self-esteem is perhaps the single most powerful agent.

In Chapter 30 we listed the stress factors that supervisors affect and the supervisor's role in reducing the stress of his or her staff members. Now we turn our attention to the stress and burnout that affects supervisors.

Managers who practice management by crisis or who try to do everything themselves are especially prone to burnout. Their stress load is high because their plans, priorities, and management of time are flawed. They react to problems only when the problems become critical, resulting in panic, finger pointing, and denials.

THE FOUR STAGES OF COPING

People usually go through four stages when they are faced with a chronic stressor or a constant barrage of multiple stressful situations:

1. They do nothing, anticipating that the stress will go away.
2. They seek fast relief, gulping down analgesics or tranquilizers and increasing their intake of coffee, alcohol, or cigarettes.
3. They take their anger out on others, usually family members, subordinates, colleagues, or even patients.
4. They get help or suffer burnout.

THE IMPORTANCE OF FRUSTRATION AND NEGATIVE EMOTIONS

Stress, which is produced by a constant feeling of frustration, leaves people drained and exhausted at the end of the day. Any negative emotion can shake our confidence and self-esteem. The most important emotions are anger, fear, and guilt.

Anger

There are three popular but questionable strategies for coping with anger:

1. The *"get it out of your system"* strategy, at best, provides only transient relief. Angry confrontations can lead to tempestuous scenes that only make matters worse.
2. The *"grin and bear it"* philosophy, as taught in Sunday school class, only results in emotional hurts being stored up (gunnysacking). This invariably leads to eventual eruptions of intense anger.
3. *Constantly mulling over an irritating incident,* or repeatedly relating it in detail to anyone who will listen, seldom provides true insight. It is more likely to lead to a victim or martyr complex.

Here are six intervention measures that work:

1. Analyze your anger by asking yourself what you are really angry about. Identify the provoking stimulus, such as criticism or time pressure. Perhaps the only time people pay attention to you is when you get angry. Fear often lurks in the background as the real villain. Writing down an objective description of your feelings of anger and your analysis of it often helps develop insight.
2. Discuss your anger with a trusted supporter or counselor.
3. Anticipate the next situation that triggers your reaction. Prepare what you will say or do (or not say or do) the next time.

4. When you feel anger welling up inside, use cooling off thoughts or humor to deflate it.

5. Walk away if you think that you cannot handle the situation. If the anger persists, divert your thought process by doing something distracting (e.g., exercise, games, sports, hobbies, a walk in the woods, or reading an inspirational book).

6. Learn relaxation or meditation techniques. Not only do these relieve tension, they also have a beneficial effect on our metabolism, cardiorespiratory functions, and endocrine system, and they may stimulate our immune system by decreasing blood levels of noradrenalin (stress hormone) or by making our bodies less susceptible to that hormone.

Fear

The most common fears are fear of failure, fear that we will not be liked, and fear of loss of control over our daily routines or over other people.

Fear of loss of control may be the most powerful fear among health care supervisors. The high incidence of burnout among nurses has been attributed in part to what the nurses perceive as lack of control over their daily activities. They feel like puppets on strings, jerked around by patients, patients' families, medical staff, and administrators.

The most effective remedies are those that increase competency, confidence, self-esteem, and assertiveness. These have all been addressed throughout this book.

Guilt

Guilt, a major source of insecurity and stress, is characterized by feelings of inadequacy and by self-criticism.

Some practical coping strategies include not striving for perfection, not permitting others to make you feel guilty, not taking criticism personally, and not letting minor irritations get to you. It also helps to regard mistakes as learning experiences.

Stop right here. Before you read on, forgive yourself for everything you ever did that made you feel guilty. While you are at it, forgive everyone else for anything they did to hurt you. This is a great sign of maturity. It will make your self-esteem soar.

STRESS RESISTANCE

Stress resistance is largely a matter of high self-esteem. To have high self-esteem, we must believe in ourselves and deliver a constant flow of positive messages to our unconscious mind to neutralize all the negative ones that reside there.

Enthusiasm is so important. It must be founded on a perception of high self-worth. Enthusiasm replenishes our stores of energy, forces optimism, attracts winners, builds networks, improves persuasion, and impresses superiors.

Here are some great ways to increase stress resistance:

- Expect only success. You are what you think you are.
- Keep a brag sheet of your accomplishments. Refer to it when negative thoughts get you down. These documents are also useful when you are preparing for performance reviews or updating your resume.
- Surround yourself with optimistic, energetic, enthusiastic doers. Stay away from negative or complaining people.
- Maintain optimism by regarding yourself as a problem solver. Refer to problems as challenges or opportunities.
- Look for the good, not the bad, in situations.
- Use success imagery. For example, picture a successful presentation starting with your introduction and opening statement, continuing with each step of your lecture, and ending with the audience giving you ear-splitting applause and flooding you with questions.
- Use powerful self-affirmations. Affirmations are brief, positive declarations. They state what you are (at your best) or what you aspire to be or to achieve (e.g., "I like people and people like me," "I am losing weight," or "I am a great listener"). These statements must be repeated frequently on a daily basis. They work because they convince our unconscious mind that they are true.
- Update your professional and managerial skills. Increase your job security by making yourself more marketable.
- Expand your supportive network (see Chapter 37).
- Take care of your body: Exercise regularly; eat a balanced diet; avoid alcohol, drugs, tobacco, excessive caffeine; and practice deep breathing before entering a stressful arena.
- Take care of your mind: Take breaks away from the work area, engage in pleasurable outside activities, listen to music, give yourself a few minutes of quiet time each day, get involved in a research project, or write an article for publication.
- Be a proactive manager. Proactive leaders plan ahead, maintain a reserve of time and energy, delegate, and seek help when needed. They are good team players. Because they plan ahead and anticipate problems, they prevent problems or attack them while they are still minor or reversible.

BURNOUT

Burnout is the emotional and physical state that accompanies an overload of stress in a work environment. Employees who have burnout feel that they have given and given and there is nothing left.[1]

Anyone who is stressed severely over a long period of time may succumb to burnout. Burnout victims tend to be idealistic or self-motivating achievers who often pursue unrealistic goals. They regard problems as frustrations, not challenges.

Nonwork problems also play a role, often adding to the difficulty of unraveling the etiology of individual burnout situations.

Burned-out people's associates may observe the following:

- emotional outbursts
- high-pitched laughter
- increased irritability
- trembling, tics, or stuttering
- decline in performance
- absenteeism
- complaints about working conditions
- lack of flexibility
- resistance to change
- decreasing participation in meetings
- loss of enthusiasm
- escalation of complaining and loss of sense of humor
- increase in procrastination
- talk of getting away from the job or community
- start of, or increased, use of alcohol or drugs

These are the common medical signs and symptoms of burnout:

- anxiety or depression
- chronic fatigue
- insomnia and nightmares
- headaches and/or backaches
- premenstrual syndrome
- loss of appetite
- compulsive eating
- duodenal ulcers
- difficulty getting up to go to work

• high blood pressure
• cardiac irregularities
• loss of interest in work, hobbies, friends, and family

Typical Reactions to Burnout

A person initially does nothing or responds with frustration or anger. Aggressive emotions gradually give way to despair and depression. Damage is both physical and psychological.

The victim seeks symptomatic relief through alcohol, drugs, cigarettes, or other nostrums, which only aggravate the condition. Associates or family members may be avoided or subjected to abuse. Eventually most victims seek help, but unfortunately often only after having given up their jobs.

The Two Critical Steps

1. *Recognize that you are experiencing burnout.* Victims are sometimes the last to know. As with all medical conditions, prevention or early detection is the best approach. Burnout is easily confused with other things, such as intense dissatisfaction with changes in one's job or associates, drug or alcohol abuse, or psychiatric disorders.
2. *Get professional help without delay!*

NOTE

1. A.J. Bernstein and S.C. Rozen, *Dinosaur Brains* (New York, N.Y.: Wiley, 1989), 83.

SUGGESTED READING

Donnelly, G.F. 1983. *RN's survival sourcebook: Coping with stress.* Oradell, N.J.: Medical Economics.
Tavris, C. *Controlling anger.* Boulder, Colo.: CareerTrack. Audiotapes.
Trager, M.J., and S. Willard. 1988. *Transforming stress into power: The energy director system.* Chicago, Ill.: Great Performance.

Chapter 37

Your Career Development

- the five criteria of success
- characteristics of achievers and nonachievers
- who is responsible for your career development?
- hard work is not enough
- risk taking
- how to get ready to move up
- what superiors look for
- the nine steps to success
- goals, objectives, and actions
- your educational needs analysis
- getting ready to ask for a raise
- how to increase your promotability

THE FIVE CRITERIA OF SUCCESS

Most of us would be happy if we could meet these five indicators; goals, plans, and effort help us move in the right direction:

1. peace of mind
2. health and energy
3. a loving relationship
4. freedom from financial worry
5. achieving all we are capable of (self-actualization)

CHARACTERISTICS OF ACHIEVERS AND NONACHIEVERS

- Achievers set goals and document them. Nonachievers do not.
- Achievers accept responsibility for their lives and their actions. Nonachievers talk about their bad luck and what others do to them.
- Achievers are willing to take risks. Nonachievers play it safe.

- Achievers combine hard work with competency and political skill. Nonachievers think hard work alone is enough.
- Achievers build effective personal networks. Nonachievers try to do it all alone.
- Achievers plan and execute their career development programs. Nonachievers wait for their employers to provide these programs.

WHO IS RESPONSIBLE FOR YOUR CAREER DEVELOPMENT?

Supervisors are often promoted from the ranks without any preparation for their new responsibilities. This is a hangover from our educational system, in which students pick a vocation and the system does their planning for them. If they work hard they are promoted each year, graduate, and find employment.

Most of these graduates wait for their employers to do what their schools always did: lay out a program for future promotion. Educators and employers must do a better job of informing these new employees that it is the employees' responsibility to plan and execute their future development.

HARD WORK IS NOT ENOUGH

Hard work alone rarely earns promotions or gets big raises. Promotions are given with the expectations of future performance. The boss is thinking "How will promoting this person help me?"

Past performance does help determine who gets selected. Previous accomplishments are not the only factors, however. In the next chapter we will discuss the importance of office politics and networking, two activities that affect job advancement and rewards.

RISK TAKING

When we speak of risk taking, we are not talking about the kinds of risks that health care providers do their best to avoid, such as failing to check on the credentials of job candidates, neglecting safety procedures, or experimenting with unproven treatments. Risk managers shudder when you mention risks.

The risks we are talking about here are career risks: the kind we take when we accept responsibility, make decisions, or delegate authority. When we select an expensive apparatus, provide a new service, or recommend something innovative, we are taking a risk. To take the initiative is to take a risk. Entrepreneurs are great risk takers; procrastinators and bureaucrats are notorious risk avoiders.

Risks can be minimized if we have confidence in ourselves and our team, set achievable goals, obtain sufficient data, prepare carefully, and execute skillfully. We must be prepared for some failures and setbacks. The absence of failures usually means insufficient tries.

HOW TO GET READY TO MOVE UP

Always Be Ready for an Opportunity

The myth that opportunity only knocks once is ridiculous. Opportunity is knocking all the time, if people would only listen. Because opportunities often present themselves without any warning, we must always be prepared to grab the brass ring when it comes around.

Learn all you can about the job you would like if it already exists. Look, sound, and act as someone who is already qualified. You want your boss to feel comfortable when he or she tries to picture you in that slot.

Interview Yourself

Visualize yourself as an applicant for the kind of job you want. Ask questions that an experienced and knowledgeable interviewer would ask, and answer them. This is an excellent way to supplement your educational needs analysis.

Find Out about Future Plans

What is being contemplated by your employer and your department? Reflect on how you can benefit from these changes. Still better, suggest some changes of your own. Maybe you can create a new and better job for yourself. Consider possible new services or customers, marketing strategies, satellite operations, or restructuring.

WHAT SUPERIORS LOOK FOR

Here are the qualities that superiors prize:

- confidence, optimism, enthusiasm, and energy
- willingness to accept delegation and to take the initiative
- trustworthiness, credibility, and loyalty (the most important traits)
- communication and other interactive skills

- ability to solve problems
- living up to promises

For more about getting the support of the person to whom you report, go back to Chapter 18.

THE NINE STEPS TO SUCCESS

1. Start with a vision.
2. Formulate and prioritize your goals.
3. Prepare a list of objectives for reaching each goal, and set target dates.
4. Inventory your strengths and weaknesses.
5. Prepare a training needs analysis.
6. List potential or real barriers, and describe how each can be overcome.
7. Implement your program.
8. Evaluate your progress, and enjoy the journey.
9. Celebrate each step toward your goal.

GOALS, OBJECTIVES, AND ACTIONS

It is essential that you have written goals. Several studies have shown that business school students who had written goals at the time of their graduation were much more successful financially years later than their classmates.

Before you select a goal that requires much time and expense, consider what you must do to reach that goal. If the journey is painful and your motivation is limited to that of reaching the goal, you are less likely to do so. It is hoped that you will enjoy most of the trip.

When you set major goals—the ones that require large expenditures of time and money—do not consider your career goals apart from those of other members of your family or apart from other kinds of goals. These should be negotiated with your family members.

Ask each member of your family to prepare a wish list that includes career or educational wants and personal pleasure wants (e.g., hobbies, workshops, sports, or music). Add a list of joint goals, such as a new house, a second car, or a long vacation. The list is then trimmed down, and the items are prioritized.

The reason for considering all these goals simultaneously is that there are always limits of time and money. If you focus only on career goals, you might end up with plans that could not be carried out or plans that are not accepted on the homefront.

When you consider all these goals at the same time, a more practical selection emerges. For example, there may be agreement that the children's college education goes to the head of the list and is followed by your spouse's goal of having the nursery converted into an office, so that your goal of taking courses at the local university drops to third spot.

Objectives are the minigoals needed to reach a goal.

Goals and objectives should be specific, challenging, relevant, achievable, and measurable. Here is an example:

- **Goal:** *To be promoted to unit manager*
- **Objectives:** to meet professional requirements by [date]; to meet administrative requirements by [date]; to meet supervisory requirements by [date]
- **Actions:**
  1. Complete courses needed to get MBA:
     —get support of family
     —seek financial support
     —enroll in local university
  2. Study administrative functions of unit:
     —computer information system
     —quality improvement program
     —budget preparation and use
     —routine and special reports
     —participation in next inspection by Joint Commission on Accreditation of Healthcare Organizations
     —procedure manuals and employee handbook
  3. Educate self about supervisory functions
     —read at least one book on supervisory skills for new supervisors
     —attend at least one seminar, workshop, or college course on the topics of leadership, planning, counseling, interviewing, writing skills, delegating, negotiating, empowering, and career development
     —volunteer to serve on a cross-functional team or a quality improvement committee
     —find a mentor, and expand professional network by at least one new person each month

EDUCATIONAL NEEDS ANALYSIS

Before you develop action plans, determine what additional skills or knowledge you need. You may want to use the Table of Contents of this book to select the areas in which you think more knowledge or experience is needed.

HOW TO GET READY TO ASK FOR A RAISE

There is an old myth that if you work hard you will be rewarded. Many employees earn big raises, but few get them. In a typical health care institution a person whose performance is rated as outstanding receives a salary increase that is 2 to 3 percent above that of the average worker. Big deal!

If you never ask, you are not likely to get what you are worth. To get a significant salary boost, you usually must negotiate, or even threaten to leave. If you are as good as they say you are, they should take these talks seriously.

Nevertheless, you do not just walk into the boss' office and demand more money. The preparation and the timing are important.

Your performance must be outstanding, or there must be a shortage of individuals who have your expertise. You should know your market value. Research the pay scale for your kind of work, know what competitors are paying, and be sure that these jobs are available.

Do not keep your talents under cover. Being quiet may work with some bosses, but in most instances you must market yourself. It helps if you have a mentor or a colleague who serves as your public relations agent.

Some tricks of the trade include the following:

- making a list of your accomplishments, and bringing it with you to performance reviews
- revising your resume, and asking your boss for comments
- making frequent progress reports or sending out memos about project completions (ideally, these represent the results of a group that you led)
- giving verbal reports at staff meetings
- passing on to your boss compliments you receive from customers (do not overdo this; it makes some bosses nervous)

The timing of your request is critical. Delay any kind of increased expense when your employer is in financial difficulty, is downsizing, or is experiencing work, health, or family problems. Never approach bosses when they are busy (Mondays usually), emotionally upset, or in the middle of an important project or crisis. Sometimes during a reorganization or an expansion is a good time, or right after you have received a glowing performance appraisal.

HOW TO INCREASE YOUR PROMOTABILITY

- Activate your success mechanism by formulating and documenting goals.
- Shake off your fear of failure.
- Increase your professional and technical competence.

- Increase your administrative and supervisory skills.
- Use time wisely.
- Develop a reputation as a problem solver and innovator.
- Become an activist for better customer service.
- Be assertive, and become stress resistant.
- Make your boss look good, and be a supporter for your employer.
- Become indispensable to the organization, but not to your job. Bosses are reluctant to promote employees who do not have back-ups in place.
- Market yourself using multiple modalities.
- Expand your personal support network, and include at least one mentor.
- Seek leadership roles.
- Earn the loyalty and support of your team.
- Be willing to make sacrifices and to compromise
- Avoid being dumped on or asked to do unethical deeds. Resist requests to perform personal tasks for superiors (i.e., tasks that deprive your employer of your full-time service).
- Always be alert for and prepared to respond to opportunities where you are and elsewhere.

For more about career development, review Chapter 18 (Managing Your Boss), Chapter 30 (Career Development of Staff), and Chapter 38 (Office Politics and Networking).

SUGGESTED READING

Dellinger, S. 1987. *Political savvy.* Boulder, Colo.: CareerTrack. Audiotapes.

Kennard, K. 1991. *How to manage your boss.* Shawnee Mission, Kan.: National Press.

Sher, B., and A. Gottlieb. 1979. *Wishcraft: How to get what you really want.* New York, N.Y.: Ballantine.

Waitley, D. 1992. *Denis Waitley live on winning.* Boulder, Colo.: CareerTrack. Audiotapes.

Chapter 38

Office Politics and Networking

- definition and importance of politics
- political games people play
- manipulation
- ethical issues
- positive political scripts
- benefits and potential negative aspects of networking
- barriers to networking
- network participants and how contacts are made
- what skilled networkers do and do not do

Politics is the pursuit of power. The original meaning of the word was to act in the service of society: a high form of public service. It has been reinterpreted to mean service to oneself.[1] This self-empowerment usually carries a negative connotation.

Corporate politics is playing the game, or using other than good performance to improve one's stance in an organization.[2] This includes trying to influence superiors and gaining a competitive edge over one's peers. If the political script is a positive one, you play the game fairly and ethically.

Career failures can result from political as well as professional incompetence. Unwillingness to address the political components of a job has snuffed out many a promising career.

Managers who are rewarded or promoted must possess political savoir faire. Employees who lack political grace refuse to accept the fact that political influence is a fact of modern organizational life.

What winners call interpersonal relationships losers call politics. The losers make no effort to acquire mentors or to build personal networks. Instead, they grow resentful toward their employer, their superiors, and their colleagues. Often they become chronic complainers or shrill negativists.

In other words, at one end of the scale politics is selfish, unethical, or illegal. At the other end political behavior supplements professional competency. It is beneficial not only to the practitioner but also to his or her subordinates, superiors, teammates, and employer.

THE INFORMAL ORGANIZATION

Every organization has an informal structure. Unions are officially sanctioned informal organizations. Cliques represent informal coteries that discriminate against fellow workers. The informal organization selects its own leaders and communicates via the grapevine.

Powerful informal work groups determine productivity norms. They may introduce initiation rituals that sometimes include such severe hazing that new hires quit. The culture of the informal organization may permit disloyalty, insubordination, and even sabotage.

Politics overlaps the formal and the informal organizations. Political scripts are flexible because there are few if any documented guidelines. In fact, the first rule of politics is that nobody will tell you the rules.[3]

NEGATIVE POLITICS

Negative politics may be dysfunctional, unethical, or even illegal. It gets blamed for almost everything: bad communication, inappropriate behavior, unpopular promotions, discrimination, and favoritism.

Block claims that organizational politics is partly based on the time-honored bureaucratic wish to be blameless and safe.[4] *Terrell identifies the following factors as the breeding grounds for politics*[5]:

- lack of clear organizational goals or lack of communication of the goals
- autocratic or bureaucratic leadership
- multiple layers of management (the more layers, the more politics)
- minimal upward communication
- frequent changes
- controversial management shifts of power
- poor relationships between workers and managers

These are some of the political games that subordinates or colleagues play:

- taking advantage of being indispensable
- abusing friendships
- probing for weaknesses of others and then revealing those weaknesses
- undermining operations or new services
- starting unfounded rumors or providing misleading information
- creating crises or discord

- displaying undue emotional distress to achieve selfish gains
- discrediting teammates in public or undermining them in private
- intimidating new employees and provoking sensitive people

Here are some political games that bosses play:

- stealing ideas or credit
- excluding others from meetings or information
- eliminating or downgrading the jobs of employees whom they dislike or distrust
- assigning unpleasant tasks
- delegating work that places delegates at risk or that prevents them from handling their regular work
- pitting one employee against another
- giving unfair or false performance appraisals
- not hiring anyone who could be threatening to them

Manipulation

Manipulators invoke the names of high-level people to get their way. They curry favor of those who outrank them, sometimes to a degree of obsequiousness. They take advantage of friends and colleagues. Threats or even bribes may be part of their strategy. Promises are forgotten.

Political savvy to these folks means passing the buck, procrastinating, and saying what they do not mean. They are always cautious about speaking candidly.

You know you are being manipulated when someone leads off with something such as: "You don't value my service anymore, do you?" or "You owe me one," or "The boss will back me on this."

Ethical Issues

Major areas of ethical conduct are loyalty to customers, employers, superiors, and peers; honesty in human relations (treating people fairly and without manipulation); and honesty in work process and results. This means not cutting corners, endangering the safety of others, or cheating customers.

Political scripts often carry people across the line into unethical waters. Here are some such activities:

- divulging confidential information

- blaming others for one's mistakes or taking undeserved credit
- authorizing subordinates to violate rules, policies, or laws
- not reporting violations
- placing personal interests above those of the organization, its stakeholders, or its employees
- discriminating or showing favoritism
- cutting corners, especially in matters of safety or quality
- giving or receiving gifts or favors in exchange for preferential treatment

POSITIVE POLITICAL SCRIPTS

Healthy political scripts call for authentic attitudes, honest and open communication, networking and mentoring, coping honestly with bosses, and earning the support and respect of co-workers and subordinates.

Direct and authentic political tactics benefit the organization, the work unit, and the employees. For example, a supervisor who is politically skilled and has a large supportive network is much more able to obtain the resources needed to improve services, products, and morale.

POLITICAL TACTICS

Positive as well as negative political maneuvering involves tactics. The selection and implementation of tactical actions must be based on a thorough understanding of not only the mission, philosophy, and values of your organization but also its traditions and culture. Also important are ethical sensitivities and the availability of information.

Buskirk describes more than 120 political tactics that can be used on the job.[6] These include the fait accompli (doing something and then telling a boss who procrastinates instead of asking permission first), displaying righteous indignation, testing the waters, and knowing when to give in quickly. This is must reading for middle managers and executives.

RAPPORT WITH SUBORDINATES

"One of the first things employees notice is whether 'the score' is being kept equitably."[7(p.2)] The score refers to how individual achievement is evaluated, how each employee is treated, and how rules are enforced.

Political power is short circuited when employees feel that they are being manipulated or hoodwinked. On the other hand, if there is mutual trust and respect, and if they perceive you as their champion, your personal power will skyrocket.

Positive negotiating skill resolves sticky interpersonal conflicts and leads to win-win solutions. Negative political statements and unfulfilled promises lead to resentment, anger, and loss of trust.

COPING WITH BOSSES

Positive political acts require trust in the people we work with. The worst scenario is when we feel that our boss is an adversary. A sound, helpful relationship with superiors is the best kind of organizational politics.

Loyalty is the trait most highly prized by executives. Thousands of managers have lost their jobs or their power because their bosses had some real or imagined perception of them as being disloyal.

Bosses are often insecure because they do not really know much about what you do. If you clarify this situation by ensuring that your priorities are what he or she thinks they should be, rapport is strengthened. The chief will also be in a better position to offer more specific support.

Know your boss' priorities and idiosyncrasies. Learn the problems that he or she has with his or her boss, and provide whatever support you can. Do everything you can to make him or her look good to upper management.

For more on boss handling, see Chapter 18.

COMPETING WITH COLLEAGUES

Gain competitive advantages by upgrading your technical, managerial, and positive political skills. Avoid shifting blame, taking credit for other people's work, denigrating peers, or being a poor team player.

Self-aggrandizers regularly exaggerate their accomplishments or political clout. Look objectively for discrepancies between what a person says and what you see happening.

Logic and factual information are the best weapons against rational antagonists. The backing of your support group often tips the scales in your favor.

Irrational opponents assume their negative stances because they dislike, fear, or distrust you. Logic and facts usually do not sway them. You must get to know them better so that they can learn that your motives are benign and that you do not represent a threat.[8]

NETWORKING

Luebbert defines a network as "an informal group of contacts who share advice, facts, techniques, job leads, plans and dreams, and who lend each other moral support."[9(p.39)] Networking used to be referred to as the old-boy system or having connections. We still hear the old (and true) cliche "It's not what you know but who you know that counts."

Networking is building informal relationships. It is internal and external, informal team building. Your network is your invisible team or your favor bank. Mastering networking is largely a matter of knowing how to be helpful to the people with whom you interface and how to ask them for help in return.

BENEFITS OF NETWORKING

Networking is the fast track to personal growth. People who build connections within and outside organizations are much more likely to succeed. Through active networking, you can:

- obtain technical, professional, and fiscal data
- obtain advance information about trends, new projects, or organizational changes
- get second opinions on proposals, ideas, speeches, and reports
- get psychological support
- learn about job opportunities (more than 85 percent of good available jobs are never advertised[10])
- indicate your availability for a new job
- solicit recommendations or support
- recruit good job candidates
- enhance your career via mentoring or counseling

POTENTIAL NEGATIVE ASPECTS OF NETWORKING

Colleagues may resent networking peers; they call them brownnosers. Some managers perceive networkers as threats. Confusion may result from getting conflicting advice from different members. Alliances may prolong or escalate group conflicts.[11]

Relationships suffer when there is not reciprocity, that is, when a member is a taker and gives nothing in return. When the networks are political or activist groups, there is strong opposition.

BARRIERS TO NETWORKING

Many health care workers feel uneasy about reaching out to others. They may have been taught early in life that asking for help is a sign of weakness.[12] Autocratic and bureaucratic managers are less likely to participate in networking. Lack of goals or ambition is not conducive to networking.

NETWORK PARTICIPANTS

In Chapter 13, we discussed the importance of mentors. Mentors represent the crown jewels in most networks. Other potential participants include the following:

- other employees, especially those who precede or follow you in work flows, those who are members of support departments (e.g., materiel management, data processing, housekeeping, engineering, etc.), and those whom you serve as an internal service provider; never underestimate the power of secretaries, security guards, or housekeeping personnel
- in-house specialists, consultants, training specialists, and coordinators
- professional colleagues
- customers and suppliers

HOW CONTACTS ARE MADE

Make use of your Rolodex or address book, files of correspondence and business cards, and computer databases.

Professional contacts are made not only at meetings, seminars, workshops, committee meetings, and other professional groups but also at churches or synagogues, schools, clubs, and hobby groups and in neighborhoods. The networking at meetings may be more valuable than the meetings themselves.

Raise your visibility by giving talks, holding office, becoming a spokesperson, and earning a reputation as a recognized expert in some professional or technical aspect of health care.

Use your present network to get information about, or contacts with, people whom you would like to get to know.

GREAT NETWORKERS IN ACTION

Effective networkers set goals (e.g., to meet one new person each week, to join a community association, or to visit another department each month). When they help get people promoted, the latter may join their network and return the favor. They know that a network is like a bank account: Depositors must put in as much as they take out.

Here are some more characteristics of these winners:

- They know how to communicate with people.
- They keep in touch with their contacts.
- They express appreciation for favors.
- They are great joiners.
- They circulate at parties and meetings, where they introduce themselves rather than wait for someone else to do the honors.
- They are cordial and courteous to all but are somewhat selective about the people with whom they develop special rapport.
- They often volunteer for committees and other groups. They agree to help teach and to hold office.
- They share clippings, reports, articles, and other information.
- They use coffee breaks and lunch times to chat with different people.
- They quickly establish relationships with newcomers.
- They develop friendly relationships with individuals who work for competitors.
- They send out lots of thank-you notes and remember birthdays and other special occasions.
- They are not afraid to ask for help.

Skilled networkers do not:

- confuse networking with manipulating or posturing (e.g., trying to get a request approved by implying that they have the support of someone at the top)
- use networking as an excuse for excessive socializing, neglecting their responsibilities, or dumping on others
- overuse people's time or take unfair advantage of alliances
- neglect old members of their networks

NOTES

1. P. Block, *The Empowered Manager: Positive Skills at Work* (San Francisco, Calif.: Jossey-Bass, 1987).
2. L.W. Rue and L.L. Byars, *Supervision: Key Link to Productivity* (Homewood, Ill.: Irwin, 1982), 324.
3. Block, *The Empowered Manager,* 5.

4. Block, *The Empowered Manager,* 45.

5. R.D. Terrell, The elusive menace of office politics, *Training* 26 (1989): 48–54.

6. R.H. Buskirk, *Frontal Attack, Divide and Conquer, the Fait Accompli and 188 Other Tactics Managers Must Know* (New York, N.Y.: Wiley, 1989).

7. T. Rendero, Editorial, *Personnel* 67 (1990): 2.

8. W. Giegold, *Practical Management Skills for Engineers and Scientists* (Belmont, Calif.: Lifetime Learning, 1980), 168.

9. P.P. Luebbert, Networking for survival and success, *Medical Laboratory Observer* 19 (1987): 39.

10. Job Opportunities, *Intellingencer Journal* (August 20, 1990): 1–2.

11. B.E. Puetz, *Networking for Nurses* (Rockville, Md.: Aspen, 1983).

12. Luebbert, *Networking for survival,* 40.

Index

About the Author

William Umiker, M.D., is Adjunct Professor of Clinical Pathology at the Hershey Medical Center of Pennsylvania State University. He holds an M.D. from the University of Buffalo and received his postgraduate training at the University of Michigan.

Dr. Umiker is a health care administrator with more than 40 years of experience. Subsequent to service in the U.S. Navy and Veterans Administration hospitals, he was laboratory director at St. Joseph Hospital in Lancaster, Pennsylvania until his retirement in 1985. He has served as an inspector of blood banks, clinical laboratories, and schools of medical technology.

Dr. Umiker has been widely published and is the author of six books about health care management.